Trees

TIME
LIFE
BOOKS
®

LIFE WORLD LIBRARY

LIFE NATURE LIBRARY

TIME READING PROGRAM

THE LIFE HISTORY OF THE UNITED STATES

LIFE SCIENCE LIBRARY

GREAT AGES OF MAN

TIME-LIFE LIBRARY OF ART

TIME-LIFE LIBRARY OF AMERICA

FOODS OF THE WORLD

THIS FABULOUS CENTURY

LIFE LIBRARY OF PHOTOGRAPHY

THE TIME-LIFE ENCYCLOPEDIA OF GARDENING

THE AMERICAN WILDERNESS

FAMILY LIBRARY
   THE TIME-LIFE BOOK OF FAMILY FINANCE
   THE TIME-LIFE FAMILY LEGAL GUIDE

THE TIME-LIFE ENCYCLOPEDIA OF GARDENING

Trees

by

James Underwood Crockett

and

the Editors of TIME-LIFE BOOKS

TIME-LIFE BOOKS, NEW YORK

THE AUTHOR: James Underwood Crockett is an eminent horticulturist and writer on gardening subjects. A graduate of the University of Massachusetts' Stockbridge School of Agriculture, he has lived in—and cultivated a wide variety of plants in—California, New York, Texas and New England and has served as a consultant to many nurseries and landscapers. His monthly bulletin, "Flowery Talks," is distributed to more than a million customers annually through florists' shops. Mr. Crockett lives in Massachusetts.

GENERAL CONSULTANTS: William Flemer, III, Princeton Nurseries, Princeton, New Jersey. Albert P. Nordheden, New York City. Dr. Donald Wyman, Horticulturist Emeritus, Arnold Arboretum, Harvard University. Staff of the Brooklyn Botanic Garden: Elizabeth Scholtz, Acting Director; Robert S. Tomson, Assistant Director; George A. Kalmbacher, Plant Taxonomist; Edmund O. Moulin, Horticulturist.

THE COVER: Its branches flung wide against the sky, a venerable sugar maple spreads a welcome green canopy over a summer day. This species is one of the most popular shade trees native to North America, partly because it provides a bonus of brilliant autumn color (pages 65 and 74-75)—and it is also the source of the sap from which maple sugar is made. It is the state tree of five states—New York, Rhode Island, Vermont, West Virginia and Wisconsin—and its leaf is the centerpiece of the Canadian national flag.

TIME-LIFE BOOKS

FOUNDER: Henry R. Luce 1898-1967

Editor-in-Chief: Hedley Donovan
Chairman of the Board: Andrew Heiskell
President: James R. Shepley
Chairman, Executive Committee: James A. Linen
Editorial Director: Louis Banks

Vice Chairman: Roy E. Larsen

EDITOR
Jerry Korn
Executive Editor
A. B. C. Whipple
Planning Director
Oliver E. Allen
Text Director
Martin Mann
Art Director
Sheldon Cotler
Chief of Research
Beatrice T. Dobie
Director of Photography
Melvin L. Scott
Assistant Text Directors: Ogden Tanner, Diana Hirsh
Assistant Art Director: Arnold C. Holeywell

PUBLISHER
Joan D. Manley
General Manager: John D. McSweeney
Business Manager: John Steven Maxwell
Sales Director: Carl G. Jaeger
Promotion Director: Paul R. Stewart
Public Relations Director: Nicholas Benton

THE TIME-LIFE ENCYCLOPEDIA OF GARDENING

SERIES EDITOR: Robert M. Jones
EDITORIAL STAFF FOR TREES:
EDITOR: Ogden Tanner
Picture Editor: Sheila Osmundsen
Designer: Leonard Wolfe
Staff Writers: Marian Gordon Goldman, Gerry Schremp
Chief Researcher: David L. Harrison
Researchers: Gail Cruikshank, Helen Fennell, Bea Hsia, Catherine Ireys, Nancy Jacobsen, Mary Kay Moran, Lyn Stallworth, Sandra Streepey, Penny Zug
Design Assistant: Anne B. Landry

EDITORIAL PRODUCTION
Production Editor: Douglas B. Graham
Quality Director: Robert L. Young
Assistant: James J. Cox
Copy Staff: Rosalind Stubenberg, Reese Hassig, Heidi Sanford, Florence Keith
Picture Department: Dolores A. Littles, Barbara S. Simon

Portions of this book were written by Henry Moscow. Instructional drawings are by Vincent Lewis. Valuable assistance was provided by the following individuals and departments of Time Inc.: Editorial Production, Norman Airey, Nicholas Costino Jr.; Library, Peter Draz; Picture Collection, Doris O'Neil; Photographic Laboratory, George Karas; TIME-LIFE News Service, Murray J. Gart; Correspondents Maria Vincenza Aloisi (Paris), Jane Estes (Seattle), Margot Hapgood (London), Elisabeth Kraemer (Bonn), Sue Wymelenberg (Boston).

74-3713

CONTENTS

Lindenbaum.

The right tree in the right place 1

The story goes that a wise man, asked what he would do if he knew that he had but one day left to live, replied, "I would plant a tree." The importance he attached to trees must be widely shared, for millions are planted every year in the United States alone—to provide shade and ornament, to increase real estate values, to add the sense of home they bring to a house and yard. Sometimes we plant them symbolically, as the wise man suggested, for trees outlive us, linking us with generations yet unborn. In my yard in Massachusetts stands a handsome Manchurian walnut placed there for me by an uncle who died many years ago. Although he is gone, his memory remains as fresh as the new leaves that clothe the tree's branches each spring. When I look at that tree I sometimes think of earlier New Englanders who used to plant a new tree to mark every family milestone—the birth of a child, a marriage, a death. And I think of the men who a century ago felt impelled to found Arbor Day in tree-scarce Nebraska; many Americans still celebrate that day in spring by planting new trees in their communities, trying in the face of modern urban pressures to maintain a link with nature through these giants of the plant world.

Perhaps our deep affinity to trees is atavistic—our prehuman forebears, in the dim past, were tree dwellers. And since the earliest times men have depended on trees: they have provided shelter from sun and rain, protection from enemies, wood for fires, houses and furniture, food for the table and, perhaps above all, the pleasure of simply looking at them. It is not surprising that our primitive ancestors actually worshiped trees, which towered toward the sky, sprang into new life each year and, compared to mortal men, seemed to live forever.

Even today those American Indians who observe ancestral ways refuse to cut down a living tree. And in Indonesia there was a tribe, the Mandelings, that customarily declined to accept responsibility for chopping down a tree, respectfully blaming the act on the government—before an ax was swung the Mandelings absolved

A favorite everywhere today, the linden was long the most familiar tree in German hamlets. Beneath its boughs villagers frolicked—as shown in this 16th Century woodcut—and dragons were thought to live.

TREES FOR POSTERITY

Arbor Day, a day set aside for tree planting in many communities across the nation and in several foreign countries, was launched a century ago by a Nebraska newspaper editor and political leader, J. Sterling Morton. The holiday grew out of a local campaign —conducted in Morton's newspaper —to plant trees on Nebraska's treeless prairie. Morton practiced what he preached. When he moved to Nebraska in 1855 with memories of the lush landscape of his Michigan home, he bought 160 acres of barren land and immediately began planting a grove. Today his home, transformed into a park known as Arbor Lodge, contains 150 different varieties of trees and shrubs. Morton passed on his fervor for tree planting to his son, Joy, who in 1922 founded the 1,500-acre Morton Arboretum in Lisle, Illinois. The Morton family's legacy is considerable: the Arboretum, with about 4,800 different types of plants, is among the largest of its kind, and Arbor Day, which falls on the elder Morton's birthday, has brought the beauty of trees to bare lands around the world.

themselves by reading to the trees an imaginary official proclamation commanding that the ground be cleared.

If trees do not quite possess the powers that primitive men ascribed to them, they are remarkable organisms nevertheless, the biggest and longest lived of all the plants. As their marvelously intricate mechanisms lift nutrients and water from the soil to make food for continuing growth *(pages 16-23)*, they help keep the earth's ecology in balance, transforming carbon dioxide into the vital oxygen that we breathe, tempering the effects of sun and wind, and anchoring the soil against erosion. They make the world livable and, on a more homely scale, they make a garden livable too. Of the almost numberless kinds of trees, the ones that are most generally useful to homeowners in many parts of the country are the deciduous trees, which lose their leaves each fall, bursting into growth again each spring. Those discussed in this book are used primarily for shade and ornament, are raised in nurseries for these purposes, and differ in characteristics and requirements from evergreens and orchard trees. Properly chosen and located, deciduous trees can frame and flatter the design of a house, complementing its lines and providing a welcoming approach. At the side or back they can shade a terrace or patio, screen out unsightly views and provide privacy for outdoor living; they can attract birds with their berries, create a beautiful backdrop for a flower garden or become flowering focal points in themselves. There are over 2,000 species and varieties of deciduous trees that will grow in various parts of North America; more than 250 of the best of these for home landscapes are described in detail in the illustrated encyclopedia starting on page 89. Not all of these species and varieties, however, are suited to all landscaping purposes; the trick lies in choosing the kinds of trees that will best do the specific job you have in mind and that will grow well in the area where you live.

Before you go any further in considering a tree you may have heard about, there are some basic questions to consider. First you should make sure that the species, or a variety of the species, will survive the winter cold and summer heat of your general area and that it will also thrive in the special climatic and soil conditions of your garden. More than one homeowner has lost a tree because he did not pay sufficient attention to these matters, and attempted to grow an exotic species outside the limits of its climatic tolerance. The areas in which each tree will grow successfully are noted in the encyclopedia by letters keyed to a map of growing areas on page 150. But even within areas, environments vary surprisingly, and it is wise to drive around your neighborhood to see if you can find a healthy example or two of a preferred species growing nearby and then to note the conditions under which they are growing. My home in Massachusetts happens to be on the northern edge of the growing range of flowering dogwoods. They do well there in sheltered locations, but in wind-swept spots and low-lying frost pockets the flower buds of the dogwood frequently fail to survive the winter. In such locations one of the varieties of a crab apple or other flowering tree that is notably resistant to cold and blossoms unfailingly each springtime would be a far better choice.

A second matter to consider is pests. Neither bugs nor diseases seem to bother the ginkgo, for example, wherever it grows. Other trees are notoriously susceptible to a particular disease—the Bechtel crab apple, for example, to apple rust. The vulnerability of others depends on location: the honey locust suffers from the mimosa webworm in Pennsylvania but is untroubled by this pest in New York, partly because the webworm cannot survive the slightly colder New York State winters.

Third, find out if the tree is messy, likely to litter the yard with fruit, seed pods or broken branches. The silver maple has such brittle wood that the lawn beneath it must be raked regularly to remove twigs that break off in the breeze and interfere with grass mowing. The horse chestnut is a lovely tree but showers its inedible nuts over a wide area; if you like the tree, plant it where the nuts will not be a problem, or be prepared to rake them up. Still better, plant the Baumann horse chestnut, which does not bear nuts. The tree of heaven, an indomitable tree that will grow out of a crack in a sidewalk, is a welcome touch of green to many city dwellers but spreads so vigorously it is a weed to others; moreover, the male of the species bears malodorous flowers. Honey locusts that have not been bred for seedlessness produce long, sinuous pods some people find objectionable in appearance. One woman who bought a honey locust later telephoned the nurseryman in a rage. "That tree you sold me is full of snakes," she screamed. "Take it away!"

TREES THAT GROW TOO BIG

Probably the most common mistake people make in choosing trees, however, is not the purchase of a minor nuisance, but the selection of trees that sooner or later grow too big for their settings and thus outlive their usefulness. Probably the second most common mistake is a corollary of the first: planting trees too close together or too close to a house, driveway or street for their eventual size. To be sure, trees in a home landscape do not become as tall as their brethren in the forest, where all trees are forced to reach upward in constant competition for sunlight. But even domesticated specimens of certain forest trees can reach a size out of all proportion to a suburban lot and, because they grow broader in the open garden than in the forest, they can soon encroach on patios and windows, sidewalks and roads; to keep them within bounds, so many branches may have to be removed that their beauty is lost. A sugar maple growing wild in the woods, for example, may become 120 feet tall; on an open lawn it will seldom exceed 75 or 80 feet, but that height may still be enough to overwhelm a one-story ranch house. Big trees are also difficult to feed, prune and spray, and their maintenance may require a professional's often costly services. And finally, the bigger the tree, the more it costs to remove if disease or disaster strikes.

Even tree experts have had to learn this lesson the hard way. Only 20 to 30 years ago park departments and shade-tree commissions around the United States were still lining local roadways with the tall-growing trees—elms, maples, oaks—that our ancestors had so proudly planted along their village streets two centuries earlier. In many towns today such trees have become so large that they interfere with telephone and power lines and in a windstorm endanger houses and cars. In the case of the American elm this drawback of size is compounded by the tree's susceptibility to Dutch elm disease. Though few men can look at a noble, arching elm without some admiration, municipal tree men now think of this tree mainly as a costly removal problem and they, like homeowners, are turning more and more to low-growing, trouble-free species.

Fortunately, many trees that are desirable but for their height have low-growing relatives that are small enough so they will not overwhelm even a modest house and garden. You do not have to settle for the common tall-growing Norway maple, which eventually may reach 75 feet or more; instead, you can use the globe Norway maple, a nicely rounded tree that seldom grows to a height of more than 20 feet. Or you can plant a paperbark, trident, hedge, Japanese, vine or Amur maple, none of which exceed 25 feet when mature. Rather than plant a species of ash that may become 60 to 80 or more feet tall, you can select a Modesto ash or a Moraine ash, both of which grow 20 to 40 feet tall.

The other common mistake gardeners make, particularly if they buy very young trees of large-growing species, is planting too many trees for the space available. After all, small maple, oak or linden trees 3 to 4 feet tall seem insignificant no matter how closely they are placed in the yard. Set 20 feet apart, they look lost, and yet even that separation is not enough; they should actually be spaced 40 to 60 feet apart. If they are not given enough room to grow, within a few years they begin to compete with one another, then to crowd one another and form a solid mass of foliage during the summer. At this point, half the stand of trees might have to be removed. But all too few gardeners have the courage to cut down every other tree so that the remaining ones will have room to develop to their full beauty. To help you choose and locate trees that will stay in bounds, both in relation to streets and houses and to one another, the encyclopedia gives for each type the average height and spread it can be expected to attain when it is fully grown.

When maximum shade is the objective, of course, tall-growing species of oaks and maples are still excellent choices if you have room for them. But along with other shade trees that grow beyond 50 feet tall, such as lindens and tulip trees, they are best located at least 30 feet from the street and the house, where they have room to grow, where their fallen leaves will not clog gutters and where storm-broken branches will cause minimum damage. If you do not have the space on your lot, and need only a pool of shade on a patio exposed to summer afternoon sun, consider a medium-sized tree, such as a yellowwood or a ruby horse chestnut, whose spreading branches provide shade yet whose mature height of 35 to 50 feet does not overpower the house. Or consider still smaller trees such as crab apples, dogwoods or cherries, which are normally thought of as flowering lawn ornaments but can also provide shade without ever growing more than 30 feet tall. Unlike larger trees, which stand best alone, they look good in clusters of two or three with branches intermingled; used this way next to a patio, they can provide not only shade but a feeling of intimacy, screening out unwanted views and displaying their flowers and berries at close range.

In choosing shade trees, bear in mind that different trees provide different kinds of shade. The big or heavily overlapping leaves of yellowwoods, catalpas and Norway maples, for example, cast a deep shade that is cooling on the hottest summer day but is so dark that grass or flowers will not grow in it. Silk trees, Jerusalem thorns and thornless honey locusts, on the other hand, have finely divided foliage that casts a filtered, dappled shade; this open shade is adequate where summer sun is not intense, and it permits you to grow shade-tolerant types of grass and plants close to the tree. The thornless honey locust, in fact, is one of my favorites as an all-round shade and lawn tree; it has a graceful airy look, grows reasonably rapidly to a height of 35 to 70 feet, and has been bred so it does not have the prickly thorns and messy seed pods of other locusts; in addition, its fallen leaves are so fine that they sift down into grass and decay with practically no need for raking them up.

Whatever tree you pick for shade, make sure you plant it where it will indeed shade the area you want at the time of day you need it most. Generally this requirement is met by locating the tree to the south and west of a patio or house windows; there the leaves will intercept the hot afternoon sun in summer. If you are not sure where to place a tree in relation to the position and angle of the sun, you can experiment with a long pole; hold it upright between the sun and the area to be shaded on an August afternoon and move it about until its shadow falls in the direction you want. The pole may not be long enough to simulate the mature height of the tree you have in mind, but that height can be gauged by eye.

Another helpful trick in locating a shade tree—or any tree, for that matter—requires only a tall stake to stand in for the tree. Drive the stake into the ground at the spot where you think the tree should be planted, then mark a circle around the stake with a diameter equal to that of the tree's mature spread. This circle immediately shows how much room the tree needs. The stake also helps you check and adjust the proposed location of the tree from as many angles as possible. Could the tree be made visible from the dining-room window, for example, by shifting it a few feet to the right? And if it were shifted, would the shade pattern move away from the spot where it is needed? Would the tree help frame the house attractively or give it a background when viewed from the street? Would it blot out an unpleasant view or, conversely, would it obscure a pleasant vista as it grows? If you have a swimming pool in your backyard or plan to build one some time in the future, be sure you do not locate a tree where it will eventually shade the pool, and do not plant the tree on the windward side of the pool, to clutter it when the leaves fall in autumn.

Shade is the often-welcome by-product of any tree, but many trees also offer purely ornamental value in several seasons. Some have bright flowers followed by colorful fruit; many have handsome autumn foliage; others have richly patterned bark or bold and distinctive branching habits that make them nearly as appealing in winter as in summer.

HOW SHADE TREES GROW IN 10 YEARS

The wide variation in growth rates among shade trees is indicated in the diagram below. It shows silhouettes, in scale, of six popular kinds of shade trees at the average heights they would achieve 10 years after they had been planted as 8- to 10-foot nursery specimens.

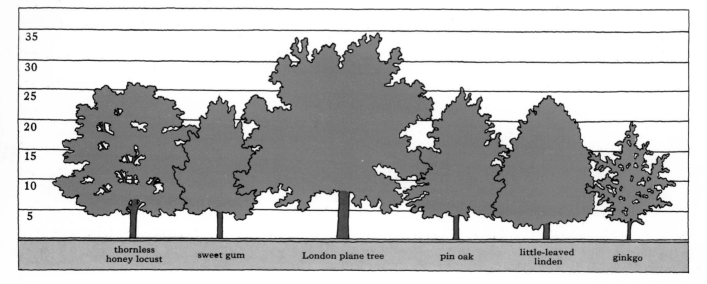

35					
30					
25					
20					
15					
10					
5					

thornless honey locust   sweet gum   London plane tree   pin oak   little-leaved linden   ginkgo

Among the ornamental trees that are most popular with today's homeowners are flowering crab apples, dogwoods, hawthorns and redbuds. But there are others rapidly climbing in popularity. One is the Bradford pear; like other trees bred specifically for today's tastes and small suburban lots, it grows fairly rapidly to a manageable height of 30 to 50 feet, and it puts on an almost year-round show. In spring it bears masses of white blossoms, in summer its glossy green foliage and upright branches make it a handsome lawn ornament, in fall it turns a brilliant red. It is pest resistant, and it also withstands the polluted air, poor soil and crowded growing space that are common to many city locations.

As there are trees that will grow well under city conditions, there are trees that have special merits in other situations. If there is a low, damp spot on your property that cannot be kept properly drained, consider a pepperidge, a sweet gum or one of the alders, all of which tolerate wet soil. If you have poor dry alkaline soil, try a locust or honey mesquite; they tolerate even desertlike conditions. If you have a house near the sea, choose trees that are sand and salt tolerant, such as mulberries and locusts, the sycamore maple and, again, the sweet gum. A fine sweet gum specimen occupies a place of honor in my own backyard, although I do not live by the ocean; it is one of the handsomest and most adaptable trees in many parts of the country.

Considerations of use and growing conditions narrow the choices among trees. Then one specific characteristic may sway the decision: rate of growth. One of the things many homeowners want most to know about any tree, particularly if they have a treeless lot

TREES FOR SPECIAL SITES

HOW FLOWERING TREES GROW IN FIVE YEARS

Popular flowering trees grow faster than shade trees and generally reach useful heights after five years. Unlike shade trees, which may grow for decades, many flowering types mature at this stage. An exception is the Bradford pear, which grows to reach 50 feet.

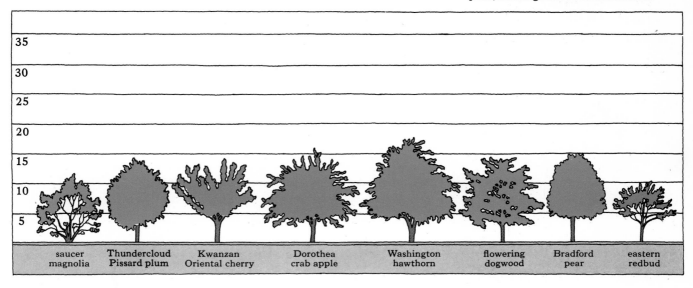

35							
30							
25							
20							
15							
10							
5							
saucer magnolia	Thundercloud Pissard plum	Kwanzan Oriental cherry	Dorothea crab apple	Washington hawthorn	flowering dogwood	Bradford pear	eastern redbud

and need a landscape in a hurry, is how fast the tree will grow. A fast-growing tree such as a plane tree or silver maple can add 3 feet or more a year, growing from 8 to 10 feet at plantingtime to 20 to 35 feet in 10 years (some fast growers such as poplars and willows may put on as much as 5 to 8 feet annually when young). A moderate rate of growth, in contrast, is about 1 to 2 feet a year; horse chestnuts and European hackberries planted at 8 to 10 feet become 15 to 25 feet high in 10 years. A slow-growing tree such as a hornbeam or ginkgo adds about 8 to 12 inches annually, reaching 15 to 20 feet in 10 years. But, like human beings, trees do not grow at the same rate throughout their lives. Most spend their first year or two getting reestablished after transplanting; then, for about the next 10 years, they add a great deal of height before slowing down and attaining their mature shape and size.

Whether you should pick a tree that grows at a relatively fast rate or at a slow one depends on a number of factors. The slow growers, because they must be cared for longer in a nursery before they reach salable size, are more expensive than fast growers and, once planted in a home landscape, take longer to reach maturity. These are the trees we are fortunate to inherit when buying an older house, but they can also be planted as a long-range investment and as a heritage for children. Most slow-growing trees are long lived as well as handsome, and their dense, fibrous wood makes them resistant to breakage in wind and ice storms.

Faster-growing trees, in contrast, do not have time to develop such strong fibers and for this reason are more brittle; you will almost always see more broken twigs and branches under a willow or poplar than you will under a little-leaved linden or oak, particularly after a blustery winter. Moreover, many fast growers have spreading roots that can plug sewer lines and buckle sidewalks if planted too close to them, and they have more than normal susceptibility to fungus diseases and insects. But fast growers have their advantages too; they represent the most tree for the money on a short-term basis. They are less expensive, they put on a show sooner after planting and, despite their drawbacks, many are graceful additions as shade trees or ornaments. For all of these reasons fast-growing trees are often the favored choice of young couples with new homes on treeless lots.

Many fast-growing trees are so vigorous, in fact, that new ones can be acquired simply by cutting off and rooting a branch of a larger tree. When I was building a new house some 20 years ago, that is precisely what I did; I took two 8-foot branches from a willow that was growing in the yard where I then lived and went over to the new property to plant them. It was early spring and the ground was so wet in the low spot I had chosen that I simply stood on an embankment and threw the sharpened willow sticks as though they were spears. They took root where they stuck in the ground, I later straightened them up, and today I have two 50-foot willows with trunks that are 2 feet in diameter. The parent willow not only supplied me with trees I could soon enjoy from the windows of my new house; that same spring I cut another branch and gave it to a 77-year-old uncle for his own yard. He lived long enough to sit in his willow's shade and never failed to point out the tree to me proudly whenever I came to visit.

I would not recommend fast-growing trees for all situations, however, nor would I suggest them as the sole trees on a lot. Because of their brittleness, proneness to disease and relatively short lives, they should be supplemented by plantings of slower-growing, more permanently desirable trees. Once they begin to outlive their usefulness or inhibit the growth of the permanent trees, you should put aside sentiment and have the courage to cut them down.

An often difficult decision to make when choosing a tree is what size to buy. If you are considering a tree mainly for ornamental purposes, such as a flowering dogwood, cherry, redbud or crab apple, I recommend that you start with a relatively small specimen, not over 6 to 8 feet tall. Not only are small trees less expensive than larger ones, but they are easier to plant yourself, a further saving. Moreover, most small flowering trees grow rapidly, and they begin to blossom at an early age, even the first season they are planted. And, too, there is something special about a tree you have planted yourself; you can watch it increase in beauty from year to year with pardonable pride.

Choosing the initial size of a shade tree, however, involves other factors, the most important of which is the buying of time. The purpose of a shade tree is to provide shade, and as soon as possible. Unlike a purely ornamental tree, it must have some height and spread to do its job. At minimum it should be an 8- to 10-foot tree. But an 8- to 10-foot tree of even a fast-growing species may take 8 to 10 years before it becomes large enough to shade a picnic table and chairs. By that time your children may have grown up and left home without having enjoyed its shade with you—or like many mobile Americans you may already be looking for another house. If you want shade so that you can begin to enjoy living outdoors in summer right away, I urge you to consider investing in a substantial tree, one that is 20 to 25 feet tall with a spread of 15 feet or more. A tree of this size can be moved by three or four men from a nursery without the use of special equipment, and the total cost will probably be no more than that of a new refrigerator. And that is a small investment to make for such a large return.

WHAT SIZE TREE TO BUY

The amazing machinery of the tree

Quietly operating pumps, valves, filters, pipelines and processing cells of an efficiency surpassing any conceived by man, a typical 40-foot-tall tree every day takes in 50 gallons of dissolved nutrients from the soil, raises this mineral brew to its topmost leaves, converts it into 10 pounds of carbohydrate food and releases about 60 cubic feet of pure oxygen into the air. It is small wonder that this intricate mechanism has for centuries inspired awe among scientists and dirt gardeners alike. But only now are the mysteries of these workings becoming more fully understood, providing basic principles to guide the homeowner in caring for his trees.

The process by which a tree lives and grows starts with the microscopic feeder roots, which collect water and minerals needed for food production, and the larger roots, which carry these nutrients to the trunk where they are piped up and out into the branches and leaves. In support of this chain, the tree sends down a taproot to anchor the trunk and braces it with a swelling of the roots at the base, called flare. Meanwhile the trunk, tapering upward to its highest point, the leader, supports the primary branches, secondary branches and twigs that together form the crown and expose the food-manufacturing leaves to air, which supplies the carbon dioxide needed as a raw material, and to sunlight, which powers the machinery.

Though many people believe that a tree's spreading superstructure is matched by its underpinnings, in fact the two are not mirror images; the roots may run out as far as three times the spread of the crown. In one sense, however, crown and roots are coequal: the total surface of the leaves must be balanced by the total surface of the roots supplying the leaves —which is why a tree that has lost some roots should always be pruned of some leaf-bearing branches as well. Despite such superficial differences as bark texture and leaf shape, all types of trees follow this same operating pattern. What is true of the function of the roots, trunk and crown of the red oak, the subject of the detailed explanations on the following pages, is true of every other deciduous tree as well.

A full-grown red oak, half its leaves removed and all its roots exposed, illustrates the major parts of a tree.

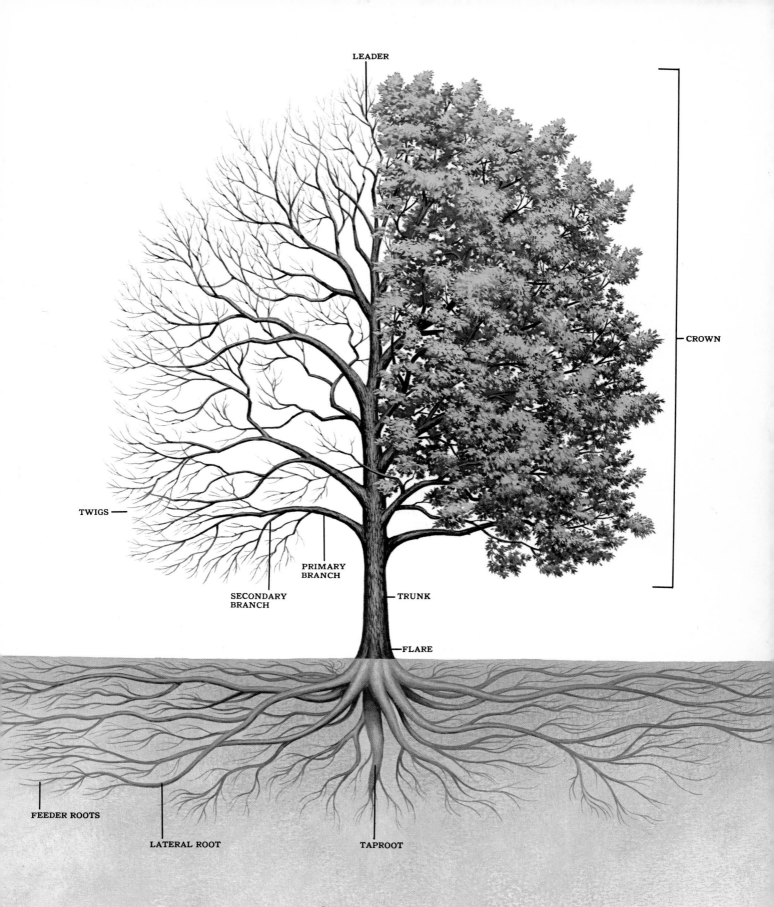

LEADER

CROWN

TWIGS

PRIMARY
BRANCH

SECONDARY
BRANCH

TRUNK

FLARE

FEEDER ROOTS

LATERAL ROOT

TAPROOT

THE BUSY ROOT TIPS

The most active part of a tree's root system lies at the very tip ends of its feeder roots. Capped by thin, slippery membranes of new cells, the tips slide and wiggle through the soil. Behind each short rootcap are fast-growing cells in a so-called zone of elongation. The rest of the feeder root is covered with delicate filaments called root hairs, which filter and draw in a steady supply of the nutrients needed to feed the tree. Root hairs function only a short time. As the tip burrows forward continuously, new hairs are being formed while the old ones die.

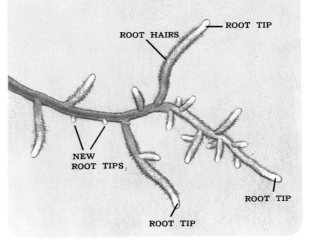

ROOT HAIRS — ROOT TIP

NEW ROOT TIPS

ROOT TIP

ROOT TIP

TAPROOT

1. *From its youthful role as both anchor and feeder, the carrotlike taproot gradually becomes anchor alone. In some species the taproot may grow 14 feet deep; in others, like the red oak, it stops growing when the lateral roots are large enough to take over.*

Roots: anchors and foragers

Out of sight and underground, the roots of a tree constantly perform their twofold task of feeding and supporting the aerial structure overhead. The vertical taproot and the network of lateral roots branching from it anchor and brace the trunk; in time the three largest of the lateral roots usually form a natural tripod around the tree's base. Cellular pipelines just below the roots' barklike sheaths act as conduits, carrying nutrients from the feeder roots back to the trunk.

The nutrients themselves, a mixture of water and minerals, are absorbed by the roots' smallest parts, the microscopic root hairs that surround the growing tips of the feeder roots. Even a young tree has billions of these root hairs, taking in tens of gallons a day of nutrients to nourish its growth.

3

LATERAL ROOTS

2. *Dividing and redividing, the lateral roots form a mat as much as 4 feet deep and from one and a half to four times the reach of the crown. They stay near the surface to obtain oxygen and moisture—which is why trees suffer if soil is compacted over them.*

FEEDER ROOTS

3. *From spring to fall, the feeder roots push outward through the soil as much as an inch every day. Sometimes they mingle with roots of adjacent trees, sharing their nourishment—as well as their diseases and any chemicals applied to these neighbors.*

BARK

1. *Wrapping the tree like a protective overcoat, the bark is made up of several layers. The thickest is the cork layer, waxy and waterproof, which gradually hardens into the tough, often-fissured outer shell.*

PHLOEM

2. *Just beneath the main part of the bark lies the phloem, a fibrous, moist sleeve that carries food from the leaves to the rest of the tree. The phloem's tubular cells age to a fibrous sheath lining the bark.*

CAMBIUM

3. *Only one cell thick, the cambium layer is the life-giving inner sheath of the tree, manufacturing cells from spring to frost. Those along the outside become phloem; those inside become xylem (below).*

SAPWOOD

4. *The young xylem tissue that carries water and minerals from the roots to the leaves makes up the sapwood. Its open-ended cells, stacked one on top of another, form rows of continuous cylinders.*

HEARTWOOD

5. *As xylem cells age they clog and harden into heartwood, which makes up the central core of the tree and lends support for its branches. Deposits within the heartwood eventually darken it.*

Trunk: prop and pipe

The trunk of a tree is composed of concentric rings of cells that form distinct layers, each having its own function. Most of the cells originate in a single layer, the cambium, which lies below the tree's surface. Cells generated by the cambium become either phloem or xylem, the two layers that make up the tree's pipelines.

Dissolved minerals are conducted upward through the xylem for conversion into food; the phloem carries the finished product downward to provide nourishment to all parts of the tree, including the roots. As the phloem cells die, they become the inner lining of the bark, the tough outer skin of the tree—a skin that may stretch as the trunk expands or, as on the red oak shown here, crack into deep fissures. The xylem cells, in maturity, join the parade of annual rings that make up the heartwood, the tree's dark core. Vascular rays cut across these rings to carry food laterally and, in fall, deposit the food in the sapwood for storage—to be released in spring to prime the arboreal pump.

5

TERMINAL BUD

First year's growth

Second year's growth

Third year's growth

TERMINAL BUD

LATERAL BUD

LATERAL BUD

BUD SCALE SCAR

BUD SCALE SCARS

BUD INTO BRANCH

At the points where leaves, lost in autumn, were joined to their branches lie the leaf buds, embryos of new growth. In spring each bud swells and a branch emerges, telescope fashion; a bud scale scar marks each year's growth.

The crown: factory for food

Every spring new branches emerge to extend the height and spread of the crown, and leaves open along them to manufacture the tree's food supply. By the process called photosynthesis the leaves use energy from the sun to create the carbohydrate glucose, a type of sugar the tree uses for food. The raw materials for this process are carbon dioxide, taken in from the air, and the mineral solution that rises through the tree's internal plumbing; the waste products are oxygen, given off in the process of forming the sugar, and most of the water used to carry the nutrients up from the roots. To make photosynthesis work, the top of a leaf must be exposed to sun and its bottom surface must have access to cool, clean air. Nature takes care of the first requirement with a hormone that tips the leaf toward the light; gardeners can help keep air unfouled by refraining from burning fires near the tree.

PALISADE LAYER

2. *Below the upper epidermis, a layer of tubular cells—the palisade—houses chloroplasts, tiny particles saturated with the green pigment, chlorophyll, that absorbs the solar energy needed to produce food.*

RIBS AND VEINS

3. *Stout ribs and a delicate tracery of veins hold the leaf tissue spread out to sunlight and air. The same lacy mesh also carries both raw materials and manufactured food inside its miniature pipelines.*

SPONGY LAYER

4. *Unlike the regimented array of palisade cells, the cells in the spongy layer are loosely arranged. Air circulates freely among them, bringing carbon dioxide into contact with water and minerals.*

LOWER EPIDERMIS

5. *Millions of tiny valvelike pores called stomata cover the bottom skin of the leaf. Each is flanked by two banana-shaped cells that open and close to let carbon dioxide in, water and oxygen out.*

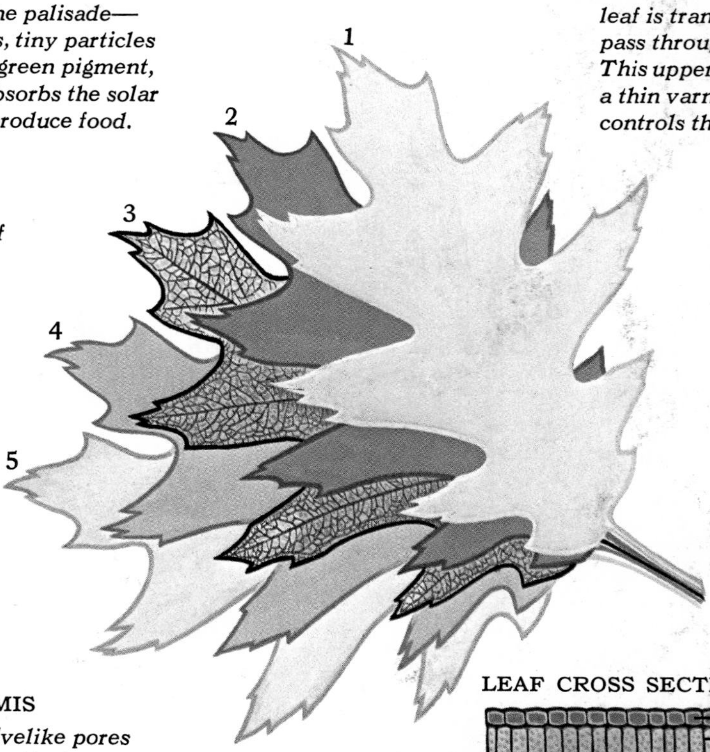

UPPER EPIDERMIS

1. *The skin covering the top of the leaf is transparent, so sunlight can pass through to the cells beneath. This upper epidermis is sealed with a thin varnishlike cuticle that controls the evaporation of water.*

LEAF CROSS SECTION

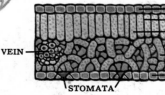

— UPPER EPIDERMIS
— PALISADE LAYER
— CHLOROPLASTS

VEIN —

— SPONGY LAYER

— LOWER EPIDERMIS

STOMATA

Choosing, buying and planting 2

There is a story in the nursery trade about an itinerant peddler who for years made a good thing of selling trees at bargain prices off the back of a truck. Each of his trees came with its base in an impressive ball wrapped in burlap, like many of the trees reputable nurseries sell; the peddler urged his customers to plant the trees as is, without even loosening the burlap. Every one of the trees died. But it was a while before anyone discovered why. The peddler had been sawing off forest trees and setting them in globs of concrete and a little dirt; he would sell as many trees as he could in one town, pocket the cash and move his one-man assembly line to another unsuspecting town before anyone was the wiser. Though the story may be apocryphal, many a tree still is sold from a truck or in a bargain-sales lot. Such trees usually have been gathered by so-called collectors who dig them in the woods, and although the trees may look healthy and have their roots they might as well be fixed in cement, because the collectors rarely prepare them properly for transplanting. If the trees do survive, they seldom amount to much.

Stories about the wrong ways to acquire trees are practically endless. The right ways are fewer. You can indeed be a collector and dig up trees yourself—from a wooded area on your own or a friend's property—and replant them in your yard; it certainly is the cheapest method, and many people use it, but successful collecting requires some knowledge and effort. First, you should pick a relatively young tree, not over 6 to 8 feet tall; it is more likely to survive the shock of transplanting than an older one. Second, you will have better luck with trees like maples and lindens, which have shallow root systems; they are much easier to transplant than deep-rooted trees such as oaks and dogwoods. Third, you must prepare the tree by pruning its roots six months to a year before the actual transplanting (drawings, page 27), and finally, after planting, you must be sure to wrap the trunk with protective tape as shown on page 31; trees that have grown up shaded by larger trees in a woodland need such wrapping even more than others do, for they have

Moving 25-year-old sugar maples from a Connecticut woodland, workers use a power digger, winch and flat-bed truck, but the method of wrapping the roots in burlap is basically the same one used for young trees.

thin bark and are especially susceptible to sunscald, which is very much like the sunburn a fair-skinned person gets when abruptly exposed to a large dose of unaccustomed sunlight.

Rather than go to all that work, most people find it simpler to buy from nurserymen, who know how to raise and prepare trees so they have the best chance to survive in home landscapes. Mail-order nurseries can be a good source for trees, particularly if you want a number of small specimens of one kind; the prices are often low, and some houses specialize in newly developed varieties of trees that are not yet widely available in local nurseries. But you will be limited to rather small sizes, for trees more than 5 to 6 feet tall cannot be shipped by mail, and it is up to you to be sure the species you order will thrive in your particular climate and soil. You should, of course, consider the reliability of the mail-order house from which you are thinking of buying. I am wary of firms that promote trees supposed to grow miraculously high in no time at all, and I generally have more confidence in companies that belong to trade associations such as the American Association of Nurserymen or the Mailorder Association of Nurserymen, which establish uniform standards for their members.

CHOOSING A NURSERY   Perhaps the simplest way to get trees, particularly if you are in the market for only one or a few, is to go to a good local nursery. A nurseryman doing business in your area knows what trees will grow best there. Generally he will not even have for sale a tree that is a poor bet for local conditions of climate or soil. In addition to helping you select the right tree, many good nurseries offer free landscaping advice and will send a man to look over your yard and make suggestions. They will also plant your purchases, if you wish, for a fee that usually runs about 50 to 60 per cent of the tree's cost (higher if the crew cannot get a truck close to the site, or if special rock or drainage problems are encountered). Many nurseries guarantee for a year any tree they plant and replace it if it dies; they also guarantee the good health of a tree they deliver for you to plant yourself, and take it back if it proves to have been diseased.

Choosing a good nursery is not difficult. Ask friends and neighbors for recommendations and visit several local nurseries. If a place appears orderly and well kept, if its trees are labeled with their botanical and common names and their prices, if they seem well watered and free of broken branches and wilted leaves, and if guarantees are cheerfully given, you probably will be in good hands.

HOW TREES ARE SOLD   Trees are sold in three forms. One is, in nurserymen's lingo, bare-rooted, that is, with the soil removed from the roots. If you buy from a mail-order house, the tree will be shipped in this fashion,

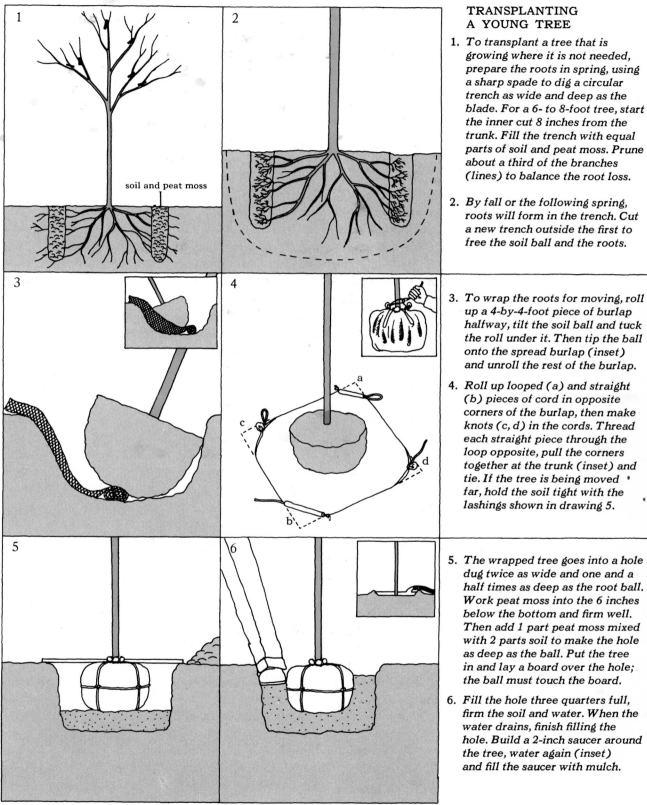

TRANSPLANTING A YOUNG TREE

1. *To transplant a tree that is growing where it is not needed, prepare the roots in spring, using a sharp spade to dig a circular trench as wide and deep as the blade. For a 6- to 8-foot tree, start the inner cut 8 inches from the trunk. Fill the trench with equal parts of soil and peat moss. Prune about a third of the branches (lines) to balance the root loss.*

2. *By fall or the following spring, roots will form in the trench. Cut a new trench outside the first to free the soil ball and the roots.*

3. *To wrap the roots for moving, roll up a 4-by-4-foot piece of burlap halfway, tilt the soil ball and tuck the roll under it. Then tip the ball onto the spread burlap (inset) and unroll the rest of the burlap.*

4. *Roll up looped (a) and straight (b) pieces of cord in opposite corners of the burlap, then make knots (c, d) in the cords. Thread each straight piece through the loop opposite, pull the corners together at the trunk (inset) and tie. If the tree is being moved far, hold the soil tight with the lashings shown in drawing 5.*

5. *The wrapped tree goes into a hole dug twice as wide and one and a half times as deep as the root ball. Work peat moss into the 6 inches below the bottom and firm well. Then add 1 part peat moss mixed with 2 parts soil to make the hole as deep as the ball. Put the tree in and lay a board over the hole; the ball must touch the board.*

6. *Fill the hole three quarters full, firm the soil and water. When the water drains, finish filling the hole. Build a 2-inch saucer around the tree, water again (inset) and fill the saucer with mulch.*

ODD JOBS FOR TREES

Many of the trees ordinarily thought of as garden ornaments are also valuable sources of wood with special qualities. The flowering dogwood is an essential in textile weaving—virtually all the shuttles on looms are made of its densely textured wood, which retains a glossy smoothness that causes almost no wear to thread. The wood of the persimmon is used for the heads of golf clubs because its interlocking grain resists splitting. Chopping bowls, gunstocks and rollers in glass factories are made of the tough pepperidge, or black tupelo. The bark of the canoe birch is no longer used to make canoes, but its wood is turned into spools, laundry clothespins and toothpicks.

wrapped in protective materials such as damp sphagnum moss and plastic. Bare-rooted trees are the least expensive and, because of their light weight, the easiest to ship and to handle for planting when they arrive. But bare-rooted trees can be shipped and planted only when they are leafless and dormant, and in many areas this requirement limits the times they are available. Moreover, their roots must never be permitted to dry out, even for a few minutes, or they will die.

Because bare-rooted transplanting limits the selling season so drastically, many local nurserymen have all but stopped offering bare-rooted trees, selling their trees instead in one of the two other forms, called container grown and balled and burlaped. Container-grown trees look like potted plants; their roots are in soil in containers—metal or plastic cans or wooden baskets—and they may be actively growing rather than dormant. They are started in open fields and shifted to containers when close to salable size, or started in small containers and transplanted to larger ones as they grow. One of the advantages of trees in containers is that their roots are not in danger of drying out, so if planting has to be delayed, they can remain safely in their containers for an indefinite period. Another advantage is that they are transplanted into the garden along with the soil in which they have been growing, and for this reason suffer little shock from being moved.

But the containers limit their size: a tree in a container small enough for easy handling, described by nurserymen as 1 gallon sized, will not be more than 3 to 4 feet high—if it is larger, its roots are probably seriously overcrowded. Bigger containers hold bigger trees but are more difficult to transport—a 15-gallon container requires two strong men and a truck.

In the third form in which trees are sold, balled and burlaped, they are dug from the nursery field with a ball of soil around their roots and this ball is tightly wrapped in burlap. Balled-and-burlaped trees cost about the same as container-grown trees, but have a special advantage: large trees, as the frontispiece picture of this chapter shows, can safely be moved B&B, as the nurserymen call it. You can get a good-sized shade tree—one that will give adequate shade almost immediately—but the planting job will be more than you can handle yourself. Even a small ball of moist soil —one 18 inches across and a foot deep usually accompanies a tree 8 to 10 feet high—weighs over 150 pounds, enough to give a strong man a sore back if he is inexperienced. Any balled-and-burlaped tree over 10 to 15 feet tall is best planted by nurserymen, who have the know-how and equipment for working with heavy loads. If you do bring home a smaller balled-and-burlaped tree for planting yourself and find that you cannot get it into the ground right away, protect the ball of earth from drying out by heaping a mulch of wood chips or peat moss up around the sides and watering the mulch occasionally to keep it lightly moistened.

In shopping for trees, regardless of how they are sold, reject any with broken branches—usually a sign of improper handling—or any with injured bark, which is an open invitation to disease. If the trees are in leaf, pass up those with wilted leaves—they have been inadequately watered or the root systems are poor—and also refuse trees with leaves smaller than those the variety usually bears, for abnormally small leaves are another indication of inadequate roots. Look at the color of the leaves; on a good tree they will be a healthy green, a vigorous shade unmistakable even to a neophyte.

If it is at all possible, examine the roots themselves to make doubly sure they are growing in a thick, unbroken tangle. On bare-rooted trees, pull aside the moss packing and look at the roots. If the tree is in a small container, ask the nurseryman to lift it out far enough so that you can see the roots; he can do so by inverting the container. A good root system will fill the can's soil. If the container is too big to invert, have the nurseryman tilt it; roots visible through the drainage holes indicate a well-developed root system. When examining a balled-and-burlaped tree, feel the ball of soil. If it is loose

PROVIDING DRAINAGE THROUGH HARDPAN

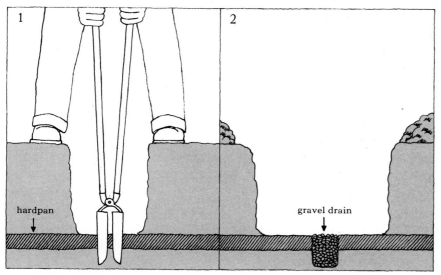

If you encounter impermeable soil —hardpan—at the bottom of a planting hole, use a post-hole digger to break through for a drainage hole. Cut a 6- to 8-inch-wide opening into the looser soil beneath.

Fill the hole through the hardpan with coarse gravel; after the tree is planted, water will drain through the gravel into the subsoil rather than collect on top of the hardpan, where it could rot the roots.

and soft instead of tightly packed and hard, some of the tree's roots are probably broken and others are loose in the soil; the air pockets formed around roots when they lose close contact with the soil make them dry out easily, and any tree with dried-out roots is likely to die. Ask to see another specimen or go to another nursery.

WHEN TO PLANT

Properly balled-and-burlaped and container-grown trees may be planted at almost any time of the year, including winter in areas where the soil does not freeze too hard to be dug. Bare-rooted trees, because they can be planted successfully only when they are dormant, must be set in the ground when bare and leafless; in northern areas frozen ground usually prevents winter planting, so they can be planted only in spring or fall. Exceptions to these general rules are noted in the encyclopedia section.

Even if you have a choice of several seasons for planting a tree, there are advantages to spring or fall planting. A tree planted in spring has many months in which to establish itself before harsh winter weather arrives. On the other hand, many gardeners prefer fall. The soil is then more likely to be easy to dig—moist, but not muddy and sticky—so that the hole-making chore is lightened. Equally important is temperature. The soil is still warm and new roots will sprout even after the tree has ceased summer growth and has lost its leaves; the following spring these new roots will give the tree a head start over trees being planted at winter's end.

MATCHING TREE TO SOIL

The trees offered by a reliable nursery will generally meet the requirements described above. But there are other requirements that the nursery can only advise you about; they relate to the suitability of particular kinds of trees to the soil in your yard. Two soil characteristics are often ignored: acidity and moisture.

Most trees grow best in a soil that is slightly acid, with a pH of 6 to 7 (measured on a scale that runs from 0 for extremely acid to 14 for extremely alkaline, with 7 as the neutral point). The exceptions to this rule, again, are noted in the encyclopedia entries. You can generally determine whether the soil in your area is suitable for a particular species of tree simply by going around the neighborhood and seeing whether or not trees of that type have been planted and are in good health. If you cannot find any specimens locally, ask a nurseryman or make a soil test, either with a simple kit available at garden centers or by sending a soil sample to your county agricultural extension service for testing.

If the soil is unsuitable for the species you have chosen and you have your heart set on growing the tree anyway, you can adjust the pH of the soil, raising it by working in ground limestone or lowering it by adding ground sulfur. But to do the growing tree any good you will have to dig the limestone or sulfur into the ground to a depth of at least 18 inches, over an area wide enough to accommodate the spreading roots. You will also have to test the soil every few years and add more limestone or sulfur if the pH reverts to its natural level. Most people are satisfied to pick suitable species in the first place and save all this trouble.

It is also best to avoid buying trees whose moisture requirements are not suited to the location you have in mind for them. Soil drainage can be modified, however, and although the job is a difficult one—generally requiring professional help to lay composition piping underground—once completed it is permanent. Most trees like moist but well-drained soil, though willows, red maples and certain others thrive in wet spots. But be wary of willows and poplars if you must place them near a sewer line, septic field or well; their far-ranging roots will seek out such water sources and may clog or break pipes, necessitating costly repairs.

When you have picked a proper spot, follow the nurserymen's adage and dig a "$10 hole for a $5 tree," that is, one twice the diameter of the root ball and one and a half times its depth (*drawings, page 27*). If you should encounter hardpan, a layer of clay soil that is almost rock hard, at the bottom of the hole, you will have a drainage problem—water will accumulate in the hole and eventually drown the tree's roots. You can remedy this situation fairly easily, as I have on occasion: simply dig through the hardpan and put in a core of coarse gravel as a drain (*drawings, page 29*). Whether there is hardpan or not, improve the drainage at the bottom of the hole by adding organic material. Work peat moss or leaf mold into the 6 inches below the bottom of the planting hole and firm the soil well with your feet so that the tree will not settle; it must not rest any deeper than it grew at the nursery.

At this stage it is far better to add no fertilizer than to use the wrong kind, for young tree roots are very sensitive to injury from fertilizers. For fast, vigorous growth, however, you can use a judicious amount of slow-acting, nonburning fertilizers such as bone meal, cottonseed meal or a chemical tree or lawn fertilizer that has 50 per cent or more of its nitrogen in slow-release form (*Chapter 3*). My favorite fertilizer for a newly planted tree is bone meal, which is entirely organic and high in phosphorus, a stimulator of strong roots. I dig it in deep into the bottom of the hole and mix some into the soil alongside the root ball, using a total of ½ pound for an 8- to 10-foot tree and 1 pound for larger trees. If you use cottonseed meal, also organic, apply about twice that amount; if you use slow-acting chemical fertilizers, apply a total of ½ cup of a formula such as 10-6-4 to an 8- to 10-foot tree, 1 cup to a larger tree.

The proper planting procedure for a balled-and-burlaped tree

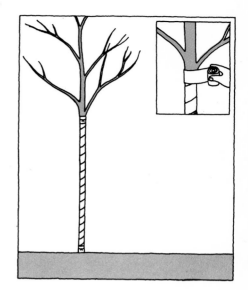

WRAPPING A YOUNG TREE

To protect the tender bark of a young tree from the drying effects of sun and from the nibbling of insects, mice and rabbits, wind tree-wrap tape up the trunk after planting. Take a couple of snug turns around the base of the trunk and spiral the tape upward, overlapping layers by about an inch (inset) so that rain will run off. Wrap the trunk as far as the crotch of the first branch, then cut the tape off the roll. Tie cotton cord at the top and bottom to secure the ends of the tape. The tape, available in 3- or 4-inch-wide rolls at garden stores, is made up of two layers of kraft paper with asphalt between and is both stretchable and waterproof. Leave the wrapping on the tree trunk for about two years.

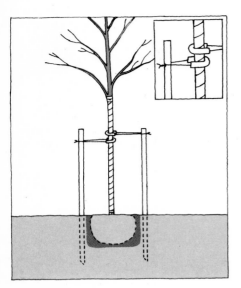

STAKING A YOUNG TREE

To help a newly planted tree stand straight and resist wind, brace it between a pair of wooden stakes about 6 feet long driven 2 feet into the ground a few inches beyond the root ball at either side of the trunk. Fasten the trunk to each stake separately, using lengths of flexible heavy-gauge wire threaded through short lengths of old garden hose to protect the bark (inset). Loop each length around the trunk, then twist one end of the wire to hold it in place; secure the other end around a notch near the top of the stake. Leave the stakes in place for two or three years until the root system becomes well enough established to anchor the tree in the ground.

is shown in the drawings on page 27. The planting of a container-grown tree is almost identical, except that you must make sure to remove the container (it is surprising how many people neglect to do this and wind up strangling their trees). If the tree is in a metal container, have the nurseryman cut its sides and tie them temporarily with twine; when you are ready to plant, cut the twine and pull away the two halves. If the tree is in a plastic container or basket, ask the nurseryman to loosen the soil ball so that it will slide out easily when the container is turned on its side. After taking a tree from its container and setting it in the prepared hole, straighten out and spread any tangled roots so that they will not constrict the tree as it grows. Always handle a container-grown or balled-and-burlaped tree by the soil ball. Never use the trunk as a handle, for you may seriously injure the tree by breaking off fragile feeder roots or loosening the whole root system in the soil ball.

The planting of a bare-rooted tree is similar to that of a container-grown or balled-and-burlaped tree, except that you must keep the roots moist until the moment they go into the soil. As soon as you remove the wrapping, plunge the roots into a pail of water or, if they are too large for a pail, cover them with wet burlap or a mound of wet hay or soil. Then set the tree in the hole on a base of prepared soil—no harm is done if you hold a bare-rooted tree by its trunk. Next trim off any broken roots and spread the rest. Have someone hold the tree upright while you toss a few shovelfuls of topsoil and peat moss into the hole, then work the mixture in with your hands—under, around and over the roots. As with container-grown and balled-and-burlaped trees, make sure the tree is planted at the precise depth it grew in the nursery (on a bare-rooted tree the soil line is marked by a difference of coloration on the bark, and this point should be made level with the surrounding ground). Add or remove some of the topsoil and peat-moss mixture until the tree is at the right depth, and jiggle the tree up and down to settle the mixture around the roots. Firm the soil with your feet, being careful not to press hard enough to break any roots. Then add and firm more topsoil mix a little at a time, until the hole is filled to within 3 to 4 inches of ground level. Fill the rest with water, and when the water has soaked in, fill in with more soil to ground level and firm gently. The last steps in the planting process are the same for all trees: the building of a low dike or saucer around the tree to hold water, as shown in the drawings, and the mulching of the surface to conserve moisture in the soil and discourage the growth of weeds.

COMPLETING THE JOB   At this point the job may look finished, but it is not quite. Three important steps remain to be taken, the first of which is an initial pruning to get the tree off to a proper start. Any tree that is moved bare-rooted or balled and burlaped has lost part of its root system in the process. To counteract this loss, cut away at least one third of the tree's top growth, bringing the top growth into balance with the remaining roots; otherwise, the roots will prove inadequate to their burden and the tree will die back from the top. Do not simply remove one third of each branch; instead, totally remove weak or poorly placed branches making up about one third of the tree's top growth, but be careful not to cut off the top main stem, or leader. Container-grown trees do not require this type of survival pruning at plantingtime, since they suffer virtually no root damage when they are moved.

A second essential task is the wrapping of the young tree's trunk to conserve moisture and protect the bark, both from strong sun and wind and from insects and rodents. Garden centers sell special tree wrap, a type of waterproof corrugated paper that expands as the tree grows. Wrap the trunk from the ground to the crotch of the first major branches *(drawing, page 31)*, then tie the top and bottom ends of the material with cotton twine, but not too tightly or you will restrict the flow of sap. Leave the tree wrap in place for about two years, then remove it.

The third step is the staking of the tree to hold it steady until the roots are established in their new soil. For the average young tree, one under 2½ to 3 inches in diameter, the best supports are a pair of 2-by-2-inch wooden posts 6 feet long. Drive these stakes into the ground parallel to the tree just beyond the roots, then lash the tree to the stakes with wire and protective pieces of garden hose *(drawing, left)*. For trees larger than 3 inches in diameter, a firm anchoring system can be made by driving into the ground three short wooden stakes, spaced equally around the tree, then running wires at 45-degree angles from the stakes to the tree, and finally looping the wires, sheathed in hose, around the trunk above a low branch. Whether you use stakes or guy wires, remove them after they have done their job, which will be in about two years.

When the tree wrap and the stakes have been removed, you can continue to protect the lower trunk of a young tree from such hazards as a misguided lawn mower and tricycles—as well as from nibbling rabbits and mice that sometimes make the tender bark a part of their winter diet—by wrapping a loose collar of wire mesh around the base *(drawing, right)*. For the first year after planting, it is advisable to water the tree once a week during the growing season, especially if a substantial rain has not fallen, and to check occasionally to see if the stakes and wires are still firmly in place. Aside from that, you can leave your new addition alone to get settled in its surroundings, until it is ready to be trained into the kind of mature tree you want *(Chapter 3)*.

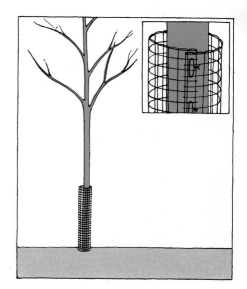

PROTECTING A TREE TRUNK WITH WIRE MESH

A mesh collar will prevent the bark of a young tree from being damaged by lawn mowers or bark-chewing rabbits and mice, particularly after the tree wrap has been removed. Make the collar from a 2-foot-wide roll of the ½-inch wire mesh known as hardware cloth, cutting a length to form a collar big enough to stand an inch or 2 away from the tree on all sides. Secure the collar at intervals with short lengths of wire threaded through the mesh and twisted into tight loops (inset). If the tree is ringed with a permanent mulch, push the mesh into the soil. If grass grows right up to the trunk, let the collar stand loosely so that it can be raised for hand-clipping around the base of the tree.

The special beauties of trees

Everyone who has looked more than once at trees has at least a few favorite images tucked away in the back of his mind: the fluffy burst of crab apple blossoms in spring sunshine *(right),* the exclamation points of a row of poplars ascending a hillside, the dappled pattern of maple leaves softly moving in the summer breeze outside a window. A list of such visual pleasures could be endless, for each tree creates its own particular appeal; the differences among species are multiplied by the individual pattern of growth, by the setting, by the time of day and the season of the year.

All trees have their virtues—few tree lovers consider any tree downright ugly—but there are certain species that over the years have proved superior choices for their beauty and usefulness in home landscapes. One of the favorites—in fact the most popular flowering tree in the United States—is the crab apple, beloved in many species and varieties for its combination of many desirable attributes. It is relatively small as trees go, most types reaching a height of 15 to 25 feet moderately rapidly, and thus fits soon and well into the small-scaled settings of surburban gardens. Its masses of fragrant flowers are a breathtaking event of spring; its attractive leaves in summer can be used to shade a small terrace; clusters of colorful red or yellow fruit ripen early and last on the tree well into fall. Although most varieties do not present as notable a blaze of autumn leaf color as some other trees *(pages 64-79),* their spreading branches lend grace to the winter scene.

Many-faceted though it is, the crab apple cannot, of course, be an all-purpose tree; no tree is. The best gardens contain several kinds of trees, each chosen for its special virtues—flowers, foliage color in fall, attractive bark or branches in winter. Some of the species most noted for a particular attribute—form, leaves, flowers, fruit or bark—are shown in photographs on the following pages; accompanying each group of pictured examples are lists of other trees notable in that respect. Where and how to grow them—and many other fine trees—are described in the encyclopedia beginning on page 89.

For two weeks in spring the Japanese crab apple is a cascade of pink blossoms that nearly hide its branches.

Japanese flowering cherry

Shapes for form and function

Trees come in all shapes and sizes, from conical to rounded to spreading, from stiffly upright or columnar to the downward-arching form known as weeping. And the shape a sapling develops as it matures is often a key to its best use. Weeping trees such as willows, for example, make graceful accents on a lawn or near a pond or stream. Spreading types like the silk tree can emphasize a long, low roof line or provide a terrace with shade. Slim-growing species like poplars, on the other hand, are better suited for vertical accents and narrow sites.

WEEPING SHAPE: Babylon weeping willow

WEEPING SHAPE

BABYLON WEEPING WILLOW

CHINESE ELM

COCKSPUR HAWTHORN

CUT-LEAVED EUROPEAN WHITE BIRCH

GOLDEN WEEPING WILLOW

RED JADE CRAB APPLE

WEEPING EUROPEAN BEECH

WEEPING HIGAN CHERRY

WEEPING MULBERRY

WISCONSIN WEEPING WILLOW

YOUNG'S EUROPEAN WHITE BIRCH

SPREADING SHAPE

AMUR CORK TREE

CHINESE CHESTNUT

DOROTHEA CRAB APPLE

FLOWERING DOGWOOD

JAPANESE CRAB APPLE

KATHERINE CRAB APPLE

KOUSA DOGWOOD

KWANZAN ORIENTAL CHERRY

ROYAL POINCIANA

SILK TREE

WHITE OAK

SPREADING SHAPE: silk tree

CONICAL SHAPE: sorrel tree

COLUMNAR SHAPE: Lombardy poplar

ROUNDED SHAPE: Rivers purple beech

CONICAL SHAPE

AMERICAN HOP HORNBEAM

CUCUMBER TREE

EUROPEAN WHITE BIRCH

KOREAN MOUNTAIN ASH

LITTLE-LEAVED LINDEN

MERRILL MAGNOLIA

PACIFIC DOGWOOD

PEPPERIDGE

PIN OAK

SORREL TREE

SWEET GUM

COLUMNAR SHAPE

AMANOGAWA ORIENTAL CHERRY

BOLLEANA POPLAR

COLUMNAR NORWAY MAPLE

COLUMNAR RED MAPLE

LOMBARDY POPLAR

PYRAMIDAL ENGLISH OAK

PYRAMIDAL EUROPEAN HORNBEAM

PYRAMIDAL EUROPEAN WHITE BIRCH

TEMPLE'S UPRIGHT SUGAR MAPLE

ROUNDED SHAPE

AMUR MAPLE

ARNOLD CRAB APPLE

EUROPEAN BEECH

FLOWERING ASH

GREEN ASH

JAPANESE MAPLE

NORWAY MAPLE

RIVERS PURPLE BEECH

RUBY HORSE CHESTNUT

SAUCER MAGNOLIA

WHITE ASH

WHITE MULBERRY

Leaves for pattern and color

Botanists categorize leaves as simple, meaning one blade on each stem, and compound, meaning many leaflets arranged along or around a single stem, and sometimes add as a subdivision leaves that are edged with lobes. The technical terms have practical consequences, for simple types generally cast dense shade, while compound leaves break up sunlight into dappled shade. But shade is not the only factor to consider; colors vary, too. Even in summer some trees have silver or yellow leaves, others red, purple or almost-black ones *(far right)*.

SIMPLE LEAVES

DOGWOOD

GINKGO

LINDEN

MAGNOLIA

PEPPERIDGE

REDBUD

SOURWOOD

LOBED LEAVES

HAWTHORN (most varieties)

MAPLE

OAK (most varieties)

PLANE TREE

SASSAFRAS

SWEET GUM

COMPOUND LEAVES

ASH

HONEY LOCUST

HORSE CHESTNUT

KENTUCKY COFFEE TREE

SILK TREE

TREE OF HEAVEN

YELLOWWOOD

COLORFUL LEAVES

Red to purple

BLIREIANA PLUM

FASSEN'S BLACK NORWAY MAPLE

JAPANESE MAPLE (most varieties)

LEMOINE PURPLE CRAB APPLE

PISSARD PLUM

RIVERS PURPLE BEECH

SCHWEDLER NORWAY MAPLE

White-edged

SILVER-LEAVED BOX ELDER

VARIEGATED NORWAY MAPLE

Silvery

SILVER LINDEN

SILVER MAPLE

WHITE POPLAR

LOBED LEAF: Japanese maple

SIMPLE LEAF: eastern redbud   **COMPOUND LEAF:** common horse chestnut   **COLORED LEAF:** Fassen's Black Norway maple

LOBED LEAF: thread-leaved Japanese maple   **SIMPLE LEAF:** ginkgo   **COMPOUND LEAF:** silk tree

Flowers to welcome spring

Spring-blossoming trees are the prize ornaments of many a garden, whether set off alone or used like the Kwanzan Oriental cherry below to mirror a planting of spring flowers. Many begin to bloom at an early age, some crab apples when they are only 3 to 4 feet tall. And though most blooms last for only two weeks or so, it is possible to have trees in flower all spring by planting both early kinds such as eastern redbuds and later ones such as ruby horse chestnuts. As a bonus, several add a notable fragrance to the visual delights of their blossoms.

SPRING-FLOWERING TREES

White flowers
BRADFORD PEAR
COMMON HORSE CHESTNUT
CRAB APPLE (fragrant)
DOUBLE-FLOWERED MAZZARD CHERRY
FLOWERING DOGWOOD
FLOWERING PEACH
HAWTHORN (most varieties)
MERRILL MAGNOLIA (fragrant)
SERVICEBERRY (most varieties)
SILVER BELL (most varieties)
STAR MAGNOLIA
YOSHINO CHERRY (fragrant)
YULAN MAGNOLIA (fragrant)

Pink flowers
BLIREIANA PLUM (fragrant)
CRAB APPLE (fragrant)
FLOWERING PEACH
HIGAN CHERRY
ORIENTAL CHERRY
PINK FLOWERING DOGWOOD
RUBY HORSE CHESTNUT
SARGENT CHERRY
SAUCER MAGNOLIA

Yellow flowers
JERUSALEM THORN
LABURNUM
TULIP TREE

Red flowers
CRAB APPLE
CRIMSON CLOUD HAWTHORN
FLOWERING PEACH
PAUL'S SCARLET HAWTHORN

Purple flowers
CHINABERRY
EASTERN REDBUD
EMPRESS TREE
SHARP-LEAVED JACARANDA

Kwanzan Oriental cherry

Scheidecker crab apple

pink flowering dogwood

eastern redbud

Waterer laburnum

ruby horse chestnut

Flowers for summer and fall

Though many gardeners associate flowering trees with spring-time, almost as many species blossom in summer and a few flower in fall. Most of these late bloomers grow fast—a notable exception is the slow-maturing Kousa dogwood *(right)*, cherished because it extends the blossoming season of dogwoods an extra month—and are primarily planted as shade trees; flowers may be an unexpected dividend. Many of them have white flowers that lend a cool note to a hot day, and as a group they are even more fragrant than spring-flowering types.

Chinese chestnut

western catalpa

fringe tree

Kousa dogwood

SUMMER-FLOWERING TREES

White flowers

BLACK LOCUST (fragrant)

CHINESE CHESTNUT (fragrant)

COMMON CATALPA

CRIMEAN LINDEN (fragrant)

FRAGRANT EPAULETTE TREE (fragrant)

FRINGE TREE (fragrant)

JAPANESE SNOWBELL (fragrant)

JAPANESE TREE LILAC

KOUSA DOGWOOD

LITTLE-LEAVED LINDEN (fragrant)

SILVER LINDEN (fragrant)

SORREL TREE (fragrant)

WESTERN CATALPA

YELLOWWOOD (fragrant)

Yellow flowers

CUCUMBER TREE

GOLDEN SHOWER (fragrant)

GOLDEN-RAIN TREE

HONEY MESQUITE

TREE OF HEAVEN

Pink to purple flowers

IDAHO LOCUST (reddish purple)

ROYAL POINCIANA (red)

SILK TREE (pink)

FALL-FLOWERING TREES

White flowers

FRANKLINIA (fragrant)

JAPANESE PAGODA TREE

Pink flowers

AUTUMN-FLOWERING HIGAN CHERRY

yellowwood

Japanese pagoda tree

An array of ornamental fruits

The myriad fruits that hold the seeds of trees are often as eye-catching as the flowers they follow. Some, like the Amur maple's winged seeds, cling to the branches until late fall; the bright red fruit of the hawthorn often remains colorful all through the winter. A few are even decorative enough to bring indoors: the lanternlike pods of the golden-rain tree, for example, are prized in dried winter bouquets, and some gardeners spray-paint the spiked balls of the sweet gum to make gold or silver ornaments for Christmas trees.

WINGED SEEDS

ASHES (green to brown)

CHINESE WINGNUT (green to brown)

HORNBEAM (brown)

LINDENS (green to brown)

MAPLES (red to green)

TREE OF HEAVEN (orange red)

BERRY OR BERRYLIKE FRUIT

AMUR CORK TREE (blue)

CHINABERRY (yellow)

CRAB APPLE (red, yellow, green)

DOGWOOD (red)

FRINGE TREE (blue)

HAWTHORN (red)

MOUNTAIN ASH (yellow, orange, red)

MULBERRY (pink, red, purple)

SERVICEBERRY (red, purple)

POD OR PODLIKE FRUIT

CATALPA (brown)

GOLDEN SHOWER (brownish black)

GOLDEN-RAIN TREE (pink, orange)

JAPANESE PAGODA TREE (yellow)

LABURNUM (brown)

REDBUD (pinkish brown)

SILK TREE (brown)

YELLOWWOOD (brown)

BALL- OR NUT-LIKE FRUIT

BEECH (brown)

BUCKEYE (brown)

CHINESE CHESTNUT (brown)

CHINESE PISTACHE (red, turning purple)

HORSE CHESTNUT (brown)

OAK (brown)

OSAGE ORANGE (yellowish green)

PECAN (brown)

PLANE TREE (brown)

SWEET GUM (green, turning brown)

WALNUT (brown)

WINGED SEED: Amur maple

BERRY: chinaberry

POD: golden-rain tree

BALL: sweet gum

BERRY: mountain ash

BERRY: Zumi crab apple

The unexpected beauty of bark

Birches and cherries are the trees that are most often chosen for their bark, but many others have decorative trunks and branches—an asset especially worth notice in winter when leaves, flowers and fruits are gone. On most species the bark becomes richly textured as it stretches and breaks with the trunk's increasing girth. Some barks become deeply furrowed, like the black locust below; others, like the Chinese elm, flake off in patches to produce a mottled effect; still others, like the canoe birch, peel off in sheets, leaving horizontal ridges.

THORNY BARK

CASTOR ARALIA

HAWTHORN

OSAGE ORANGE

FURROWED BARK

AMUR CORK TREE

BLACK WALNUT

MULBERRY

SASSAFRAS

SWEET GUM

TULIP TREE

FLAKING OR PEELING BARK

CANOE BIRCH

CHINESE ELM

PAPERBARK MAPLE

PERSIAN PARROTIA

PLANE TREE

RUSSIAN OLIVE

SMOOTH BARK

BEECH

ENGLISH WALNUT (when young)

KOREAN MOUNTAIN ASH

SAUCER MAGNOLIA

SERVICEBERRY

YELLOWWOOD

COLORED BARK

BEECH (gray)

CANOE BIRCH (white)

CUCUMBER TREE (gray)

EUROPEAN WHITE BIRCH (white)

GRAY BIRCH (white)

KENTUCKY COFFEE TREE (black)

PAPERBARK CHERRY (red)

SARGENT CHERRY (red to brown)

SAUCER MAGNOLIA (gray)

WHITE ALDER (white to brown)

WHITE POPLAR (greenish white)

THORNY: castor aralia

COLORED: paperbark cherry

FURROWED: black locust

FLAKING: paperbark maple

FLAKING: Chinese elm

COLORED: European white birch

COLORED, PEELING: canoe birch

Feeding, pruning and spraying 3

Not long ago in Virginia I visited friends who lived in a well-planned development: the curving streets conformed to the contours of the countryside and the trees that lined them had been wisely chosen—they were willow oaks, easy to grow and suited by nature to the region. The trees had been planted in front of all the houses in the development at the same time, about five years before, and you would have expected them to look pretty much alike. They did not. Some were pathetic—they were hardly taller than when they had been set out and they extended thin, shriveled branches sparsely clothed with yellowish leaves, or bare and dead ones, victims of an ice storm many months earlier. Other trees were more vigorous, but resembled big, rambling bushes rather than well-groomed shade trees —branches sprouting close to the ground had become competing trunks, and low-growing branches obscured driveways or walks, posing traffic hazards.

But some homes had trees that were straight and tall, with fresh, healthy leaves and strong new growth, already giving shade and an aura of settled stability to a site that had been a bare field a few years earlier. My old horticulture professor could have used the place for a field demonstration in a course in tree culture. The condition of each tree strikingly reflected the care—or lack of care—that the tree had received from the householder whose property it fronted (neither the developer nor the town had assumed the responsibility, leaving it up to individuals). The healthy, handsome trees had been fed, watered and pruned for their appearance as well as their health. The vigorous but unkempt trees had been fed and watered, but never pruned. The starvelings had been left to fend for themselves. Even if someone went to their rescue and began to give them the attention they so sorely needed, they would be a long time catching up with their luckier fellows, for the first five years of a tree's life after planting can be as important as the first five years of a child's.

The situation I saw along the streets near my friend's house

Trees in a New York garden are given a dose of dormant oil to smother scale insects and the eggs of other pests. The oil is applied in early spring with a spray rig like the one shown or a garden hose and siphon sprayer.

is typical of neighborhoods everywhere. Most gardeners lavish care on their roses and petunias, but all too many believe trees can get along on their own. A friend to whom I commented on this neglect recently replied, "But who feeds and waters trees in a forest?" In a forest, where survival is more important than beauty, trees live —and die—by what nature provides. If a tree cannot compete with others for sunlight, it succumbs and no one minds very much; if a limb breaks off in a storm, a tree heals itself if it can or ends up a rotting mass on the ground, to be replaced by others. But domesticated trees are grown by homeowners for their beauty and each one is expected not merely to survive but to become a splendid specimen. It is true that garden trees get more beneficial sunlight than those in a forest, but they encounter handicaps that their wild counterparts do not. Trees in a forest grow with a permanent blanket of leaves beneath them that insulates the soil from winter cold and summer heat, conserving moisture and creating a stable environment for root growth. The leaves, as they decay into leaf mold or humus, also become a source of nutrients that gradually become available to the feeder roots. Trees planted on a suburban lawn, however, have little natural organic matter to nurture and protect them— gardeners rake away the fallen leaves to save their lawns from suffocation as well as to keep them neat. Trees close to sidewalks and roads also lack adequate soil, water and air for their roots. Living under such unnatural conditions, they can attain beauty and health only if they are properly fed and watered and knowledgeably pruned to maintain their vigor as well as their looks.

WATERING TREES   To get young trees off to a good start, they should be watered once a week during the growing season of the first year after planting. In hot, arid regions such as the Southwest, older, established trees may also need occasional watering. Elsewhere, established trees usually do not require added moisture except during a summer dry spell that lasts a month or more, when watering will give them a fresh, healthy look and build up their moisture reserve to carry them through the winter.

Whenever you water any tree, do it thoroughly, soaking the ground so that the moisture will penetrate deep down to the feeder roots. Repeated superficial sprinkling may cause the roots to grow closer to the surface, resulting in a shallow root network that loses its effectiveness as an intake system and anchor; in extreme cases gradual erosion may expose these shallow roots. The best tools for watering are canvas soil-soaking hoses or perforated plastic hoses, both of which release a steady, diffused flow of water that can penetrate deep. Let the water run at low pressure until the soil is saturated down to a level of 1½ to 2 feet—which may take several hours, particularly in the case of hard clay soils. If you use a perforated plastic hose, face the holes down so the water will seep directly into the soil instead of shooting upward wastefully. Ordinary garden hose may be used alone if you keep the flow slow enough so that the force of the stream will not bore a hole in the ground, washing away the soil and exposing roots.

But be careful not to overwater, for too much moisture is as bad as too little. Some homeowners overwater their trees inadvertently in the course of watering their lawns, particularly if they leave lawn sprinklers going all day or have sprinklers that turn on and off by the clock. A long "on" setting may keep the grass lush, but if the soil's drainage cannot cope with the flood, tree roots may eventually drown and rot. If you use a sprinkler, watch out for standing pools of water around the bases of your trees and reduce the length of the watering period if they persist.

Although most trees will get along in reasonably fertile soil without special feeding, they will grow better, look better and stay healthier if you give some attention to their nutritional demands. Undernourished trees, like undernourished people, get sick faster and oftener than well-fed ones. The fertilizer sprinkled on the lawn to nourish the grass seldom does the trees any good; the grass gobbles up the food long before it can seep down into the deeper feeding zone of the trees' roots. So once a tree has been planted, it should be fed regularly and the food should be placed down in the ground deep enough so it can do the job.

FEEDING TREES

Trees, like other plants, need nitrogen, phosphorus and potassium. Nitrogen encourages rapid growth of the trunk and branches and the production of healthy, dark green leaves. Phosphorus stimulates vigorous root growth, which is why I particularly recommended it in Chapter 2 for newly planted trees; it also induces the formation of flower buds and increases resistance to cold. Potassium helps strengthen trees, enabling them to withstand wind and ice breakage and diseases. All three elements are provided in fertilizers sold in garden supply centers. My favorite fertilizer for established trees is cottonseed meal. I like it because it releases its nutrients slowly, making them available to the roots over an extended period, and is unlikely to burn the roots. But the so-called complete chemical fertilizers, which are more generally available, are perfectly adequate if 50 per cent or more of their nitrogen content is in a slow-release form such as urea; the label on the bag specifies what form the nitrogen comes in. A good tree fertilizer is one marked 10-8-6 on its label—10 per cent nitrogen, 8 per cent phosphorus and 6 per cent potassium in various compounds—but you need not buy a special tree fertilizer if you have some lawn fertilizer left over in your tool shed or garage; most of the better grades of lawn fertilizers have their nitrogen in slow-release form, and the ratio of nitrogen to phosphorus and potassium in many such fertilizers is also satisfactory for trees. A typical formula printed on the label is 10-6-4. Any formula that is roughly in these proportions—23-19-17, for example—will provide a good balance of nutrients.

The best time to feed an established tree is early spring. The nutrients will then be available to the tree for the greater part of its growing season but will be largely used up by late summer. If too much nitrogen remains in the soil near the end of the season, it will push the trees to keep on growing; late growth never gets a chance to mature fully and thus is far more vulnerable than established growth to winter cold and wind.

HOW TO FEED A TREE
There are three ways to apply fertilizer to a tree: punch holes around it and drop in dry fertilizer, squirt nutrients into the soil with a needlelike device called an injector, or spray liquid fertilizer on the leaves. Which method or combination of methods you should use depends on the tree's situation and health as well as the amount of energy you are willing to expend.

Punching holes, the traditional method, can be hard work but in many ways it is still the best method. The dry fertilizer placed in the holes is made available to the tree steadily over an exceptionally long period, a year or more. To make the holes, you can use an ordinary crowbar or a soil auger, which resembles a giant drill bit with a T-shaped handle; both are available at larger garden supply centers or hardware stores. Professional tree men often use a heavy-duty, two-handed electric drill, which works much faster, but unless you have a lot of trees you would probably not use such a drill often enough to warrant buying one.

Before you start making the holes, prepare your fertilizer mixture. For a tree with a trunk that is less than 6 inches in diameter, allot a total of 1 to 2 pounds of dry fertilizer for each inch of diameter; for bigger trees, use 2 to 4 pounds per inch. Mix it with an equal amount of soil, sand or peat moss, or a mixture of any two of these; diluting the fertilizer in this fashion not only makes it easier to distribute evenly in each hole but also provides extra protection against burning the roots.

Feed your trees on a day in early spring when the soil is moist —it will be easier to punch holes in the ground then, and better for the trees because even the gentlest fertilizer may sometimes burn roots in dry soil. If the ground is dry and hard when you plan to feed, soak the soil thoroughly several days in advance; this will soften it, but not leave it too wet to work with. To put the fertilizer within the reach of the most roots, you will need about 10 holes for every inch of the tree's diameter. Each hole should be 18 to 24 inches deep to get the fertilizer down into the root zone. When you are ready to dig, visualize a circle around the tree at a point about one third of the way from the trunk to the outer reach, or drip line, of the branches. Visualize another circle an equal distance beyond the branches' spread. Roots sometimes reach out far from the tree, but most of the feeder roots will be concentrated in the area between the two circles, so this is where you should punch your holes, as shown in the drawings below.

Before making a hole, lift a tab of sod with a shovel and flop it aside; when you have filled the hole, the sod can go back into place, leaving the lawn unmarked. If you are using a crowbar, plunge the tool into the soil, rotate it with a stirring motion, lift it

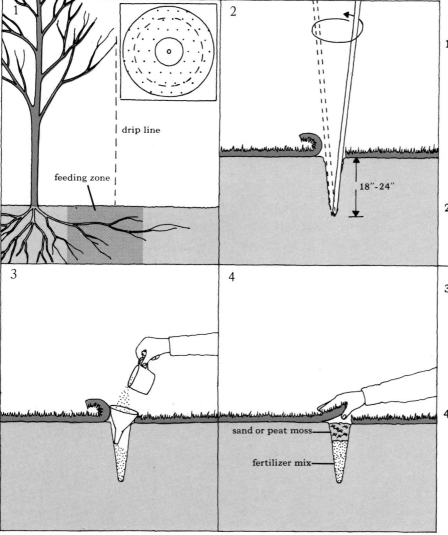

FEEDING TREE ROOTS WITH DRY FERTILIZER

1. *To get dry fertilizer down to as many roots as possible, plot a circular feeding zone that starts about a third of the distance from the trunk to the drip line and extends an equal distance beyond the drip line. Allow at least 10 feeding holes for each inch of trunk diameter, and space the holes 18 to 24 inches apart inside the feeding zone (inset).*

2. *After rolling back a tab of sod with a shovel, drive a crowbar into the ground and rotate it to make a hole 18 to 24 inches deep.*

3. *Using a large funnel, pour about a cup of fertilizer mixture into each hole—10-6-4 mixed with an equal amount of soil, coarse sand or peat moss is suitable. The funnel will guide the food into the hole, preventing it from spilling and overfertilizing nearby grass.*

4. *After filling the rest of the hole with plain peat moss, sand or soil, fold the grass tab back into place and tamp it down firmly with your foot. The tree's root system will absorb the nutrients from the dry fertilizer gradually over a period of a year or two.*

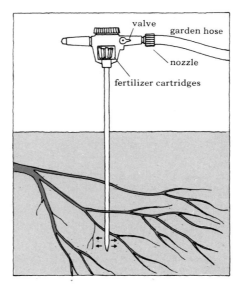

An injector-fertilizing attachment uses water from a garden hose to dissolve fertilizer from cartridges in the handle and carry the solution directly to tree roots underground. The long pipe is inserted into the ground with the valve turned on low —the water from the nozzle will help ease the pipe into the soil. The valve is then set on full for large trees but kept on low if a young tree is being treated, since a strong flow could injure tender roots. Because the water provides some lateral flow of nutrients through perforations near the tip of the pipe, the holes can be spaced 2 to 3 feet apart within the feeding zone of the tree (page 53).

and poke it in again until the hole is the required depth. If you use an auger, simply turn it in the ground and lift out the soil the screw displaces. Then use a large kitchen funnel to channel no more than a cup of the fertilizer mixture into each hole. Fill the remaining space at the top of the hole with soil, sand or peat moss—this material will prevent the fertilizer from stimulating the grass over each hole to grow into a rich green plume—and finally replace the tab of turf, tamping it down with your foot.

USING AN INJECTOR

As an alternative to filling holes with dry fertilizer, many gardeners find it easier to squirt nutrients into the soil with an injector, sometimes called a needle probe, root feeder or root-zone applicator. The injector, which is sold in inexpensive homeowners' models as well as heavy-duty professional ones, is essentially a hollow, pointed shaft, 3 to 4 feet long, topped by a cylinder into which you fit cartridges of concentrated fertilizer *(drawing, above)*. Then you attach a garden hose, turn on the water and stick the needle nose of the injector into the soil at 2- to 3-foot intervals in the tree's feeding zone. The flow of water slowly dissolves the fertilizer and the solution comes out of holes near the bottom of the needle, helping to soften the soil for easier penetration; the flow also loosens the soil laterally, spreading the fertilizer to more roots than does dry feeding in punched holes. (If you leave out the fertilizer cartridge, the injector can also be used for deep watering of tree roots.)

The main disadvantage to injector feeding is that the nutrients in the cartridge, having been dissolved in water as they were applied, drain out of the soil faster than does dry fertilizer, and a second and even a third feeding may be advisable in late spring or early summer. Do not, however, feed the tree any later than about mid-July or you may run the risk of stimulating late growth that will be vulnerable to cold weather and wind.

FOLIAR FEEDING

The third method of fertilizing a tree, called foliar feeding, consists of spraying nutrients on the leaves. The method works fast because the leaves absorb the nutrients directly instead of having to wait for them to come up from below, and it often produces dramatic results. In fact, I have known wealthy homeowners who called in tree surgeons to spray-feed all the trees on their estates a week or so before a garden party, just to give the trees a fresh glow of health. Any gardener can use this method too, and I recommend it especially in combination with punch-hole feeding or injector feeding for trees that are seriously undernourished. It is also particularly helpful for trees whose roots spread under paving and cannot be reached by punched holes or injectors.

A convenient device for foliar feeding is a siphon-type sprayer about the size of a fruit jar. The jar is filled with concentrated liquid fertilizer and attached to a garden hose, the nutrients are drawn up into the hose stream and sprayed out in dilute form. With average water pressure, the hose will reach foliage 20 to 25 feet high. The results often become evident within a week. But they will not last long because the leaves absorb and use up the nutrients so fast. Foliar feeding, unless supplemented by root feeding, may have to be repeated several times in a growing season if the tree is weak and sickly. Foliar feeding can be done at any time of the day. If manufacturer's directions are followed carefully, the concentration of chemicals in the water solution will be so diluted that it will not burn the foliage. It is normal for leaves to show a slight grayish covering of dried fertilizer after foliar sprays have been applied.

WHY AND WHAT TO PRUNE

Just as important as feeding and watering to a tree's health and appearance is proper pruning. In front of my house, where I can enjoy it from the window of my study, stands a Kentucky coffee tree. Although it is only about 20 feet tall, it casts a wide circle of shade without interfering with passersby and it does not block the view of the lawn and lower shrub plantings beyond. The tree means a great deal to me because it grew from a seed that my son, now grown, picked up beside the Mississippi River when he was six years old. But it gained its utility and attractive shape from careful pruning. It grew about a foot a year and put out many low branches during its early years. I cut off the low-growing ones as higher ones formed so that now the lowest branches are 8 feet aboveground, and I can walk under the tree and sit under it when I have a mind to.

Many trees, for lack of this kind of pruning when young, act

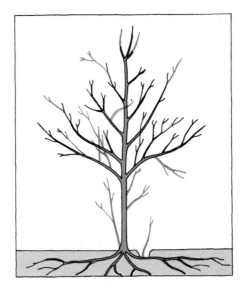

BASIC STEPS IN PRUNING

To prune a tree for health and symmetry, remove suckers and competing sprouts at the base. If you will be walking beneath the tree, cut off low-growing branches and downward-pointing ones that may eventually interfere. Next, trim away weak limbs angling close to the trunk as well as crossing branches. Also remove any upward-growing suckers, called water sprouts, which will eventually sap the tree's strength. Eliminate inward-growing branches and, on trees that normally have a single leader, or main upper stem, cut back any competitor. Finally, prune branch tips that protrude beyond the tree's basic outline.

a bit like the overgrown children of parents who were too busy to give them the proper guidance when they were young. They become annoyances if not outright hazards—their low or heavily bent branches slap you in the face every time you try to push a lawn mower under them, or they obscure a view from a terrace or they keep you from enjoying a picnic spot because there is no room under them for a table. Near a sidewalk or road the problem is even more serious; in those locations low-slung branches not only get in the way of pedestrians but may also block the view for motorists unless there is sufficient clearance; in many communities the required minimum is 12 feet for residential streets and 16 feet for roads used by trucks. You will have to remove any such low branches, because the tree is not going to raise them up for you.

A tree trunk does not grow from the bottom up, as some people think, lifting its branches as it grows. A tree develops vertically only at the top while increasing its girth below to support the weight of its growing crown; the points at which the branches spring from the trunk stay at the same levels. You can see this fact demonstrated if you drive along a country road where pastures are fenced with barbed wire nailed to trees. The fencing may have been nailed up so long ago that the trunks now envelop the wire, but it is still at the height at which it was originally placed, as you can verify from the height of wires on nearby fence posts.

The upper branches of a tree sometimes need pruning too, particularly to keep them from tangling with power and telephone wires overhead or to remove the effects of damage from wind or ice storms. The best way to handle problems such as these, of course, is to prevent damage before it happens. The key to all pruning is time-liness—it should be done early enough to prevent difficult and costly problems from developing later on in the tree's life.

The first rule of good pruning is to remove broken or diseased branches as soon as you spot them, at any time of the year, not only for appearance' sake, but also to prevent decay from entering the wound or disease from spreading. For most trees, all other pruning can be done at any time it is convenient for you without injury to the tree, although I prefer to do my routine pruning in early spring just before the buds begin to swell; at this time of year the cut spots will begin to heal immediately and will have the whole growing season in which to replace tissue.

WHEN TO PRUNE

Some trees, however, cannot be pruned in early spring without creating a mess. Maples, birches, walnuts and beeches, as well as yellowwood, bleed profusely—that is, they exude sap when cut. Bleeding does not seem to do the trees much harm—after all, sugar maples are deliberately bled year after year for maple sugar and they continue to thrive—but the exuded sap is unsightly and sticks to your pruning tools, making the job harder. So it is usually better to prune such trees in late summer of early fall when their sap runs less freely. Among other exceptions to the spring-pruning rule are such flowering trees as deciduous magnolias, which form their buds the year before they bloom. Spring pruning will reduce the number of flowers, so it is better to prune them just after they have bloomed and before new buds form. There are a few additional trees that should not be pruned in spring; their special requirements are noted in the appropriate entries in the encyclopedia section.

Successful pruning depends not only on knowing when to cut, but on using the right tools. For branches within easy reach up to ¾ inch in diameter, you can use ordinary hand pruning shears. Branches between ¾ inch and about 1¼ inches thick can be cut with long-handled lopping shears or with a pruning saw. For thicker branches you will have to use a pruning saw. A carpenter's saw is not satisfactory—it has fine teeth that make thin cuts and it will stick in live wood. The coarser teeth of pruning saws are angled outward more widely so that they make wide cuts, lessening the chance of binding. For shaping the ragged edges of larger cuts to promote healing, you will also need a sharp knife; a pruning knife, which has a hooked blade, is the most effective and easiest to use for this purpose (drawings, page 61). For cuts larger than an inch in diameter you will also need tree paint to guard against infection (do not use ordinary house paint; it is likely to be toxic to the tree).

To trim branches beyond easy reach from the ground or a

TOOLS FOR PRUNING

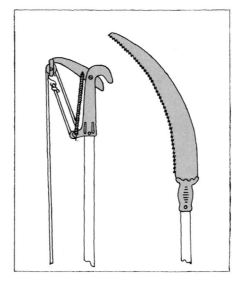

TOOLS FOR HIGH PRUNING

Special pruners and saws mounted on extension poles make it possible to remove branches high above normal reach without using a ladder. A pole pruner (far left), used for cutting branches up to an inch in diameter, has a lever-and-pulley-operated blade that cuts when the attached cord is pulled, springing open when the cord is released. A pole-mounted pruning saw (left) is used to remove larger branches. In the one illustrated, the blade has downward-facing teeth that cut on the pulling stroke. Some models have pruner and saw on one pole that can be telescoped or have sections added to extend to 12 feet.

low ladder, there are special tools mounted on extension poles. Branches up to about an inch thick can be removed with a device called a pole pruner, thicker branches with a pole-mounted pruning saw *(drawings, above)*. Pruning of any branches beyond the range of such tools, which is generally 12 to 18 feet, should be left to professional tree men. There are two tools that should not be used for pruning. Hedge shears are not designed to cut through anything larger than small hedge twigs and are useless for precise limb pruning. Neither should a chain saw be used, for it is heavy enough to become dangerous when used at the long reaches and awkward angles involved in pruning. Save your chain saw, if you have one, for cutting down whole trees, thinning out a stand of trees or cutting up firewood.

Whatever tools you acquire, buy good ones, keep them dry and oiled to prevent rusting and keep them sharp. If you know or suspect that a tree you want to prune is diseased, disinfect tools by wiping the cutting parts with 70 per cent denatured ethyl alcohol before moving from that tree to another, and again before putting the tools away. If you rent or borrow tools, you would be well advised to disinfect them the same way before using; the tree they pruned the day before for someone else may have harbored a fungus you would just as soon not inherit for your own trees.

HOW TO PRUNE   The initial pruning of a young tree at the time it is planted *(Chapter 2)* gives it a good start in life, but its second pruning—usually after it has been in the ground for a year—determines what it will look like when it is mature and how much of an asset it will be to you. There are three major objectives: to shape the young tree to your needs, to bring out the natural beauty of the species and to strengthen the structure. Before you do any cutting, try to visualize the effect on the tree's eventual appearance. Most flowering crab apples, for example, are naturally low, spreading trees, so aim to trim out crossing branches and avoid shortening wide-spreading branches too much. A Lombardy poplar, on the other hand, is naturally tall and columnar and generally will grow that way; any irregularly spreading branches that occur should be trimmed off to enhance their basic shape.

To strengthen and shape any tree, remove suckers, the fast-growing upright sprouts that appear at the tree's base or along lower branches; also cut off any branches that are so low on the trunk that they will eventually be in the way and any that threaten to become competing trunks. Two or more competing trunks make a tree particularly vulnerable to wind damage when it is mature because the crotches between such trunks are usually formed at so shallow an angle that there is little or no growing wood to bind the trunks together—in fact a growing layer of bark inexorably forces them apart. There is always the possibility that a high wind may someday break loose one trunk, destroying the tree's symmetry and leaving a gaping wound.

Higher on the trunk, decide what branches will make the best main limbs. Like competing trunks, branches with narrow crotches are vulnerable to wind, snow and ice; if possible get rid of branches that grow at narrow angles to the trunk and save those that jut out more. Shorten branches that reach out so far that they spoil the tree's symmetry. In doing so, look carefully for buds before cutting; trim the branch back to the outermost bud that points in the direction you want the tree to grow. At the top of the tree, shorten all but one of the nearly vertical stems that professional tree men call leaders. Trees with two or more leaders of equal height generally are unsightly and susceptible to storm damage. But you should not cut the main and tallest leader of a young shade tree of a tall-growing species—cutting it will only encourage growth of competing tops. (There are a few exceptions to this rule—some trees such as certain types of maples and birches, particularly those that are normally grown with multiple trunks, have several leaders that constitute part of their natural shape.)

If a tree has been properly pruned when young, it will require less maintenance pruning later on. But of course no one can foretell exactly how a tree will grow, and from time to time you will probably have to remove deadwood or wayward branches. If live wood must be trimmed, approach the job as you would the shaping of a young

MULBERRY'S SILKEN PROMISE

The profitable sound of silkworms munching on tender young mulberry leaves—a sound that has been likened to rain falling on a roof—has been heard for 2,500 years in China and briefly at various times in the United States. The silkworm's favorite, the white mulberry (Morus alba), was first introduced into Georgia and South Carolina in the 18th Century, but this and later efforts to promote commercial silk growing in America failed, primarily because of high labor costs. One of the last—and most ambitious— attempts was made in 1945, when a group of businessmen in Mineral Wells, Texas, planted 130,000 white mulberries with hopes of producing 40,000 pounds of silk a season. The advent of nylon and other synthetic fibers put them out of business.

PRUNING OLDER TREES

tree, considering the impact—immediate and future—on the appearance and health of the tree. A low-hanging bough that threatens to break off under the weight of the next wet snow may seem a prime candidate for removal. But visualize first how the tree will look without it and ask yourself if you will be happy with the result. If the limb can be eliminated with no esthetic loss, cut it off at the trunk. If you decide the bough is essential to the tree's good looks, thin out the smaller branches to lighten the burden; treated this way, the bough will be less likely to snap off and, instead of hanging low, it will rise and reach out closer to the horizontal, restoring the tree's natural symmetry.

Where two branches rub, the rubbing may open a wound in the bark through which insects and diseases can attack. Cut away one of the two, saving the branch that contributes most to the appearance of the tree. Eliminate any inward-growing branches, whether they are rubbing against one another or not; their loss will not be noted, and one day they will probably die from lack of sunlight anyway. High branches or main stems that threaten to tangle with power or telephone lines also must be removed or shortened. You should have the job done before the utility crew arrives and does it for you to protect the wires; if they are in a hurry they may butcher the tree. Do not attempt this kind of high pruning yourself. Call in a professional tree man, for the job is dangerous and requires special skill to train the tree away from the wires without damaging its looks.

Whatever you prune off, one rule always holds true: cut close to the trunk or main branch and leave no stub. The wound will heal better. All healing, like all growth, originates in the tree's cambium layer *(pages 20-21)*. The cambium on the edges of a cut grows toward the cut's center to cover it up and heal the wound if it can. But the cambium cannot grow around to enclose a protruding stub; as a result, decay is likely to enter the stub and work its way deep into the interior of the tree.

There is a special technique for removing big branches and there is more to it than just cutting close to the trunk. Some people learn about it the hard way. They are in the process of sawing through a large limb, close to the trunk, when they hear a ripping, cracking sound. The branch falls of its own weight before the cut is complete, pulling with it a long strip of wood from the trunk. The result is a long ugly wound that is easily infected. To avoid such damage when cutting off a large branch, follow the procedure shown in the drawings at right, starting with a "safety" cut about 2 feet out from the trunk on the underside of the branch. Next, remove the branch with a top cut farther out; you can then deal with the stub, making a second safety cut from underneath if the stub itself is a thick, heavy one, and completing the job with a clean top cut as close to the trunk as possible. Before it is sealed with tree paint the last cut should be shaped with a knife to ease the growth of protective cambium and guide water away from the wound.

One of the main purposes of tree care, be it feeding, watering or pruning, is to fend off the ills that can beset trees. Well-tended trees are less susceptible to pests and diseases than neglected trees and, if attacked, recover faster. A good example is the flowering dogwood, whose natural enemy is the dogwood borer. As long as the tree remains healthy and has sufficient moisture, the borer is no great problem. But if the tree weakens, the borer moves in. The health of a flowering dogwood and its resistance to borer damage depend chiefly on its site in the garden. Trees planted where the soil be-

DISEASES AND PESTS

REMOVING A LARGE LIMB

1. *To remove a branch several inches thick without tearing bark and wood from the trunk, make an initial cut with a pruning saw a foot or 2 away from the trunk; saw upward into the branch until the blade binds. Then make a downward cut a few inches farther from the trunk, sawing until the limb snaps off.*

2. *The stub is removed without tearing bark by making a shallow cut from underneath, flush with the trunk, then sawing away the stub down from the top as close to the trunk as possible.*

3. *With a sharp pruning knife, clean away ragged or loose edges of bark. Shape the wound into an oval, pointed at both ends; this helps the bark shed water that might lead to rot and also speeds the growth of healing callus tissue.*

4. *Coat the entire exposed surface with tree-wound paint, available at garden centers, to protect the cut from insects and wood-rotting fungi while it is healing. For occasional pruning jobs, use tree paint in a spray can, which saves clean-up time and also cannot spread disease, as a brush might.*

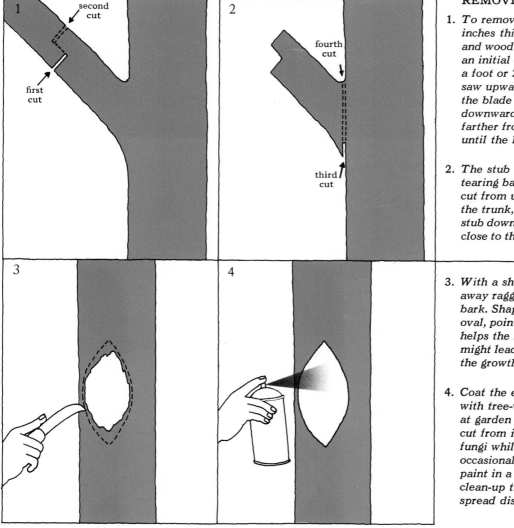

THE SYRUP TREE

If you are lucky enough to have sugar maple trees on your property, you can tap them for home-produced pancake syrup. Early in spring, before the buds begin to swell, drill a hole about 3/8 inch in diameter and 2½ inches deep into the sapwood. A tree 10 inches in diameter can take one taphole; larger trees can handle as many as five. Hammer a galvanized iron spout into the hole and hang a bucket on it; cover the bucket to keep out rain and twigs. The clear, colorless sap will begin to drip into the bucket on the first warm day, often producing a daily take of up to 12 quarts of sap. The efforts of one tree in one day will not get you very far, however. In order to end up with one gallon of maple syrup, you need 45 to 50 gallons of sap, strained and boiled slowly in shallow pans.

comes excessively dry in the summer are more apt to be attacked than are those that have not been weakened by drought.

Not every tree that looks sick, however, is actually a victim of disease. If a young, newly planted tree puts out only a few pale small leaves, chances are simply that somebody did not prune its top growth to compensate for the roots it lost when being removed from the nurseryman's field. The remaining roots cannot cope with the demand of its leaves for food, and the top starts to die back to restore the balance. The treatment is simple. Prune off some of the weaker branches, shorten the others by about a third, feed the roots lightly (or give the leaves foliar feeding) and, most important of all, make sure the tree gets enough water. If the tree is an older, established one and exhibits the same symptoms, it is possible that a construction or landscaping job has piled too much earth above the roots and they are suffocating, or that digging near the tree has severed the roots on one side; in either case the effects become visible first in the foliage. The best first-aid treatment is foliar feeding, but if the roots are suffocating, special measures are needed to get air and water to them *(Chapter 4)*.

But a sickly look often means that the tree is indeed diseased. The wise gardener watches for the first signs of the troubles described on the chart on pages 148 and 149 and takes remedial action. Usually the cure requires spraying (materials and methods of control are prescribed on the chart). You can spray a tree up to 20 or 25 feet in height with a garden-hose siphon attachment of the kind used for foliar feeding. For trees taller than 25 feet you need a professional tree man's more powerful spray equipment.

Sprays can also be used on healthy trees to block insect attack. A good ounce of prevention against a pound of such pests as aphids, scales, mites and the eggs of many caterpillars is provided by so-called dormant and delayed dormant sprays. Dormant spray is applied while the tree is dormant, early in spring before the buds begin to open. Delayed dormant spray is applied as soon as leaves have fully formed and opened. I prefer dormant spraying because I like to get my chores done early, but bad weather sometimes interferes, and in that case I use a delayed dormant spray. Most of these sprays, obtainable at garden centers, consist of mineral oil that is mixed with water before being applied, and gardeners concerned about ecology can use them with clear consciences. Oil sprays simply cover and smother insect eggs; they are not poisons and do not harm birds or animals. Do not use them, however, when the temperature is below 45° or above 85° F.; the sprays are ineffective when it is too cold and can injure trees during hot weather by burning the foliage.

Some oil sprays cannot be used, however, on all varieties of maples, for some types are damaged by the oil, especially during periods of high temperatures. Oil sprays should not be applied at all in close proximity to evergreen trees or shrubs; they may be injurious to them. For scale and mites in maples, and a wide range of pests and diseases in some other trees such as beeches, a spray of liquid lime-sulfur applied in late winter will generally prove effective as a preventive measure. It must be handled with care, though, because it irritates human skin and discolors paint when it is used close to houses. When insects do attack, other chemicals that are listed on the chart on page 148 and 149 may have to be used.

Because chemical sprays may harm birds, fish and beneficial insects —including bees, which are essential to the pollination of garden plants—tree lovers find themselves torn when such destructive pests as gypsy moths attack on a large scale. These periodic plagues are best controlled by extensive spraying from airplanes or helicopters, but such indiscriminate spraying also causes the greatest alteration in the balance of nature. Today more attention is being paid to the use of so-called biological controls—the employment of a pest's natural enemies to keep it in check. Ladybugs, for example, have a prodigious appetite for aphids and will consume as many as 50 apiece a day. Praying mantises—like the ladybugs, they can be bought from breeders—gobble up aphids and small flies when they first hatch and later take on beetles and large insects. Also available for purchase are lacewing larvae, known as aphid lions before they grow into gauzy-winged fluttering adults; they devour scale, aphids and other insects that feed on trees. One innovation that is just becoming available to home gardeners promises biological control of the gypsy moth, which periodically defoliates trees over wide areas, particularly in the Northeast; it is a form of bacteria, *Bacillus thuringiensis,* that attacks the gypsy moth caterpillar and certain other caterpillars but is harmless to other kinds of life. Scientists seeking substitutes for insecticides are experimenting with still other ingenious ideas. One is trapping the males of an insect species by luring them with the synthesized scent of nubile females. The males then are sterilized and turned loose. When they mate, the females with which they have coupled remain unfertilized and the population of that species falls.

But chemical treatments thus far remain, for many pests and diseases, the only practical means of defense a homeowner has. If you have to use chemicals, always do so with the greatest caution —for your own sake as well as that of birds, fish and other animals —and read the instructions that come with them carefully. Used with discretion, they may save a favorite old tree so that it can give you many more years of pleasure.

BIOLOGICAL CONTROLS

Fall's vibrant schedule of color

Each year the concentrated palette of New England's fall foliage——the reds and yellows of maples, the orange scarlet of pepperidges and dogwoods, the purplish bronze of beeches and ashes——draws as many as three million pilgrims, who drive hundreds of miles on October weekends just to see the spectacle. New England's climate stimulates the greatest number and variety of deciduous trees to do their autumn best; but trees in many other areas provide equally fine hues, and gardeners in these regions can plan their own displays.

The striking color changes that take place as deciduous trees prepare to drop their leaves are triggered by shortening days and cooling temperatures. Both stimulate the build-up of a layer of corklike cells at the base of the leaf stem that halts the flow of nutrients between leaf and tree. The manufacture of chlorophyll ceases and, as its green color fades, two underlying chemicals, carotin and xanthophyll, are unmasked, "turning" the leaves yellow. Red foliage appears only in leaves that contain certain sugars or tannins, and then only if the shortening days are sunny and the nights cool to temperatures below 45° F., forcing the corklike layer to form before the sugars or tannins drain away. Trapped in the leaf, they combine with other substances to produce the red pigment, anthocyanin, that stains the trees their glorious crimson.

Although many deciduous trees offer splendid fall color, the 22 pictured on the following pages are among the most spectacular and reliable performers and will grow in many parts of the United States and Canada (accompanying maps). They are presented in successive groups according to the weeks in which they change hue; the grouping is based on an average New England autumn lasting four weeks. Although the sequence is generally the same in other areas, the brilliance and duration of the colors vary with the region and the year; early frost can kill the foliage, and a warm, cloudy autumn can produce dull color. A gardener can only pick his trees; if nature frowns, he can always console himself with an old New England adage: "A poor fall means an easy winter."

The mellowing foliage of a sugar maple in a Vermont dooryard seems to reflect the golden glow of the lamplit windows.

CANOE BIRCH

The yellow foliage of the canoe birch, also known as paper or white birch, is one of the first heralds of autumn. This handsome clump graces a home in Reading, Vermont, in the tree's native habitat, the Northeast (darker area on map). It also provides good fall color in regions of the Midwest, Northwest and Canada (lighter area on map).

RED MAPLE

As the map indicates, the red, or swamp, maple has a wide growing range; it can be depended on for 10 days of autumn brilliance over most of the country, especially where the soil is moist. Normally the leaves change to brilliant red with paler undersides; some, however, become yellow because of genetic aberrations or alkaline soil.

DOWNY SERVICEBERRY

This tree is also called the downy shadblow because it blooms each spring at the time of the annual shad run up New England rivers. In autumn a single tree can display a rich brocade of yellow, orange and red, lasting about 10 days. The species, although native to the eastern half of North America, flaunts its colors throughout the country.

GRAY BIRCH

The leaves of the gray birch turn a golden yellow that lasts about a week. In autumn coloring as in general appearance, it closely resembles the white birch; the gray birch, however, has triangular leaves, the white birch oval ones. The gray birch will thrive and turn color in a variety of soils, from poor to rich and from wet to dry.

Second week

SOURWOOD

The sourwood needs full fall sun in order to turn the glossy red of this Litchfield, Connecticut, specimen. The change is gradual, from green to yellow to bright orange and finally to a clear red that lasts about 10 days. Native to the Southern states (darker area on map), the sourwood also grows in the Midwest, the Pacific Coast and British Columbia (lighter areas).

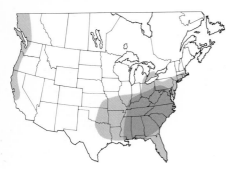

AMUR MAPLE

Imported a century ago from Manchuria, where the climate is one of the harshest in the world, the Amur maple can withstand bitter winters better than other maples and is a sturdy choice for those who live in cold wind-swept areas such as the Great Lakes region, the Dakotas and Manitoba. The leaves turn yellow or orange or, where sun is strong, the scarlet shown at left.

SWEET GUM

The distinctive star-shaped leaves of the sweet gum change from green to yellow and then, if the tree gets strong sun, to a rich red that lasts 10 days or so. In swampy areas, foliage may become a dark wine red and in other circumstances a tree may display a two-toned effect; the leaves on outer branches are brushed with red, those on inner branches are a glowing yellow.

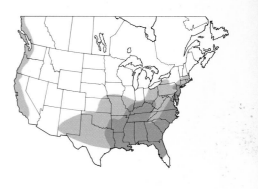

PEPPERIDGE

This tree, also known as the sour gum, black tupelo or black gum, turns a glowing orange or scarlet that lasts about 10 days. The tree has a great number of branches bearing dense foliage, so that in autumn it appears as a concentrated blaze of color. The pepperidge does best in rich moist soil throughout New England and the South. It also grows on the Pacific Coast.

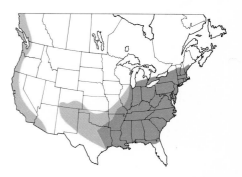

GINKGO

This magnificent ginkgo in Old Bennington, Vermont—said to be the largest and oldest in New England—rewards its owners every year with 10 days of glorious color. The leaves gradually turn from green to clear yellow (below), then drop in a quick shower of gold on the lawn (right). The whole family cheerfully assembles to pay the inevitable price for the annual display: raking up the leaves (far right).

Third week

EUROPEAN BEECH

A majestic European beech serves as an after-school rallying point for young cyclists in Orange, Connecticut. The tree is in an early state of change: the leaves at the tips of its branches have turned russet; the inner leaves, still green or yellow, will soon follow. Eventually all the foliage will become a burnished bronze, the fourth, final stage of fall color.

TULIP TREE

The tulip tree, so named because both leaves and flowers resemble stylized versions of a tulip, changes to a warm yellow in fall. Only about a week of bright foliage can be expected—each leaf is so heavy that the stalk attaching it to the twig soon snaps. The tulip is one of the largest native deciduous trees and can grow to 90 feet or more with a 40-foot spread.

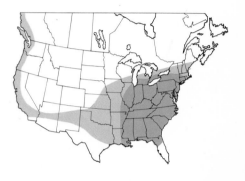

CALLERY PEAR

The glossy dark green foliage of the callery pear, best known for its variety called Bradford, turns to a dark wine red for about 10 days; the berrylike russet fruit, so tiny it is usually obscured by the leaves, hangs on the tree until midwinter or until eaten by birds. A relatively recent import from China, the callery pear thrives and colors over most of the United States.

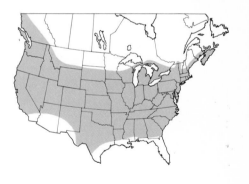

EASTERN REDBUD

The heart-shaped golden leaves of the eastern redbud last only about a week—but the bright fall coloring is a welcome bonus from a tree usually planted for its early spring blossoms. As the map shows, this tree grows over most of the country except for a few Western states; however, it cannot tolerate the extreme changes of temperature common to high altitudes.

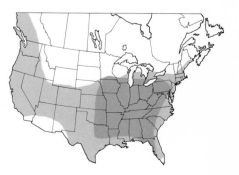

SUGAR MAPLE

*Golden sugar maples lining a roadside
are a familiar fall delight for Vermonters,
a 10-day dividend of color from trees
that earn their keep by producing sap
for maple syrup. Trees that grow close
together like these, which are cultivated
in a grove, or "sugar bush," for syrup
production, shade one another—so the
leaves generally remain yellow. The lone
fiery tree below, however, has had full
sun, stimulating leaf sugars to produce
the red pigment that dyes its foliage.*

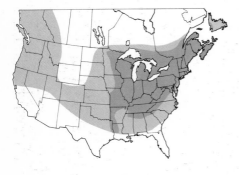

Fourth week

PIN OAK

The red foliage of a spreading pin oak in Connecticut heralds the last days of fall. After almost three weeks of color, the leaves will slowly fade to brown and remain on the tree long into winter. This tree, named for its pinlike branchlets, grows from New England to British Columbia, as shown on the map, and is the most often planted of the oak species.

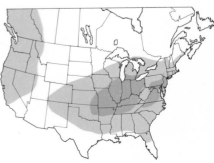

SCARLET OAK

The veins of these scarlet oak leaves still retain a little green chlorophyll; as it disappears the leaves will become a deep red, the most brilliant of the oak family. The color lasts for about 10 days. Interestingly, the spring foliage is a forerunner of autumn's glory—a protective pale red fuzz tinges the leaves in spring, disappearing as the leaves mature.

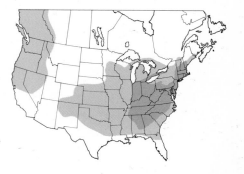

WHITE OAK

These white oak leaves, about halfway through their color change, will deepen to a distinctive purplish red for about 10 days, then turn brown and remain on the tree into winter. The white oak, so called because of its light-colored bark, is the mightiest of deciduous oaks native to North America; some specimens are 150 feet tall and more than 800 years old.

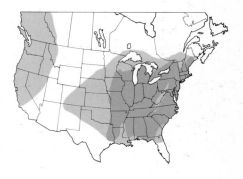

RED OAK

The leaves of the red oak become a dark red for a week or more, then slowly fade to brown, remaining on the tree most of the winter. The red oak is the fastest growing as well as the hardiest of the native oaks and is extensively planted along streets in the regions indicated because of its tolerance of pollution and the compacted soil along roadways.

FLOWERING DOGWOOD

Dogwood, prized for its lush spring blossoms, is just as lovely in fall. In this garden in Washington, Connecticut, the larger, older tree has stopped manufacturing chlorophyll and has changed to a rich scarlet. The younger tree is still functioning; the remaining green and the red being unmasked combine to give it a deep purple hue.

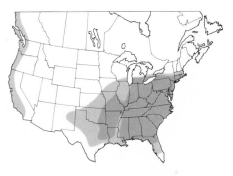

WHITE ASH

The foliage of the white ash usually turns a warm yellow, as in the picture at left, though some or all of the leaves, especially the outer ones, may become an unusual deep purple in sunny weather. The leaves drop after a week of color; happily for the busy gardener, the small leaflets disintegrate so quickly that leaf raking is usually unnecessary.

NORWAY MAPLE

One of the most popular shade trees, the Norway maple is also one of the most spectacular in autumn. Except for red- and black-leaved types, most varieties produce dense patterns of large leaves that turn a brilliant yellow for 10 days. The Norway maple in its many forms grows through most of the United States and parts of Canada.

KOUSA DOGWOOD

The leaves of the Kousa, or Japanese, dogwood keep their lustrous red for a little more than a week in late fall. Most leaves change directly from green to red, but others that are shaded go through an intermediate yellow stage. The Kousa dogwood flourishes in the Pacific Northwest and through most of the Eastern and Southern states.

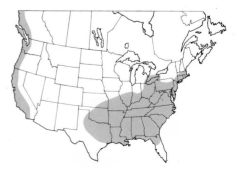

Expert tips from the professionals 4

When my parents bought a wooded site some years ago for a new house, the man who sold them the lot gave them a piece of gratuitous advice. "The first thing you ought to do," he said, "is bulldoze out all those scraggly trees." My parents, however, had learned something about trees and they quickly discarded the idea. Instead of bulldozing indiscriminately to get a clear building site, as all too many home builders do, they planned their house and garden with the trees in mind, thinning out spindly ones but preserving as many of the best specimens as they could. To be sure, long neglect had taken its toll, and many of the trees needed pruning, feeding, repair and professional help. But the carefully planned effort was well worth it; today the house, framed by fine, healthy trees, looks as though it has been part of the landscape for years.

Even a little expert knowledge of trees can repay you many times over, not only when you are faced with a big job like clearing land for a new home but in the course of many routine chores involved in taking care of a house and yard. Only if you understand some of the finer points of tree care can you get the greatest pleasure and usefulness from your trees, aiding them to grow properly and protecting them against damage. Professional tree men point out, in fact, that attractive trees are often injured by homeowners who have no notion that they may be causing harm. The most common mistakes, the experts say, are of three main kinds:

• Overzealous application of herbicides on lawns or poison ivy sickens or even kills trees.

• Work around the house—for construction or landscaping—changes the character or level of the soil around trees and interferes with their supply of food, air and water.

• Old trees are allowed to die before their time because the homeowner does not know they can be saved and, conversely, trees that should be chopped down are left standing.

Yet all these mistakes are easily avoided. The principles of protecting your investment in trees are fairly simple, and many of the

After pruning deadwood with the saw at his belt, a tree worker descends from a huge willow oak in North Carolina. He uses the long rope, looped around his waist and a sturdy limb, to "walk" up and down the tree.

steps demand nothing more than ordinary gardening skills. But it is also necessary to know when professional help is needed.

Weed killers are among the most dangerous enemies of trees, mainly because they are so easily misused. A man who prides himself on a nice green lawn notices some dandelions creeping in one summer and rushes for the weed killer. He applies twice the specified amount on the theory that he will get rid of the pesky weed once and for all. Before long the leaves on the fine old maple at the edge of the lawn begin to yellow and curl for no apparent reason. By then it may be too late; so much weed killer has been absorbed by the tree's system that it is likely to die.

Misguided attempts to get rid of poison ivy can have the same result. The most effective poison ivy killers are nonselective herbicides that are equally deadly to all broad-leaved plants, including deciduous trees. Soaking the offensive vines can administer a fatal dose to the trees they grow on. Harm may be caused even if the poison ivy does not grow right next to a tree; I know of one gardener who applied a powerful herbicide in a brush-filled corner of his lot only to have the chemical drain downhill through the soil and sicken a fine dogwood 50 feet away.

Poison ivy should, however, be removed if it is climbing a tree, and not only because it is a health hazard. Along with certain other vines such as woodbine, honeysuckle, wisteria and wild grape, it can either wrap itself around the trunk of a young tree, killing it by impeding the flow of sap just beneath the bark, or it can climb above the tree's branches, casting shade that causes the tree to lose vigor or even die.

The best way to avoid trouble with a vine like poison ivy is to uproot it (wearing gloves) and dispose of it in a trash bag. Do not burn the ivy; its virulent poison is easily carried by smoke. If you do use a herbicide, follow the directions on the package closely.

BUILDING NEAR TREES Many trees are harmed by physical rather than chemical alteration of the ground around the roots. One of the most common problems arises when a homeowner decides to build a patio around a tree so he can put some chairs and a table in the shade. If the patio is a solid layer of masonry—concrete, or flagstones set in mortar—the impenetrable surface will deprive roots of needed air and water. Unless the paving is fitted with drains at frequent intervals the tree may suffer and, if the paving extends far enough around the tree, it may die. This difficulty can be avoided if a continuous masonry surface is not used; a patio can be made of flagstones, bricks or lightweight concrete slabs laid in a bed of sand with gravel underneath, leaving gaps between the stones or bricks to allow air and water through.

Similar problems may arise when heavy construction equipment must be used near trees. A bulldozer or a truck not only can make a dangerous gash in a tree trunk but its very weight can compress the soil so much over the roots that the proper amount of air and moisture can no longer reach them. Piles of construction materials and excavated soil, if left on the ground over tree roots long enough, have a similar suffocating effect. The heat from fires built by workmen under trees can do irreparable damage to branches some distance in the air.

The best way to avoid such harm is to go over your property before construction starts, show the contractor the trees you are concerned about (you can tie rags around their trunks so there is no question) and ask him to put temporary fences around them. He can easily nail up such fences out of scrap lumber and it hardly matters what they look like as long as they accomplish their purpose, which is to keep his workmen and their heavy equipment away from the trees. Such fences should be placed to protect the roots over as wide an area as possible and they ought to be no closer to the trunk than the outermost reach of the branches.

If construction or landscaping alters the ground level around a tree by more than 6 inches, you will have to take special steps to preserve the tree's health. Both adding dirt and removing it have the same harmful result—the roots are denied their normal supply of food, air and water. The remedies involve some digging, but seldom more than a gardener can undertake on his own.

If the ground level is to be raised and the fill will be less than a foot deep, an open tree well to keep the soil away from the trunk, plus a bed of coarse gravel laid over the original surface before the fill is added, will usually allow enough air and moisture to penetrate to the roots. If the fill is to be deeper than a foot, it is advisable to install a system of perforated pipes leading to the well around the trunk, and then to cover the pipes with coarse gravel and soil (*drawing, page 84*). The pipes will act as conduits for air and moisture, as well as for supplementary watering with a hose during dry spells and for feeding with water-soluble fertilizer.

If, on the other hand, the grade is to be lowered, you should build some sort of retaining wall on one or more sides of the tree to keep most of its roots at their normal growing level (*drawing, page 85*). If the grade must be changed by more than 2 feet, the tree will probably blow over and you should seriously consider cutting it down and starting over by planting a new, young tree on the new level of the site. Such a tree will grow more vigorously because of its youth and the fact that it has ample room to establish its roots at the proper level in the soil; moreover, the total cost of the job, including that of removing the old tree and planting the new one,

ARISTOCRATS AMONG TREES

The American Forestry Association maintains a Social Register of Big Trees that admits only the biggest known tree of each species growing in the United States. The Association welcomes new nominations; if you know of a champion, send the details—height, circumference 4½ feet above ground level, spread of crown—to the Association at 919 17th Street N.W., Washington, D.C. 20006. The 13 tallest deciduous trees on the most recent list:

TREE AND LOCATION	HEIGHT	SPREAD
PECAN Mer Rouge, Louisiana	160 ft.	95 ft.
SWEET GUM Richland County, South Carolina	145 ft.	75 ft.
AMERICAN BEECH Jamaica Plain, Massachusetts	144 ft.	96 ft.
PEPPERIDGE Easterly, Texas	139 ft.	83 ft.
RED MAPLE Macomb County, Michigan	136 ft.	95 ft.
TULIP TREE Macon County, North Carolina	135 ft.	55 ft.
PIN OAK Saint Davis, Pennsylvania	135 ft.	135 ft.
EASTERN POPLAR Wayne, Michigan	131 ft.	129 ft.
CUCUMBER TREE Great Smoky Park, Tennessee	125 ft.	60 ft.
CALIFORNIA PLANE TREE Santa Barbara, California	116 ft.	158 ft.
AMERICAN LINDEN Grand Traverse County, Michigan	115 ft.	76 ft.
BLACK WALNUT Anne Arundel County, Maryland	108 ft.	128 ft.
HONEY LOCUST Big Oak Tree State Park, Missouri	105 ft.	58 ft.

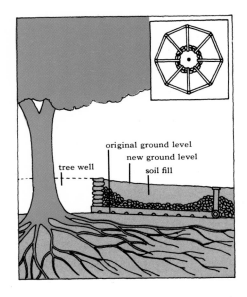

RAISING THE GROUND LEVEL

To supply air and food for roots when the ground level near a tree is to be raised a foot or 2, provide an open well at the original level around the trunk. It should extend at least 3 feet on all sides. From the well, run perforated pipes, holes down, on the original grade sloping downward to the outer limits of the branches (inset). Join the pipes together and connect them to the new ground level with vertical pipes. Cover open ends with wire mesh to keep the pipes clear, then line the well with stones or masonry. Spread ½-inch glass-fiber batting and 6 to 8 inches of coarse gravel over the pipes and cover them with soil.

original ground level

new ground level

tree well

soil fill

may well prove to be less than that of trying to save the old tree.

If you suspect that one of your trees has had soil improperly filled over its roots by a previous owner, there is a simple way to find out. The base of a tree growing at normal depth flares out at the point where it enters the ground; added soil will hide this flare line, making the trunk appear to descend straight into the ground. If you see such a situation, dig away some of the soil on one side of the trunk; eventually you will reach the original ground level, which will be marked by a layer of dead grass or a thin, dark layer of decaying leaves. If this layer is more than 6 inches down, clear soil away for 5 to 6 feet out from the trunk and build a tree well; if the fill is more than 1 foot deep, add perforated pipe.

It is generally more difficult to save a tree left above a cutaway section of the yard. I once saw a huge old oak sitting on a mound of gravelly soil above a lawn; the ground level had been lowered in the whole area except for a small island around the tree. It did not have long to live. It might have been saved by increasing the area of the mound and surrounding it with retaining walls, but again it might not, and removal was probably more practical.

THE ART OF THINNING

If you have quite a few trees around your house or on a site where you are planning to build, do not be afraid to cut some down; proper thinning can help both you and the remaining trees. Most wooded areas have too many trees competing for sun and soil nutrients for all of them to do well. Clearing out certain of them opens up views and lets welcome sunlight reach both the house and the trees, allowing each tree to grow more fully and handsomely than before.

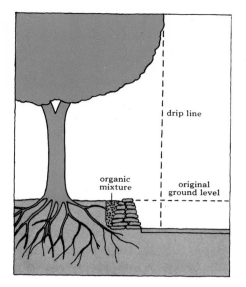

LOWERING THE GROUND LEVEL

The steps illustrated at left will protect the health of a tree when an excavation requires lowering the ground level by a foot or more. Preserve as many roots as possible, being sure to excavate no more than two thirds the distance from the trunk to the drip line of the branches, and prune the branches selectively to compensate for lost roots. Then build a retaining wall and fill the space behind it with an organic mixture of half soil and half peat moss or compost to encourage thick new root growth. If the wall is mortared, include small holes or pipe drains spaced 2 feet apart, to prevent water from accumulating behind it.

One of my neighbors who has a wooded lot makes it a practice to remove a few of his trees each year, according to a long-range plan. Just this fall, after converting a half dozen more into firewood, he confessed to me that he did not miss them at all.

There are good reasons for thinning a little at a time instead of all at once. In the first place, it prevents a sudden sparse or bare look. What is more, it gives the remaining trees a chance to adjust gradually to the changing conditions; if all the unwanted trees were taken out simultaneously, the rest would quickly become susceptible to the sunscald that burns tissues of trees whose thin bark developed in shade. To keep the thinned-out area as natural looking as possible, remove a varied selection of trees each year. Do not simply cut out all the trees under a certain size, and do not clear away all the underbrush. A wood lot is more beautiful if plants of all types and ages are allowed to grow. Leave untouched some of the more appealing natural groupings here and there; then the eye can shift from one area of interest to another across open spaces that lend a feeling of light and air to the composition.

TREES TO SAVE

In the course of thining you may be tempted to cut down a tree that looks sickly but really ought to be saved. Dying leaves may indicate a defect that can be remedied with a reasonable expenditure of effort, and even an incurable affliction can often be ameliorated to lengthen the useful life of a tree.

Among the easily misread symptoms are spindly branches on one side of a tree; they are not always a sign of disease but may indicate a remediable condition called root girdling. In such cases one wayward root has circled back around the base of the trunk, squeezing the trunk or other roots so tightly that it reduces or even stops the flow of sap on that side. If you suspect root girdling, look to see whether the trunk beneath the undersized branches descends straight into the soil instead of flaring at its base. If so, a little digging there often reveals the wayward root pressing against the trunk or another root. Enough of it must be cut away to eliminate the pressure. If you are reasonably handy, you can do the job yourself (drawings, below); if not, you can have a tree expert do it.

Old and seemingly decrepit trees may also be hastily condemned. It is true that older trees, despite solicitous care, develop problems of aging such as cavities and weak limbs. Many homeowners look upon the appearance of a cavity in a tree with the concern they feel for a cavity in a tooth; their first instinct is to have it filled. Cavities in trees, like cavities in teeth, continue to decay rapidly unless properly treated, but filling is not always the best treatment. Small cavities in a fast-growing or easily replaced tree such as a poplar or willow are best dealt with by cutting out decay with a chisel and mallet and coating the inside of the hole with tree paint. If the cavity is checked every year and fresh tree paint is applied, it can probably be kept under control. If you feel impelled to fill the hole for appearance' sake—the only purpose it will serve—

HOW TO REMOVE A GIRDLING ROOT

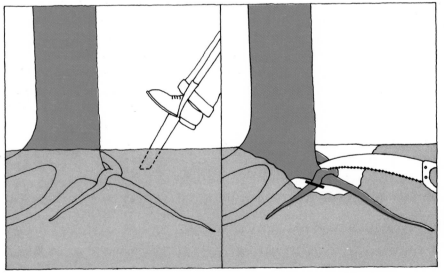

When leaves die on part of a tree, indicating that one root has girdled or strangled another, dig around the offending root. To locate it, dig where the trunk enters the ground straight, without flaring at the base.

With a pruning saw, sever the girdling root by making a cut (line) at each side of any root it covers and remove the cut section; the rest will rot away. If space is too cramped for a saw, use a chisel and mallet.

have it done by a professional. He will not use concrete, but a composite tree-filler material. Unlike concrete, which cracks easily, this material is flexible and adheres to the walls of the cavity.

Some cavities that appear small may actually extend almost from the base to the crown of the tree. In such cases it is impossible to chisel out the decay and paint the hole; the best course is to concentrate on feeding the tree and keeping it well watered during dry spells, thus fortifying it in its battle against infection. If the cavity is a large one in an old and highly prized tree, it may be necessary to brace the trunk with threaded iron rods, screwed from one side of the cavity to the other. Where large, old trees have developed weak crotches—perhaps as a result of neglected pruning in their formative stages—or have big limbs that threaten to snap off in a storm, damage can be forestalled by strengthening the joints with cables and eyebolts. Such bracing, however, requires a knowledge of stress and engineering as well as a knowledge of trees, and is best left to the ministrations of men who are professionals.

Cutting down trees and building wells and walls are arduous—occasionally dangerous—jobs. For these tasks, and others such as bracing and high pruning work, you will probably want to call in a professional tree expert. Make sure, first of all, that you get a reputable one and not an unskilled itinerant worker, who could do more harm than good. A qualified professional is not hard to find. At the very least he is listed in the classified pages of the local telephone book under "tree service" or "tree surgeons," indicating that he has a base in the community he serves and a reputation at stake. He is generally covered by liability and workmen's compensation insurance, and is not afraid to advertise the fact; in some states he will also have a license or certificate that may spell out what kind of work he is qualified to do, and he will not mind showing proof of it. It is always wise to ask specifically about the extent of his insurance coverage; tree work is often dangerous, no matter how skillfully performed, and an uninsured accident can be costly as well as tragic for all concerned.

JOBS FOR EXPERTS

From a qualified professional you can expect not only skillful workmanship but wise guidance as well. When he bids on a job, he can also tell you if the job is worth doing. The death of a badly decayed tree may be postponed for a few years, but eventually it will have to be cut down. Protecting a tree against the effects of ground-level change may cost more than replacing it with another of nearly equal size. Yet practicality is not the only consideration, and sentiment must weigh heavily. A tree is no machine to be thrown out when it no longer works perfectly, but a living thing to be cherished. It is what helps to make a house a home.

An illustrated encyclopedia of deciduous trees 5

Are you looking for a fast-growing tree to shade a picnic table? A flowering lawn ornament? A brilliant splash of autumn color? To help you select species suited to both your climate and your purpose, the following encyclopedia chapter illustrates and describes the characteristics, uses and requirements of 75 genera of deciduous trees. The areas in which each tree grows best are designated by letters keyed to the map on page 150.

Trees can usually be purchased from nurserymen in any of three ways, depending upon the species and location: bare-rooted, with the roots free of soil; balled and burlaped, with the roots in their original soil ball wrapped in burlap; or in containers, usually metal or plastic cans or wooden baskets. Unless otherwise specified, bare-rooted trees should be planted when leafless and dormant and when the ground is not frozen; for most regions this means spring or fall. Properly balled-and-burlaped trees and container-grown trees may be planted at any time the ground can be worked. Most trees grow best in slightly acid to neutral soil, with a pH of 6.0 to 7.0; variations are noted in the entries. Flowers and fruit are described only if noteworthy or visible from the ground; those particularly notable are illustrated in detail. Drawings of trees prized for their fall color show the leaves in that color.

Trees should be pruned to grow in a desired shape when young. This training, as well as the trimming of overlong branches, is usually best done in early spring but can be done at other seasons unless otherwise indicated. Dead, diseased or broken wood should be removed when the damage is noticed, regardless of season.

The trees are listed alphabetically by their internationally recognized Latin botanical names. The columnar Norway maple, *Acer platanoides columnare,* for example, is listed under the genus *Acer,* followed by the species name *platanoides* and the variety *columnare.* Common names are cross-referenced to the Latin genus names. For quick reference, a chart of characteristics of the trees described in the encyclopedia appears on pages 151-154.

Some of the ways deciduous trees beautify a garden are shown in this portrait of a colorful red oak flanked by a Lombardy poplar and a weeping willow. Above are blossoms of an *Oriental cherry and leaves of a silver-leaved box elder. Below are the red berries of a European mountain ash, English walnuts and a sprig of the variously shaped leaves of sassafras.*

VINE MAPLE
Acer circinatum

AMUR MAPLE
Acer ginnala

A

ACACIA, FALSE See *Robinia*
ACANTHOPANAX See *Kalopanax*

ACER

A. buergerianum, also called *A. trinerve* (trident maple); *A. campestre* (hedge or English cork maple); *A. circinatum* (vine maple); *A. ginnala* (Amur maple); *A. griseum* (paperbark maple); *A. negundo* (box elder, ash-leaved maple); *A. palmatum* (Japanese maple); *A. platanoides* (Norway maple); *A. pseudoplatanus* (sycamore maple); *A. rubrum* (red, scarlet or swamp maple); *A. saccharinum,* also called *A. dasycarpum* (silver, white or soft maple); *A. saccharum* (sugar or rock maple)

Maples have long been favorite choices for shade and ornament, but in the past gardeners were limited almost entirely to tall-growing species. Today a broad selection is available; of the 12 species listed here, six generally grow to a height of only about 25 feet and are excellent for planting in average-sized yards and along roadways. The tall-growing species are, of course, highly desirable where there is room for them to develop their full beauty, for they quickly create a handsome effect and cast dense shade that is welcome during the hot days of summer.

Size is not the only characteristic that varies greatly from one species of maple to another, as a glance at the paintings on pages 90-95 will prove. Even the leaf shapes differ, despite the fact that most people are sure they can recognize a maple leaf—what they usually have in mind is the sugar maple leaf, the national emblem of Canada. The foliage of all maples is relatively pest free and handsome throughout spring and summer; on most species it is spectacular in fall, when it turns brilliant shades of yellow, orange or red. The flowers and fruit are seldom impressive, but children enjoy playing with the winged seeds. The basic care of maples is similar to that required by most other deciduous trees, with one significant exception: all pruning should be done in late summer or early fall; if maples are pruned in spring, they bleed excessively.

The trident maple grows moderately fast: planted when 5 to 6 feet tall, it reaches a height of 15 to 20 feet with an equal spread in seven or eight years, eventually becoming 20 to 25 feet tall. Its 1½- to 3½-inch three-lobed leaves turn yellow, orange or red in fall. The trident maple usually has main limbs that branch out close to the ground, but can be pruned to prevent such low branching and provide a single trunk with headroom under the branches. Because of its low height and easy maintenance, a single-trunked maple is excellent for shading a patio or planting along a roadway. Trident maple grows in Areas C, D, G, I and J, and does best in full sun in nearly any well-drained soil. Trees bought balled and burlaped—that is, with their roots in their original soil ball wrapped in burlap—should be planted in spring.

Hedge maple is a European species that was known to the ancient Romans as *acer,* the Latin name that now designates the entire genus of maples. A tree widely grown in English hedgerows, it yields lumber with a prominent circular bird's-eye grain pattern that has been popular in furniture and paneling. Hedge maple grows slowly: planted at 5 to 6 feet, it becomes 15 to 20 feet tall with an equal spread in 10 to 15 years, eventually reaching a height of about 25 feet. It has a densely branched globular shape with 2-inch five-lobed leaves; in some years the leaves become yellowish in autumn, in other years they remain green until they drop. The hedge maple is often planted in city gardens and along streets because it tolerates automobile exhaust fumes and because it is so low it does not interfere with overhead wires. Hedge maple grows in Areas B, C, D, F, H, I and J, in full sun or light shade in almost any well-drained soil. It requires practically no pruning.

In the Pacific Northwest, where vine maple grows wild in the shade of evergreens, its branches are long and limber, often trailing on the ground and taking on gnarled and twisted shapes, much as a vine might. But if a vine maple is planted where it gets some sun and is shaded only during the hot part of the day, it will grow into tree form moderately quickly, a 5- to 6-foot plant reaching a height and spread of about 15 feet in six to eight years and eventually becoming about 25 feet tall. The many stems of the vine maple are attractively laced with young red twigs. Its leaves, each 2 to 7 inches across with 5 to 11 shallow lobes around the edges, are tinged with red when they first unfold in spring and turn brilliant orange and red in autumn. Vine maple is one of the few species of maple with interesting flowers; although the flowers are minuscule and form only tiny clusters, their attractive reddish purple and white coloration is clearly visible from the ground. The flowers appear before the leaves develop and are followed by seeds that turn bright red in summer and cling to the branches until midwinter or later. The low stature of the vine maple makes it more useful as a lawn or patio ornament than as a shade tree. Because of its long pliant branches and red twigs, it is especially beautiful when trained to grow flat against a wall in espalier form, even during the winter when its leaves have fallen. Vine maple grows in Areas C, D, I and J. It does best in light shade in moist soil that has been liberally supplemented with peat moss or leaf mold. Vine maples bought balled and burlaped should be planted in spring.

Amur maple, a handsome, carefree tree, is one of the most cold resistant of all maples and offers toughness and year-round beauty that is of special value to gardeners in windswept regions of the United States and Canada. Trees planted when 5 to 6 feet tall usually grow rapidly in a many-trunked shrublike form to a height and spread of about 20 feet in five to seven years. If you prefer a single-trunked tree without having to train it yourself, nurserymen also sell Amur maples that they have trained to grow with a single trunk; either type serves as a patio or lawn ornament or tall screen. Early in spring, before the leaves unfurl, the Amur maple bears tiny white flowers that are fragrant, an unusual trait in a maple. The masses of bright red winged seeds contrast with the dark green foliage from midsummer on, and in fall the 2- to 3½-inch leaves turn yellow, orange or scarlet, the reddest hues appearing on trees that get the most sun. The Amur maple grows in Areas A, B, C, F, H and I, in full sun or light shade in almost any soil, moist or dry.

The paperbark maple has one characteristic that is unusual for a maple—its light brown outer bark steadily flakes off to expose an inner bark of orange brown, adding a warm touch of color to a winter garden. Paperbark maple grows slowly, a 5- to 6-foot tree becoming 15 to 20 feet tall with an equal spread in 10 to 12 years, eventually reaching about 25 feet. Its leaves consist of three distinct leaflets, each about 2 inches long, and are whitish on their undersides but turn bright red and orange in fall. Relatively few nurserymen stock the species because it is difficult to propagate, but its colorful aspects make it worth searching for. Paperbark maples grow in Areas C, D and I, in full sun and almost any well-drained soil. Trees bought balled and burlaped should be planted in spring. Paperbark maples require practically no pruning.

Box elder is very fast growing, a 5- to 6-foot tree reaching a height of 20 to 25 feet with an equal spread in four

PAPERBARK MAPLE
Acer griseum

SILVER-LEAVED BOX ELDER
Acer negundo variegatum

For growing areas, see map on page 150.

BLOOD-LEAVED JAPANESE MAPLE
Acer palmatum atropurpureum

NORWAY MAPLE
Acer platanoides

or five years, eventually reaching 40 to 60 feet. Its branches are brittle and are easily broken by wind or ice storms. Its leaves—6 to 10 inches long, each composed of three to seven leaflets up to 5 inches long—are more like those of the ash *(page 115)* than of most other maples, and give it its other name, ash-leaved maple; the dull green leaves turn yellow before dropping in autumn. The stringlike clusters of winged seeds sprout so readily that they often bring an overabundance of young trees to the neighborhood. Box elders are very resistant to cold and also tolerate drought and poor soil. The ordinary species is widely used as a windbreak or screen in parts of the West, but varieties with multicolored foliage are preferred for ornamental plantings; the silver-leaved or variegated box elder, *A. negundo variegatum,* has dense foliage with creamy white edges and is often used as an individual ornament in the Northwest. Another widely grown variety is the gold-edged box elder, *A. negundo aureo-variegatum,* which has green leaves marked with yellow. Box elders grow almost everywhere in the United States and southern Canada, but are most valuable in Areas A, F, G, H and I, where few other maples survive. They need full sun and grow in almost any soil (established trees even stand drought), but grow fastest in moist soil.

Japanese maple is considered by many gardeners the most graceful of all maples. Although red-leaved types are most common, the true Japanese maple has leaves that are reddish only in spring, when they unfurl, and in fall, when they turn orange and deep red; in summer they are green. The Japanese have been cultivating the species for centuries, selecting dozens of varieties whose leaves, mostly red, vary widely in size, in the number of lobes and in the indentation, or laciniation, of the lobes. Most have 2- to 4-inch roundish leaves and grow at a rather slow rate, a 4- to 5-foot tree becoming about 15 feet tall with an equal spread in about 10 years, eventually becoming about 20 feet tall. Cut-leaved varieties with deeply indented leaves grow at an even slower rate, usually no more than 6 to 8 inches a year, and rarely exceed 8 to 12 feet. Excellent red-leaved varieties are the blood-leaved Japanese maple, *A. palmatum atropurpureum,* which is relatively cold resistant and has purplish red leaves throughout the season; Burgundy Lace, whose deeply indented red foliage is displayed against green stems rather than the usual red ones; the thread-leaved Japanese maple, *A. palmatum dissectum,* sometimes sold as *A. palmatum dissectum atropurpureum,* a very slow-growing variety with gnarled branches and deeply indented red leaves; and Oshio-Beni, a bright red variety with long graceful branches. Japanese maples grow in Areas C, D, I and J. In the northern parts of their growing areas they do best in open shade—that is, where the branches of taller trees block the midday sun but admit light from all sides; in the southern areas light shade is preferred at all times. Japanese maples thrive in moist soil liberally supplemented with peat moss or leaf mold. Trees bought balled and burlaped should be planted in spring. Japanese maples rarely require pruning.

Norway maples grow fast: an 8- to 10-foot tree usually becomes about 20 feet tall with an equal spread in five to seven years, eventually reaching a height of 70 to 90 feet with a spread of 40 to 50 feet. Their dense leaves, 4 to 7 inches across, resemble those of sugar maples, but the two species can easily be told apart because the Norway's leaf produces a drop of milky juice at the base of its stem when it is plucked while the leaf of the sugar maple does not. Early in spring before the leaves open, tiny yellow flowers hang in 1- to 3-inch clusters on the twigs; the leaves turn yellow before dropping in the fall. Norway maples tolerate the polluted air of cities and the wind and salt spray of the seashore. Since they grow so easily under a variety of conditions, nurserymen are able to sell them inexpensively, an advantage that often leads to their overuse and sometimes even to their misuse. Most, for instance, are poor choices for use in streetside locations—even though they are very tough—because their branches soon become tall enough to interfere with overhead wires. And they cast such dense shade and have such thick matted roots close to the surface of the soil that grass and other ground covers are difficult to grow beneath them.

A number of excellent varieties of Norway maple differ widely from the ordinary species. Cleveland is oval rather than rounded. Columnar Norway maple, *A. platanoides columnare,* is valuable where height is needed in a constricted area, eventually reaching 50 to 60 feet with a spread of only 25 to 30 feet. Crimson King, one of the best of the large-growing red-leaved shade trees, retains its color all summer; it grows more slowly than green-leaved forms, an 8- to 10-foot tree reaching only about 20 feet in 8 to 10 years, eventually becoming about 50 feet tall. Variegated Norway maple, sold as *A. platanoides drummondii* or *A. platanoides variegatum,* has green leaves edged in white. Emerald Queen has glossy leathery dark green leaves. Fassen's Black grows more slowly than other Norway maples, an 8- to 10-foot tree reaching only about 20 feet in 10 to 12 years; it has extremely dark reddish purple foliage.

Globe Norway maple, *A. platanoides globosum,* rarely grows taller than 18 feet but may spread 30 feet and is one Norway maple that is excellent for planting along streets, since it combines toughness with limited height. It is unusual in that it lacks a central main branch, or leader, and sends its branches sideways in a manner called mopheaded, but when a stem of a globe Norway maple is grafted onto a 6-foot upright stem of a common Norway maple, it forms an attractive, densely leaved tree, with the strong central leader of the species and the horizontal branching of the variety. Another variety, Greenlace, has deeply indented leaves that give a light and airy texture quite unlike that of most other Norway maples. Schwedler Norway maple, *A. platanoides schwedlerii,* has dense foliage that is deep red in spring but turns mostly green by the end of summer; it grows slowly, an 8- to 10-foot tree becoming only about 20 feet tall in 8 to 10 years and eventually reaching about 50 feet. Summershade has dark green leathery foliage and does better than most other varieties in the Deep South.

All Norway maples grow in all areas except Area E, in full sun or light shade and almost any well-drained soil. Prune regularly, removing some branches in order to reduce the density of growth; otherwise, the trees will cast too deep a shade.

Sycamore maple grows fast: planted at 8 to 10 feet, it usually reaches a height of about 20 feet with an equal rounded spread in five to seven years, eventually becoming 50 to 70 feet tall. In summer greenish bronze winged seeds hang from the branches in 5-inch stringlike clusters. The 4- to 6-inch five-lobed leaves, unlike other maple leaves, do not change color. Sycamore maple is not harmed by seashore conditions—one huge old specimen stands on the harborside lawn at the House of Seven Gables in Salem, Massachusetts. Two unusual varieties are the wine-leaved sycamore maple, *A. pseudoplatanus spaethii,* whose leaves are dark green on top and burgundy red underneath, and the yellow sycamore maple, *A. pseudoplatanus worleei,* whose leaves unfold bright yellow in spring but turn green in summer. Sycamore maple grows in Areas C, D, I and J, in full sun or light shade and almost any well-drained soil.

CRIMSON KING NORWAY MAPLE
Acer platanoides 'Crimson King'

RED MAPLE
Acer rubrum

For growing areas, see map on page 150.

SILVER MAPLE
Acer saccharinum

SUGAR MAPLE
Acer saccharum

Trees bought bare-rooted should be planted in spring.

Red maple is well named, for in very early spring, often before the snow has melted in the North, tiny red flowers brighten every red-hued twig; in late spring the flowers are supplanted by bright red winged seeds, and in early fall the foliage begins to take on autumn tints, usually red but often yellow or orange or a combination of all on a single tree or even on a single leaf. It is a fast-growing rounded or oval-shaped species—an 8- to 10-foot tree usually grows about 20 feet tall with an equal spread in five to seven years, eventually becoming 50 to 70 feet tall. Its dark green leaves, 2 to 4 inches across and usually three-lobed (some have five lobes), have silvery undersides, which create a two-toned effect in the wind. Young red maples have smooth pale gray bark; as the trees mature, the trunks turn nearly black, but the younger branches still retain the gray color. Among the outstanding varieties are three with a columnar shape—Armstrong, Columnare and Doric; of these, Armstrong and Doric have very slender profiles (trees 30 feet tall are only 6 feet in diameter), while Columnare usually grows only twice as tall as its width. Two varieties noted for their deep red autumn color and their ability to hold their leaves longer than most other red maples are October Glory and Red Sunset. The variety Tilford is densely foliaged with a broadly conical shape, and is so symmetrical that it appears sheared.

Red maples of one kind or another grow in all parts of the United States and southern Canada, but to be sure that the variety you buy is resistant to winter cold in your region, select only plants that have been growing for several years in a local nursery. Red maples tolerate almost any soil if the ground is given a good soaking during dry weather. Trees bought either bare-rooted or balled and burlaped should be planted in spring.

The silver maple grows very fast: an 8- to 10-foot tree becomes about 20 feet tall with an equal rounded spread in four or five years, eventually reaching 60 to 100 feet. Its leaves are bright green on top with silvery undersides; in autumn they take on a delicate shade of clear yellow, sometimes with an orange tinge. Because it is exceptionally cold resistant and beautiful—the tips of its branches droop gracefully, and the delicate lacy leaves cast a light shade —the silver maple is still widely planted despite serious drawbacks. Its brittle branches break easily in high winds and ice storms. And its spreading roots often cause damage if it is planted along a street; they push up pavements and, because the species normally grows in wet places, have a tendency to seek out and plug up drainage lines. Two varieties of silver maple are not so tall as the ordinary species, a fact that reduces the disadvantages somewhat—they offer less surface for the winds to damage and their roots do not range as far. Wier's cut-leaved silver maple, *A. saccharinum laciniatum wierii,* usually grows no more than 50 feet tall; its deeply indented foliage gives an extremely lacy appearance and its drooping branch tips are unusually long. The pyramidal silver maple, *A. saccharinum pyramidale,* grows 60 to 80 feet tall with a spread of only about 40 feet. Silver maples grow in all areas except Area E, in full sun or light shade in almost any soil, but grow fastest in moist soil. Trees bought bare-rooted should be planted in spring.

Sugar maple is the source of maple sugar and syrup. It grows rather slowly: planted when 8 to 10 feet tall, it becomes about 20 feet tall in seven or eight years and forms a slender oval shape that does not cast much shade. It eventually reaches about 75 feet with a spread of 40 to 50 feet. Its handsome leaves, usually 3 to 5 inches across, are noted for their brilliant fall shades of yellow, orange and red.

Because of the height of this tree and because it does not tolerate the chemicals used to melt ice on highways or the air pollution from passing traffic, the sugar maple should be planted well away from roadways, set off on a lawn where it can develop its full beauty through the years. One of the most unusual of many excellent varieties is the globe sugar maple, *A. saccharum globosum,* which has to be grafted to the upright stem of the species and then slowly becomes globe-shaped, adding about 6 inches a year until it reaches about 10 feet in height and 10 feet across. Green Mountain has tough waxy dark green leaves; it is listed by many nurserymen as a sugar maple but is believed to be a naturally formed hybrid between the sugar maple and the more drought-resistant black maple, *A. nigrum.* The cut-leaved sugar maple, *A. saccharum laciniatum,* has deeply lobed lacy-looking leaves. Two varieties that are useful as accents or in constricted areas where height is desired are Newton Sentry, also called the columnar sugar maple, *A. saccharum columnare,* and Temple's Upright, also called the Sentry sugar maple, *A. saccharum monumentale;* both grow 50 to 60 feet tall with a spread of about 12 feet. Sugar maples grow in all areas except E and J. They do best in full sun in an evenly moist well-drained soil. Trees bought bare-rooted should be planted in spring.

AESCULUS

A. californica (California buckeye), *A. carnea briotii* (ruby horse chestnut), *A. glabra* (Ohio buckeye), *A. hippocastanum* (common horse chestnut)

Many gardeners who have seen the magnificent horse chestnut trees that still line the boulevards of Paris, or who have childhood memories of horse chestnuts or buckeyes shading the streets of their hometowns, cannot help but have a soft spot in their hearts for them. They are among the first trees to unfold glistening buds in spring, and for two weeks in late spring the ends of their branches are tipped with flower spikes as much as a foot long, each thickly set with pink, red, white or greenish yellow flowers an inch across. But it must also be admitted that these coarse-foliaged trees bear poisonous leaves and nuts, drop their leaves early in fall, usually without changing color, and litter the ground in almost every season.

The dark brown nuts are about 1 inch in diameter. The husks of most buckeyes are smooth, while those of horse chestnuts are prickly; all are usually rounded, about 2 inches in diameter, and become major impediments to lawn mowing. The palm-shaped leaves measure 8 to 12 inches or more across and consist of five to seven leaflets of various sizes; the leaves provide bold accents and cast a deep shade in summer. Even when leafless, buckeyes and horse chestnuts add interest to a garden because of their dark bark and thick stems. All species tolerate urban pollution and the salt spray of seaside areas.

California buckeye grows from 6 to 8 feet to about 20 feet in 8 to 10 years, eventually reaching 40 feet with a spread of 30 to 50 feet. It begins to bear fragrant pinkish white flowers in 6- to 10-inch spirelike clusters when it is 10 to 12 feet tall and is particularly useful in seashore gardens along the Pacific coast. The ruby horse chestnut, a hybrid, makes a spectacular small tree; planted when 6 to 8 feet tall, it reaches 20 feet in 8 to 10 years, eventually reaching 30 to 40 feet with a spread of 25 to 30 feet. It begins to bear its 5- to 8-inch spikes of brilliant red flowers when only 6 to 8 feet tall. The Ohio buckeye grows from 6 to 8 feet to about 15 feet in six to eight years, eventually reaching 20 to 30 feet with an equal spread. The species is valued more for its bright orange autumn foliage than for its 4- to 7-inch spikes of inconspicuous greenish yellow

TEMPLE'S UPRIGHT SUGAR MAPLE
Acer saccharum monumentale

RUBY HORSE CHESTNUT
Aesculus carnea briotii

For growing areas, see map on page 150.

OHIO BUCKEYE
Aesculus glabra

BAUMANN HORSE CHESTNUT
Aesculus hippocastanum baumannii

flowers. The oval-shaped common horse chestnut grows from 6 to 8 feet to 20 feet in six to eight years, eventually reaching 50 to 75 feet with a 35- to 40-foot spread. It has rough brownish black bark and thick, unusually formed branches; they rise from the trunk, then descend, then rise again at their tips. The branches begin to bear great numbers of white flowers in 8- to 12-inch spikes when the tree is 15 to 20 feet tall. The Baumann horse chestnut, *Aesculus hippocastanum baumannii*, a sterile variety of the common horse chestnut—which it resembles in size and shape—has many-petaled white flowers but no fruit and is particularly recommended for cities because its lack of fruit eases the litter problem.

HOW TO GROW. California buckeye grows only in Areas I and J; the other species listed here grow in the southern part of Area A and in Areas B, C, D, F, G, H, I and J. All species grow in full sun or light shade in soil that is deep enough to accommodate the trees' long root structures and do best if the soil is moist; if the soil dries out in summer, the leaves turn brown at the edges and drop early. Prune in early spring.

AILANTHUS
A. altissima, also called *A. glandulosa* and *A. japonica* (tree of heaven)

There is a quirk that runs through the nature of many gardeners—a tendency to consider a plant that is difficult to grow as being desirable and to disdain one that happens to be easy to grow; if it is very easy to grow, it is termed "weedy." For this reason, the tree of heaven is often scorned—and unnecessarily. It is a Chinese species that grows very rapidly, thrives in almost all soils and climates, resists practically all insects and diseases, and tolerates soot and pollution better than any other tree, native or foreign. It gained fame as "the tree that grows in Brooklyn," but the name of any metropolis could be used as well.

The species grows so rapidly that a 4- to 6-foot tree usually attains its full height of 40 to 60 feet, with a spread of nearly equal size, in 10 to 15 years. It is short lived, however, and is likely to succumb to damage by wind or ice storms by the time it is 25 to 30 years old. Its leaves, reddish when they unfurl late in the spring, but soon turning green, are fern-shaped and from 1 to 3 feet in length, and each consists of 11 to 31 leaflets, 3 to 5 inches long. The leaves grow in bunches at the ends of heavy twigs, creating a pattern that allows sun to filter through to the ground below. Although scentless on the tree, the leaves have an unpleasant odor when crushed.

Because the tree of heaven grows so easily, it can become a nuisance, sending out underground shoots to sprout into a thicket and winged seeds to take root over a wide area. The unwanted seedlings are easily avoided, however, because each tree bears flowers of one sex; if you (and your neighbors) plant only female trees, they will produce seeds that are attractive—6- to 12-inch clusters, yellow to orange red in color—but, being unpollinated, cannot develop into seedlings. Female trees are also preferable because their flowers—inconspicuous clusters of tiny yellow blossoms—lack the odor that makes the male flowers objectionable. A particularly attractive female variety of the tree of heaven, *A. altissima erythrocarpa*, has bright red seed clusters that are conspicuous from late summer through late fall, clinging to the branches even after the leaves have fallen.

HOW TO GROW. The tree of heaven grows in Areas B, C, D, F, G, I and J, in almost any soil and light conditions. Underground shoots should be pruned as soon as they appear if additional trees are not desired.

ALBIZIA (ALBIZZIA)

A. julibrissin (silk tree, mimosa)

Throughout the southern and western parts of the United States, silk trees are among the most popular of all flowering trees. They grow very rapidly: planted at 5 to 6 feet, they become 15 to 20 feet tall in three to five years, eventually reaching 25 to 35 feet with a spread equal to or greater than their height. They often have several trunks but can be trained to grow with single trunks by being pruned when young. Their branches extend in horizontal tiers that make the trees ideal for shading patios or as lawn ornaments. Their 9- to 18-inch featherlike leaves consist of dozens of ¼- to ½-inch leaflets that cast a shade so delicate it does not inhibit the growing of grass. Beginning in early summer and extending until early fall, 5- to 8-inch clusters of ball-shaped pink flowers about 1 inch across are borne above the foliage, where they make a spectacular display and are very attractive to hummingbirds. The flowers are followed by flat seed pods about 5 to 6 inches long. Silk trees begin to bloom when they are only two or three years old, but start to lose their vigor when they are only 25 to 30 years old. (This tree's other common name, mimosa, is widely used for this species in the South, but in the West it is usually applied to an evergreen, *Acacia baileyana*, which has similar foliage but yellow flowers. *Mimosa* is also the botanical name of a genus that includes a somewhat similar plant called the sensitive plant.)

A variety of the silk tree, *A. julibrissin rosea*, the pink silk tree, grows from 5 to 6 feet to 10 to 12 feet in three or four years, ultimately reaching only 15 to 20 feet. It has smaller clusters of darker pink flowers than the ordinary species and is slightly more cold resistant.

HOW TO GROW. All silk trees grow in Areas D, E, G, I and J; the pink silk tree also grows in the southern half of Area C. They tolerate wind, partial shade and poor soil, including alkaline soil, but grow fastest and blossom most abundantly in full sun and well-drained soil. Buy young trees not over 8 to 10 feet tall; if they are purchased balled and burlaped—that is, with their roots in their original soil ball wrapped in burlap—they should be planted in spring. To help prevent winter injury to pink silk trees in Area C, wrap their trunks in burlap or heavy paper for two or three years, until the trees become firmly rooted. Prune both types of silk tree in winter or early spring.

ALDER See *Alnus*
ALGAROBA See *Prosopis*

ALNUS

A. cordata (Italian alder); *A. rhombifolia* (white alder); *A. rubra,* also called *A. oregona* (red alder)

Alders grow well near ponds and other wet places. Fast growers, they are sometimes used until more desirable species reach an adequate size. Alders often have multiple trunks but can be trained to grow with single trunks by being pruned when young. Their leaves open early in spring and drop late in fall. Male and female yellowish green flowers appear in scaly clusters, or catkins, on the same tree in spring, just before the leaves unfurl. The cylindrical male catkins are 2 to 6 inches long. In summer the 1-inch female catkins become brown conelike fruit that cling most of the year and can be used in dried floral arrangements.

The Italian alder grows from 6 to 8 feet to 20 feet in four or five years, eventually becoming 30 to 50 feet tall and conical with a spread of 20 to 30 feet. Its 2- to 4-inch leaves are a shiny medium green on top and pale green underneath. The white alder grows from 5 to 6 feet to 20 feet in four or five years, eventually reaching 50 to 75 feet

TREE OF HEAVEN
Ailanthus altissima

PINK SILK TREE
Albizia julibrissin rosea

For growing areas, see map on page 150.

ITALIAN ALDER
Alnus cordata

WHITE ALDER
Alnus rhombifolia

with a spread of 30 to 40 feet; its slender branches droop gracefully at the tips and are densely set with 2- to 4-inch leaves that are glossy dark green on top and pale green underneath. The red alder grows from 5 to 6 feet to 20 feet in four or five years, eventually becoming 40 to 60 feet tall and conical with a spread of 30 to 40 feet. It is often so plentiful in low-lying coastal areas of the Pacific Northwest that it is disdained as a garden tree but is quite attractive, with 3- to 6-inch dark green leaves that are rusty gray beneath and light gray-white smooth bark reminiscent of birches.

HOW TO GROW. The Italian alder grows in Areas C, D, I and J; the white alder in Areas I and J; and the red alder in Areas C, F, G, H and I. All grow in light shade or full sun in almost any moist or wet soil; the Italian alder will also tolerate well-drained soil if the soil is given a good soaking every two weeks during dry seasons. Prune in winter or early spring.

AMELANCHIER
A. canadensis (downy serviceberry), *A. grandiflora* (apple serviceberry), *A. laevis* (Allegheny serviceberry). (All also called shad-blow or Juneberry)

The serviceberries listed here are among the first native trees to blossom in spring. Slender-branched and airy, with delicate twigs and smooth light gray bark, they may have single or multiple trunks. In their first year they begin to bear short spikes of 1-inch flowers, which appear in great quantities just before the leaves unfurl, and are followed in early summer by tiny apple-shaped red or purple sweet berries. The berries were welcomed by pioneers because they ripened early, providing fresh fruit months before other tree fruits were ready for picking. They are hidden among dark green leaves, however, and birds usually eat most of them before gardeners realize they are getting ripe. The 1½- to 3-inch leaves turn yellow, orange or red in fall. Serviceberries are excellent for growing in a semiwild setting, either under larger trees or at the edge of a group of trees. Because their blossoms are snowy white, they are especially effective when seen against dark evergreens.

The downy serviceberry grows from 6 to 8 feet to 15 to 18 feet with an equal or greater spread in five to seven years, eventually becoming 20 to 30 feet tall and oval-shaped with a spread of 10 to 15 feet. New leaves are covered with soft gray hairs when they first open—hence its common name—but are smooth and green the rest of the summer. The apple serviceberry, a natural hybrid between the downy and the Allegheny serviceberries, grows from 6 to 8 feet to 15 to 18 feet in five to seven years, eventually becoming 20 to 25 feet tall with an equal rounded spread. Its flowers, slightly more than an inch across, open from buds that are pinkish on some plants. The Allegheny serviceberry grows from 6 to 8 feet to 15 to 18 feet in five to seven years, eventually becoming 25 to 30 feet tall and oval-shaped with a spread of 10 to 12 feet. Its leaves are tinged purple as they open but quickly turn dark green.

HOW TO GROW. Serviceberries grow in Areas B, C, D, F, G, H and I, in full sun or light shade and moist well-drained soil. They rarely need pruning or fertilizing.

AMYGDALUS See *Prunus*
ARALIA, CASTOR See *Kalopanax*
ASH See *Fraxinus*
ASH, MOUNTAIN See *Sorbus*

ASIMINA
A. triloba (papaw, pawpaw)

The papaw tree—not to be confused with the tropical papaya plant, *Carica papaya*, which is sometimes also called papaw—is an unusual native tree that grows from New Jersey and Illinois to the Gulf of Mexico. It grows from 3 to 5 feet to 12 to 15 feet in four to six years and eventually becomes 20 to 30 feet tall with an equal spread. Its 6- to 12-inch-long glossy leaves hang downward, trembling whenever a breath of air stirs; they turn yellow before dropping in fall. In late spring, just as the leaves become nearly full grown, 2-inch blossoms develop at the bases of the leaves; the flowers are greenish when they open but change to dull purple. They are followed by strange sausage-shaped fruit, 4 to 6 inches long and 1 to 2 inches in diameter, that ripen in fall. Dark yellowish brown, with a sweet rich flavor similar to that of bananas, the fruit are enjoyed immensely by some people and disliked intensely by others. The pulp has the consistency of creamy custard and may be eaten raw or baked or used as a pie filling. Within the flesh of the fruit are numerous brown seeds about the size and shape of lima beans.

HOW TO GROW. The papaw grows in Areas C, D and E, in full sun or very light shade in moist well-drained soil that is deep enough to accommodate its long root structure. Buy young trees no more than 3 to 5 feet tall, for larger ones are difficult to establish in the garden; many nurserymen do not stock papaws regularly.

B

BASSWOOD See *Tilia*

BAUHINIA
B. variegata (Buddhist bauhinia, mountain ebony and orchid tree)

The Buddhist bauhinia is renowned in warm climates for its dramatic, faintly fragrant orchid-shaped blossoms. The 2- to 3-inch pinkish, purple or white flowers bloom in winter and early spring before the 3- to 4-inch leaves appear, and are followed by 6- to 8-inch flat brown seed pods. The Buddhist bauhinia grows fast: planted at 6 to 8 feet, it reaches its full height of 20 to 25 feet and spread of about 15 feet in 8 to 10 years. It usually has several trunks but can be trained to grow with a single trunk by being pruned when young.

Buddhist bauhinias are excellent for shading a patio, lining a suburban street or ornamenting a lawn. In its native India, the tree has still another use—the young leaves and flowers are stewed and eaten as vegetables.

HOW TO GROW. Buddhist bauhinias grow in parts of Areas E and J where winter temperatures do not drop below 25° F. The trees may suffer dieback—that is, 2 to 12 inches of the tips of the branches may be killed by cold temperatures—but if the freezing period lasts no longer than a few nights, the trees themselves are not usually killed and the branches will sprout again below the damaged areas. Buddhist bauhinias grow in almost any moist well-drained acid soil (pH 5.5 to 6.5) and do best in full sun but must be sheltered from wind. Prune after the flowers fade only if necessary to train the tree to a desired shape.

BEAD TREE See *Melia*
BEECH See *Fagus*

BETULA
B. papyrifera (canoe, paper or white birch); *B. pendula*, also called *B. alba*, *B. verrucosa* (European white birch); *B. populifolia* (gray birch)

There are few springtime garden pictures to rival a clump of snowy-trunked birches sending out their first pale green leaves. The trees are at their best seen against a

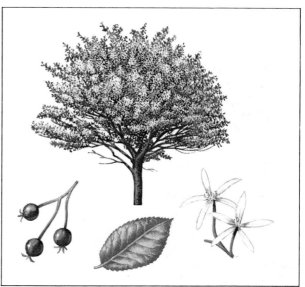

APPLE SERVICEBERRY
Amelanchier grandiflora

PAPAW
Asimina triloba

BUDDHIST BAUHINIA
Bauhinia variegata

For growing areas, see map on page 150.

CANOE BIRCH
Betula papyrifera

CUT-LEAVED EUROPEAN WHITE BIRCH
Betula pendula gracilis

dark evergreen background, not only during summer, when their own leaves are bright green, or in fall, when the leaves turn golden yellow, but in winter, when the white trunks and branches stand out boldly against the evergreen foliage. Not all birches have white bark, but the species described here do; however, even the bark of these species is not white to start with—for the first four or five years, it is brown. Birches grow rapidly: planted when 6 to 8 feet tall, all species provide a handsome effect in about 10 years, when they generally reach a height of 20 feet or more. But despite their universal appeal, it is necessary to note that birches are often attacked by two kinds of insects—the bronze birch borer, which can kill or disfigure a tree by girdling the tops of its main stems, and the birch-leaf miner, which tunnels through leaves, causing them to turn brown. Both pests, however, can usually be controlled (see pest-control methods on page 148).

A canoe birch eventually becomes 60 to 75 feet tall with a loosely rounded spread equal to about half its height. It may have either a single trunk or multiple trunks, and its leaves are 1½ to 4½ inches long. Native to the northern part of North America, it has the whitest bark of any birch and was the one used by Indians in making canoes; it is unlike the other birches discussed here in that the old outer bark shreds and peels naturally.

The European white birch, the Eurasian counterpart of the canoe birch, eventually reaches 30 to 60 feet with a conical spread of 10 to 20 feet. Although it is able to tolerate the poor growing conditions of urban areas, it is a relatively short-lived tree, declining in vigor after 25 to 30 years even in ideal locations. European white birches are available with single or multiple trunks. They have 1½- to 2½-inch-long diamond-shaped leaves, and bark marked with black ridges; their branches droop gracefully, an attribute that is especially noticeable in some varieties. One such variety, the cut-leaved European white birch, *B. pendula gracilis*, also called *B. pendula laciniata*, has long slender branches that move in the slightest breeze; its 1- to 2½-inch leaves are so deeply lobed that they appear lacy. Young's European white birch, *B. pendula youngii*, has a pronounced weeping habit of growth. The pyramidal European white birch, *B. pendula fastigiata*, is more columnar in shape than its common name suggests. Another variety, Purple Splendor, has purplish green leaves.

The gray birch is native to northeastern North America and is often the first tree to reappear after an area has been logged or burned out by a forest fire. A gray birch rarely becomes more than 20 to 30 feet tall with a conical spread of 10 to 15 feet. It has multiple trunks and 1- to 2-inch wedge-shaped leaves. The name gray birch alludes to the effect of the blending into the white trunk of the black spots that mark the places where branches have grown and been lost; the overall color seems to be white, however, unless the trees are seen beside the pristine whiteness of canoe birches. Gray birches are short lived, usually succumbing after about 20 years.

HOW TO GROW. The canoe birch grows in Areas A, B, C, F, H and I; the European white birch in Areas A, B, C, D, F, G, H, I and J; the gray birch in Areas B and C. All require full sun and do best in moist soil, either sandy or average. The European white birch and the gray birch will also grow in very wet or dry soil. Trees bought balled and burlaped—that is, with their roots in their original soil ball wrapped in burlap—should be planted in spring. Prune only in summer or fall—pruning in late winter or early spring causes the tree to bleed excessively.

BIRCH See *Betula*

BOX ELDER See *Acer*

BROUSSONETIA
B. papyrifera (paper mulberry)

The paper mulberry is a tough fast-growing tree that casts a heavy shade and does well in the grime and soot of cities and also tolerates the heat and drought of deserts. Planted when it is 6 to 8 feet tall, it often reaches its full height of 25 to 40 feet with an equal rounded spread in 8 to 10 years. It grows with one or several gray-barked trunks, which become gnarled and twisted with age. The rough-textured leaves are generally heart-shaped or lobed but vary considerably in form, and several different shapes may appear on the same branch. The undersides of the leaves, as well as the tree's twigs, are covered with woolly hairs. The paper mulberry bears male and female flowers on separate trees. The female flowers form compact rounded heads ½ inch across *(far left in illustration)*, while the male flowers appear in scaly clusters, or catkins, 1½ to 3 inches long; both are greenish yellow and appear in spring. On female trees the flowers are followed in early summer by ¾-inch red globular fruit *(right in illustration)*, which are eaten by birds. If trees of both sexes are present, the paper mulberry produces so many seedlings it may become a nuisance; even a single tree is apt to send up shoots, or suckers, from its roots, which should be cut away whenever they appear. The paper mulberry is not related to the true mulberry of the genus *Morus (page 128)*.

HOW TO GROW. The paper mulberry grows in the southern part of Area C and in Areas D, E, G, I and J. It requires full sun but grows in almost any soil, even highly alkaline soil, and endures wind and heat.

BUCKEYE See *Aesculus*
BUTTONBALL See *Platanus*
BUTTONWOOD See *Platanus*

C

CARPINUS
C. betulus (European hornbeam), *C. caroliniana* (American hornbeam)

Hornbeams have such dense foliage and tolerate close shearing so well that they are often grown as tall hedges. Their dark green leaves may drop in the fall after turning yellow, or become brown and cling to the branches most of the winter. The smooth gray tightly clinging bark seems to ripple as though it had muscles tensing beneath it. The extremely hard wood beneath the bark was used by the ancient Romans to make their chariots and by American pioneers to make yokes for oxen. Hornbeams grow slowly and are unusually resistant to pests and diseases. Planted at 5 to 6 feet, the European hornbeam becomes about 15 feet tall with a conical or oval shape in about 10 years, eventually reaching a height of 40 to 60 feet with a globular spread of about 30 to 40 feet. The leaves are 1½ to 3½ inches long and turn yellow in fall. The pyramidal European hornbeam, *C. betulus fastigiata*—which has an oval shape despite the word pyramidal in its common name—grows to an ultimate height of only about 30 feet with a spread of 10 to 12 feet. Its twigs and leaves are spaced so closely together that the tree gives the appearance of having been sheared. The American hornbeam grows from 5 to 6 feet to 15 feet in about 10 years and eventually reaches a height of 20 to 35 feet with an equal rounded spread. It often has several trunks. Its leaves are 2½ to 4½ inches long and turn orange and red in fall.

HOW TO GROW. The European hornbeam grows in Areas C, D, G and I; the American hornbeam in Areas B, C, D, E,

PAPER MULBERRY
Broussonetia papyrifera

PYRAMIDAL EUROPEAN HORNBEAM
Carpinus betulus fastigiata

For growing areas, see map on page 150.

PECAN
Carya illinoensis

G, H and I. Both grow in almost any soil, but the European hornbeam does best in full sun and the American hornbeam prefers light shade. Hornbeams are easiest to establish in the garden when they are under 8 feet tall. Trees bought balled and burlaped—that is, with their roots in their original soil ball wrapped in burlap—should be planted in spring. Pruning is rarely required.

CARYA
C. illinoensis, also called *C. pecan, Hicoria pecan* (pecan)

Pecans are justly famous for the delicious nuts they bear where summers are long and hot. In many cooler regions they are also excellent for shade, producing a filtered shadow in which grass grows well. The trees grow slowly: a 6- to 8-foot tree reaches a height of 15 to 20 feet after about 10 years, but ultimately may become as tall as 100 feet with a spread of 40 to 75 feet. In fruit-producing areas, the trees produce their first nuts four to seven years after planting and eventually bear large crops of the familiar nuts, which are usually 1½ to 2½ inches long. The nuts drop to the ground when they are ripe in fall and do not have to be picked off the tree, although squirrels do their best to harvest them before the homeowner gets around to picking them up. The enormous leaves, usually 12 to 18 inches long, turn golden yellow in fall.

HOW TO GROW. Pecan trees grow in most of Area C, as well as throughout Areas D, E, G, I and J, but there are so many varieties, some more suitable for one area than another, that it is advisable to consult your local nurseryman for the ones best suited to your region. Pecan trees need full sun and moist soil that is deep enough to accommodate their long root structures. Pecans have long vertical main roots, or taproots, which make them difficult to establish in the garden, especially if purchased balled and burlaped, with their roots in their original soil ball wrapped in burlap; because of the shape of the roots, the soil balls are usually much higher than they are wide, and deep holes must be dug to accommodate them. For easiest planting, buy the trees bare-rooted and plant them in winter or early spring. In fruiting areas it is especially important to fertilize early each spring to help produce large crops. Pruning, which is rarely needed, should be done in the winter.

CASHAW See *Prosopis*

CASSIA
C. fistula (golden shower, shower of gold, senna)

The golden shower, a spectacular flowering tree from India, is a familiar sight in southern parts of Florida and California as well as in Hawaii. Planted at 5 to 6 feet, it grows rapidly to its full height of about 30 feet with an equal spread in 8 to 10 years. It usually begins to blossom about three years after planting. From midspring until early summer it provides a splendid display of fragrant 2-inch yellow flowers that hang in clusters 12 to 18 inches long; the flowers are followed by cylindrical brown-black seed pods 1 to 2 feet long. The foot-long leaves consist of four to eight pairs of 2-inch leaflets and cling to the tree most of the year, dropping late in winter. Golden shower is often used with dramatic effect as a lawn ornament or along roadways. The blossoms are eaten as a delicacy in India, where the tree has been grown for medicinal and other purposes for thousands of years. Among its many diverse products are a tobacco flavoring, a leather-tanning agent, a cough medicine and a laxative made from the fleshy pulp of the seed pods. The hard, durable red heartwood of the tree is used in the tropics for fence posts, but is also treasured for fine cabinetwork.

GOLDEN SHOWER
Cassia fistula

HOW TO GROW. Golden shower grows in the frost-free and nearly frost-free parts of Areas E and J, in full sun or light shade and almost any well-drained soil. Pruning is rarely required.

CASTANEA
C. mollissima (Chinese chestnut)

The Chinese chestnut is a fast-growing tree. Planted at 4 to 5 feet, it becomes 8 to 12 feet tall in three or four years, at which time it begins to produce edible nuts; by the time the tree is 13 or 14 years old it will have reached a height of 20 to 25 feet with an equal spread and may produce as much as 75 to 100 pounds of nuts annually; it eventually becomes 30 to 50 feet tall. The handsome 4- to 7-inch leaves of the Chinese chestnut provide dense shade. The leaves are reddish when they first unfold, soon become a glossy dark green and in fall turn shades of yellow and bronze. In early summer masses of tiny fragrant creamy white flowers appear in 8- to 10-inch upright clusters. These are followed by 2- to 3-inch prickly seed husks that open to release two or three shiny brown edible chestnuts, each up to an inch across. Trees of at least two different varieties should be planted, for pollination of one variety by pollen from another is usually necessary if the flowers are to bear fruit.

HOW TO GROW. The Chinese chestnut grows in Areas C, D, G, I and J, in almost any well-drained nonalkaline soil (a pH of 5.5 to 6.5 is ideal). It requires full sun. The trees are easy to establish bare-rooted and should be planted in spring. It is especially important to fertilize them. Pruning is hardly ever needed.

CASTOR ARALIA See *Kalopanax*

CATALPA
C. bignonioides (common or southern catalpa), C. speciosa (western catalpa). (Both also called Indian bean)

Catalpas are such fast-growing, easy-to-establish, pest-free trees that some people consider them too commonplace to bother about. But they should not be neglected, for they provide welcome dense shade and handsome white flowers. A 5- to 6-foot tree generally grows about 20 feet tall with a spread of 10 to 15 feet in seven or eight years. The trees begin to blossom when 10 to 12 feet tall; the flowers appear in erect 6- to 8-inch-high clusters at the ends of the branches in early summer after most other trees have finished blossoming, and are followed by brown seed pods, 6 to 20 inches long and the thickness of a pencil, that cling to the trees throughout winter. When catalpas reach about 30 years of age, their trunks and branches become picturesquely gnarled. The common catalpa eventually grows 35 to 40 feet tall with an equal spread. Its leaves are 5 to 6 inches long and 3 to 4 inches wide. Each of its 2-inch flowers has two yellow stripes and numerous purplish brown spots. The western catalpa eventually grows 40 to 60 feet tall with a spread of 30 to 40 feet. Its leaves grow 8 to 12 inches long and 5 to 7 inches wide. The 2½-inch flowers have faint purplish spots and open about two weeks after those of the common catalpa.

HOW TO GROW. Catalpas grow in Areas C, D, E, F, G, H, I and J; the western catalpa also grows in Area B. Both types grow in sun or shade in almost any soil, wet or dry, and almost any climate, hot or cold; they even tolerate alkaline soil and drought. Catalpas rarely need pruning.

CELTIS
C. australis (European hackberry); C. laevigata, also called C. mississippiensis, C. integrifolia (sugarberry, southern or

CHINESE CHESTNUT
Castanea mollissima

COMMON CATALPA
Catalpa bignonioides

For growing areas, see map on page 150.

COMMON HACKBERRY
Celtis occidentalis

KATSURA TREE
Cercidiphyllum japonicum

Mississippi hackberry); *C. laevigata reticulata,* also called *C. douglasii* (net-leaved or western hackberry); *C. occidentalis* (common hackberry). (All also called nettle tree)

Hackberries are native to most of the United States and southern Canada and are extremely easy to establish, even under such trying conditions as drought, poor soil, and the soot and grime of cities. Their tough branches resist breakage by wind, and because their root systems are deep and do not disturb sidewalks and other paving, they make excellent plantings along streets. They grow moderately fast when young: planted at 6 to 8 feet, they usually reach a height of 25 to 35 feet with an equal spread in 10 to 15 years; after that their rate of growth slows. Hackberries are related to elms and have similarly shaped leaves, usually saw-toothed, that turn pale yellow in fall before dropping. Pea-sized berries appear in fall and cling to the branches into winter if they are not eaten by birds. The bark of hackberries is often covered with wartlike bumps, making the trees easy to identify.

The European hackberry eventually grows to a height of 45 to 75 feet with a rounded spread of 35 to 50 feet and has gray-green leaves 2 to 6 inches long and purple berries ½ inch in diameter. The sugarberry eventually grows 75 to 90 feet tall with a spread equal to about half its height; it has 2- to 4-inch-long smooth-edged leaves and black fruit ¼ inch across. The net-leaved hackberry ultimately reaches a height of only 25 to 30 feet with an equal rounded spread; it has 2- to 4-inch-long leaves with prominent veins and bears black fruit ¼ inch across. The common hackberry, the species stocked by most nurserymen, eventually grows 50 to 60 feet tall with a nearly equal spread; it has 2½- to 5-inch-long leaves and ¼-inch purple fruit. Its twigs are often attacked by a parasitic fungus that deforms the leaf buds and causes an abnormal bushiness known as witches'-broom. The disease is not disabling, however, and the infected twigs, which eventually die, should simply be removed when they are noticed.

HOW TO GROW. The European hackberry grows in Areas G, I and J; the sugarberry in Areas C, D, E, G, I and J; the net-leaved hackberry in Areas C, D, G, I and J; and the common hackberry in Areas A, B, C, D, F, G, H, I and J. All species do best in full sun and tolerate almost any soil, acid or alkaline, wet or dry, but they grow at a sharply reduced rate if moisture is scarce. Hackberries up to 6 to 8 feet tall can be planted bare-rooted in spring if their root system is kept quite moist. Little pruning is required.

CERCIDIPHYLLUM
C. japonicum (katsura tree)

The katsura tree, a native of Japan, is one of the most attractive and dependable of all shade trees and deserves a wider popularity than it presently enjoys. It bears inconspicuous male and female flowers on separate trees. Male trees usually grow with a single trunk in a slender conical shape, while female trees often have several trunks and usually spread their branches to a distance equal to their height. Both sexes grow quite rapidly when young, a 6- to 8-foot tree usually becoming 20 to 25 feet tall in five or six years; after that it grows more slowly, ultimately reaching a height of 40 to 60 feet. The shiny 2- to 4-inch heart-shaped leaves are arranged in such a manner on the tree that they are able to cast ample shade, yet at the same time allow air to flow through freely. They have a reddish tinge when they open early in spring, then become a deep blue-green in summer and turn shades of yellow or red before dropping in autumn. The tips of growing branches are tinged with red throughout the summer. The bark of the katsura tree is dark brown, and on old trees it shreds along the trunk and main branches to give a shaggy appearance.

HOW TO GROW. The katsura tree grows in all areas except Area A. It requires full sun in Areas B, C, D, F, H and I, and light shade in Areas E, G and J, and does best in moist well-drained soil. Pruning is seldom necessary.

CERCIS
C. canadensis (eastern redbud); *C. occidentalis* (California redbud); *C. reniformis,* also called *C. texensis* (Texas redbud). (All also called Judas tree)

Redbuds are lovely flowering trees that, in one species or another, grow wild over much of the United States. Early each spring, before their leaves unfurl, they clothe their branches and even their trunks with great clusters of ½-inch purplish pink blossoms. The two larger-growing species—the eastern redbud and the Texas redbud—grow from 3 to 4 feet to 10 to 15 feet in five or six years, eventually reaching a height of up to 35 feet. A California redbud planted at 3 to 4 feet reaches its full height of 10 to 12 feet in four or five years. A delightful white-flowered variety of the eastern redbud is *C. canadensis alba.* Redbuds begin to blossom when they are four or five years old. After their flowers fade, redbuds bear 2- to 4-inch greenish pink seed pods, which turn brown when they ripen and cling to the trees throughout most of the winter. The 3- to 5-inch glossy green leaves open late in spring and turn yellow before dropping in fall. Redbuds make a lovely combination with flowering dogwoods *(Cornus, page 106),* which blossom at the same time.

HOW TO GROW. The eastern redbud grows in all areas except Area A; the California redbud grows in Areas H, I and J; the Texas redbud in Areas D, E and G. All grow in full sun or light shade and do best in moist but well-drained soil that is deep enough to accommodate the trees' long roots. Buy young trees that are no more than 6 feet in height. Plants bought balled and burlaped—that is, with their roots in their original soil ball wrapped in burlap—or container grown should be planted in spring in Areas B, C, F, G and H; in Areas D, E, I and J, they can be planted at any time from fall to spring. During the first season after they are planted, redbuds are often slow to send out their leaves. They rarely require pruning.

CHERRY See *Prunus*
CHESTNUT See *Castanea*
CHESTNUT, HORSE See *Aesculus*
CHINABERRY See *Melia*
CHINESE DATE See *Zizyphus*
CHINESE FLAME TREE See *Koelreuteria*
CHINESE PARASOL TREE See *Firmiana*

CHIONANTHUS
C. virginicus (fringe tree, old-man's-beard)

An inexperienced gardener seeing a leafless fringe tree in midspring might well think it dead, for this tree—one of the finest of all small flowering trees—waits to open its leaf buds until late spring or even early summer, long after most other trees are in full foliage. Just after the leaves unfold, 6- to 8-inch hanging clusters of fragrant white flowers appear on the branches. Each pendant blossom has four petals about 1 inch long and less than ¼ inch wide, and from a distance their shape makes the clusters seem to be made of shredded paper. Male trees have slightly larger clusters than female trees, but the female trees bear ½- to ¾-inch dark blue grapelike fruit, which is eaten by birds; there is no other apparent difference between the sexes. The fringe tree may begin to blossom when it is only 2 to 4 feet tall, but it grows slowly. Planted at 4 to 5

EASTERN REDBUD
Cercis canadensis

FRINGE TREE
Chionanthus virginicus

For growing areas, see map on page 150.

feet, it reaches a height of only 12 to 15 feet with an equal spread in about 10 years, eventually becoming 25 to 30 feet tall. It grows with either a single or a multiple trunk and makes a most attractive lawn ornament. Its 3- to 8-inch-long leaves turn golden yellow before dropping in autumn.

HOW TO GROW. The fringe tree grows in Areas B, C, D, E, F, G, I and J, in full sun or light shade, and does best in moist soil that is deep enough to accommodate the tree's long root structure. Pruning is rarely required.

CLADRASTIS
C. lutea, also called *C. tinctoria* (yellowwood)

The yellowwood is a superb tree for many purposes: its dense branches provide cool shade for a patio, its deep roots do not disturb paving when the tree is planted along a street, and its fragrant white flowers add beauty anywhere. Planted at 6 to 8 feet, it becomes 15 to 20 feet tall with a nearly equal spread in 8 to 10 years, eventually reaching 30 to 50 feet. The 1-inch flowers are borne in 12- to 15-inch clusters that hang from the ends of its twigs. The yellowwood begins to blossom when 15 to 18 feet tall. It usually has a bumper crop of flowers every two years, and relatively few in alternate years. The flowers bloom in late spring when the leaves are fully open, and are followed by 2- to 4-inch flat brown pods that ripen and drop in fall. The bright green leaves are 8 to 12 inches long, each with 7 to 11 leaflets 3 to 4 inches long; in fall they turn shades of yellow and orange before dropping. The light gray bark is smooth except on old trunks. The bright yellow of the heartwood gives the tree its common name. Both the heartwood and the bark were used by early American settlers to make yellow dye for homespun cloth.

HOW TO GROW. The yellowwood grows in Areas B, C, D, E, G, I and J. It does best in full sun and tolerates almost any soil, including alkaline soil, so long as it is moist and deep enough to accommodate the tree's long root structure. The yellowwood will even tolerate drought if the soil is watered thoroughly for a few years until the roots are well established. Buy trees 6 to 12 feet tall. Prune only in summer—the yellowwood bleeds severely if pruned in winter or spring. Remove some branches of mature trees to make them less vulnerable to breakage by wind.

COCKSPUR See *Crataegus*
COFFEE TREE, KENTUCKY See *Gymnocladus*
CORK TREE See *Phellodendron*

CORNUS
C. florida (flowering dogwood), *C. kousa* (Kousa or Japanese dogwood), *C. nuttallii* (Pacific, Nuttall's, western or mountain dogwood)

To many gardeners dogwoods are the most beautiful of all flowering trees. These delightful garden ornaments often begin to blossom when they are only 4 to 6 feet tall, and their spectacular flowers are so tough that they often stay colorful for three or four weeks, twice as long as the blossoms on other trees. But the flowers are not the trees' only attraction, for dogwoods have other traits that extend their usefulness well beyond the flowering season. The white or pink flowers are followed by bright red fruit, which are relished by birds; the dark green leaves of summer turn deep red or orange in autumn; and the horizontal tiers of branches are attractive throughout the year. Even during winter the upturned ends of the twigs look interesting, since they are tipped with fat greenish buds that will become the next season's flowers. Dogwoods usually grow from 6 to 8 feet to 12 to 15 feet with an equal spread in about five years. They have single or multiple trunks,

YELLOWWOOD
Cladrastis lutea

PINK FLOWERING DOGWOOD
Cornus florida rubra

and mature trees usually take on a flat-topped appearance. They are at their best standing alone or in groups on a lawn. Even in city gardens, where space is usually highly restricted, dogwoods can serve as dramatic accents as well as provide shade. In nature they grow at the edges of woods or under the shade of tall deciduous trees, and when they are planted in similar situations on home grounds, they are not only most attractive but are also most likely to do well.

The flowering dogwood, a species that is native from New England to Florida and Texas, is well known to all gardeners, and it is unquestionably one of the outstanding flowering trees of America. In addition to enjoying a wide popularity as a garden tree, it has been extensively planted along highways throughout much of its native area. The flowering dogwood eventually grows to a height of 15 to 30 feet with a spread of 15 to 20 feet. Its 3- to 5-inch flowers are borne in midspring before the leaves open. The blossoms are usually white, and each petal—which is actually a petallike leaf called a bract—has a distinctive notch at its tip. Small clusters of shiny red berries ¼ inch in diameter are borne at the ends of the twigs in late summer and fall. The leaves, 3 to 4 inches long and 2 to 3 inches wide, are pinkish green when they open, then turn medium green in summer and red in fall. The bark of the flowering dogwood is also distinctive: it is nearly black and, on old trunks, is deeply furrowed in a checkerboard pattern. There are a number of particularly good white-flowering varieties of flowering dogwood. Among them are White Cloud and Cherokee Princess, both of which are known for the profusion of their flowers; Gigantea and Magnifica, whose flowers are enormous—up to 6 inches across; Pluribracteata, which has double flowers with more than the usual four bracts; Welchii, whose leaves have creamy white and pink markings; and *C. florida pendula,* a variety with heavily drooping branches. In addition to these is the pink flowering dogwood, *C. florida rubra,* whose blossoms vary from blush white to deep pink. Among its many excellent varieties are Apple Blossom and Spring Song, both of which have medium pink flowers, and Cherokee Chief, which has very dark pink flowers.

The Kousa dogwood, a white-flowering species from Japan and Korea, eventually grows 15 to 25 feet tall. It bears great quantities of 3- to 4-inch blossoms in horizontal or slightly drooping sprays when its leaves are fully open in early summer, about a month after the flowering dogwood begins to blossom. The tip of each bract is sharply pointed rather than notched in the manner of the flowering dogwood, and some trees have blossoms that are tinged with pink. The pinkish red fruit of the Kousa dogwood is about ¾ inch across and looks like a large raspberry. It ripens in late summer and is eaten by birds. The leaves, 3 inches long and 1 inch wide, turn reddish brown in fall. A variety of the Kousa dogwood, the Chinese dogwood, *C. kousa chinensis,* has flowers up to 5 inches across; a particularly fine type of the Chinese variety is called Milky Way.

The Pacific dogwood is native to the mountains that range from British Columbia to Southern California. It eventually grows to a height of 20 to 30 feet and is unusual for a dogwood in that its 4- to 5-inch white blossoms generally have six rather than four bracts; the bracts are either rounded or slightly pointed at the ends and are sometimes tinged with pink. The flowers bloom not only in spring but often again in fall, at which time they are interspersed with bright red to orange fruit clusters. Each round cluster, about 1 inch across, may contain as many as 30 to 40 small berries. The 3- to 5-inch leaves of the Pacific dogwood turn yellow and red in fall.

For growing areas, see map on page 150.

KOUSA DOGWOOD
Cornus kousa

PACIFIC DOGWOOD
Cornus nuttallii

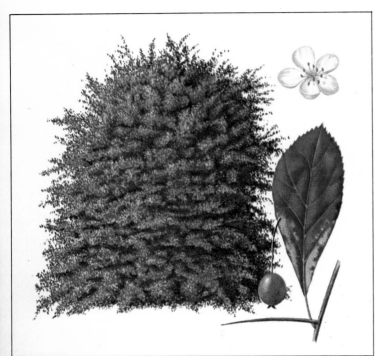

COCKSPUR HAWTHORN
Crataegus crus-gallii

LAVALLE HAWTHORN
Crataegus lavallei

HOW TO GROW. The flowering dogwood grows in Areas C, D, E, G, I and J, except for the southern half of Florida, the southern tip of Texas, southern Arizona and Southern California; the Kousa dogwood grows in all parts of Areas C, D, E, G, I and J; the Pacific dogwood grows only in Areas I and J. All do best in moist but well-drained acid soil (pH 5.5 to 6.5) that has been liberally supplemented with peat moss or leaf mold; they can tolerate neither drought, which makes them especially vulnerable to attacks by the dogwood borer *(page 148),* nor constantly wet soil. In Areas C and I, flowering and Kousa dogwoods blossom most profusely if planted where they receive full sun except during the hot part of the day. In Areas D, E, G and J, they do best in light shade. Pacific dogwoods do best in light shade in both of their growing areas. All dogwoods should be sheltered from high winds. In the cold climate of Area C, it is especially important to buy flowering dogwoods that have been grown locally because those grown from seeds of trees native to more southerly areas may not be sufficiently resistant to the severe winter cold, which if it does not kill the tree is likely to destroy the flower buds. Types with pink flowers are especially sensitive. Select young trees up to 10 feet tall. In Area C, trees bought container grown or balled and burlaped—that is, with their roots in their original soil ball wrapped in burlap —should be planted in early spring. Pruning should be kept to a minimum because dogwoods are slow to heal. To prevent lawn-mower injury to the trunk, cover an area 2 feet or more in width around each tree with a 2- to 3-inch mulch of ground bark or wood chips. To prevent injury from rodents, wrap a piece of 12-inch-wide coarse screening, called hardware cloth, around the trunks of young trees.

COTTONWOOD See *Populus*
CRAB APPLE See *Malus*

CRATAEGUS

C. arnoldiana (Arnold hawthorn); *C. crus-gallii* (cockspur hawthorn and cockspur); *C. lavallei,* also called *C. carrierii* (Lavalle hawthorn); *C. mollis* (downy hawthorn and red haw); *C. monogyna* (single-seeded hawthorn); *C. mordenensis* 'Toba' (Toba hawthorn); *C. nitida* (glossy hawthorn); *C. oxyacantha* (English hawthorn); *C. phaenopyrum,* also called *C. cordata* (Washington hawthorn and Washington thorn)

There are well over 1,000 different kinds of hawthorns, most of which are native to North America. It is no wonder, then, that there are many hawthorns that are relatively easy to grow in almost any garden. Trees planted when 5 to 6 feet tall become 15 to 20 feet tall in 6 to 10 years. Two years after planting, hawthorns begin to bear 2- to 3-inch clusters of white, pink or red flowers less than an inch across. The flowers line the branches in spring and are followed by red fruit called haws, also less than an inch across, that can be used to make jam or jelly. In most of the species listed here, the fruit is apple-shaped and clings to the branches through much of winter. Only a few birds, such as grosbeaks and woodpeckers, are fond of it. Hawthorn leaves vary in size, shape and fall coloring from species to species, but all species have very sharp thorns that become bone-hard. Because of their dense branching and a natural tendency to multiple trunks, hawthorns are sometimes left unpruned, with the branches close to the ground like the cockspur hawthorn at left; but more often they are grown as free-standing trees to decorate a lawn, shade a patio or adorn a street. Hawthorns are remarkably tough trees and can endure seasons of drought and cold as well as the soot and grime of cities.

The Arnold hawthorn eventually grows 20 to 30 feet tall, its dense zigzag branches lined with 2- to 3-inch thorns. It bears white flowers followed by fruit that ripen in midsummer and cling only until early fall. The 2- to 3-inch oval leaves have saw-toothed edges.

The cockspur hawthorn eventually grows to a height of 20 to 35 feet and has curving thorns 1½ to 3 inches long. Its distinctive horizontal branches bear white flowers and fruit that cling most of the winter. The shiny 1½- to 3-inch leaves turn orange and red in fall. Some nurserymen stock a thornless variety, the thornless cockspur hawthorn, *C. crus-gallii inermis.*

The Lavalle hawthorn is a hybrid that grows 15 to 30 feet tall and has thorns ¾ to 1½ inches long. It bears white flowers and red-to-orange fruit that cling most of the winter. The 2- to 2½-inch leaves turn coppery red in fall.

The downy hawthorn grows 20 to 30 feet tall and has stiff thorns about 1 inch long. It bears white flowers and pear-shaped fruit that ripen in late summer and drop in early fall. Its 3- to 4-inch lobed and toothed leaves are covered with soft whitish hairs when they first unfold.

The single-seeded hawthorn is a European species that grows 20 to 30 feet tall. It has very dense twiggy branches with 1-inch thorns and bears white flowers and attractive fall fruit. Its 1- to 2-inch leaves have three to seven deeply indented lobes. A relatively slender variety, *C. monogyna stricta,* the pyramidal single-seeded hawthorn, usually has a spread of only 6 to 8 feet.

The Toba hawthorn is a hybrid that is valued for its great resistance to winter cold and for its fragrant many-petaled flowers, which open white but change to pink as they age. It grows about 15 feet tall and has 1-inch thorns, 2-inch glossy three-lobed leaves and berries that cling through most of the winter.

The glossy hawthorn grows 20 to 30 feet tall and has wedge-shaped toothed dark green leaves, 2 to 3 inches long, that turn red in fall. Its relatively few thorns are 1 inch long, and its white flowers are followed by fruit that cling most of the winter.

Although the true English hawthorn is rarely used in gardens, some of its varieties are the most colorful and most widely grown of all hawthorns. They become about 15 feet tall and are thickly branched. They produce many flowers, either single blossoms, with one ring of petals, or doubles, with numerous overlapping petals; the double-flowered varieties rarely bear fruit. English hawthorns have many ½- to 1-inch thorns and three- to five-lobed leaves up to 2½ inches across. Crimson Cloud, *C. oxyacantha superba,* has bright red single flowers with white centers; its fruit cling well into the winter. Among the many outstanding double-flowered varieties are Paul's scarlet hawthorn, *C. oxyacantha paulii,* red flowers; the white double-flowered English hawthorn, *C. oxyacantha plena;* and also the pink double-flowered English hawthorn, *C. oxyacantha rosea-plena.*

The Washington hawthorn grows 25 to 30 feet tall and is one of the finest species for home gardens. Its zigzag stems are lined with 1½ to 3-inch thorns and 1½- to 3-inch glossy leaves that take on brilliant hues of orange and red in fall. Its masses of white flowers are followed by great clusters of fruit that cling to the branches through most of the winter.

HOW TO GROW. All hawthorns grow in Areas B, C, D, F, G, H and I and the northern part of Area J; Toba hawthorn also grows in Area A. Hawthorns need full sun but grow in almost any well-drained soil, either acid or alkaline. Buy trees no taller than 8 feet—larger trees are difficult to establish in the garden because of their long vertical main roots, or taproots. Trees bought balled and

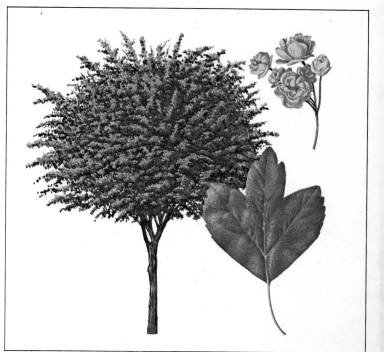

PAUL'S SCARLET HAWTHORN
Crataegus oxyacantha paulii

WASHINGTON HAWTHORN
Crataegus phaenopyrum

For growing areas, see map on page 150.

burlaped—that is, with their roots in their original soil ball wrapped in burlap—should be planted only in early spring. To remove some branches of mature trees in order to let more light pass through, or to remove side branches to provide overhead clearance, prune when the trees are dormant, in winter or very early spring. Cut away stems, or suckers, that rise from the roots at any time.

CUCUMBER TREE See *Magnolia*

D

DAVIDIA

D. involucrata (dove tree)

The dove tree is to many gardeners the ultimate exotic. A native of China, it is the only species of its genus and in this country forms a rounded tree 20 to 40 feet tall with branches spreading an equal distance. Planted when 4 to 5 feet tall, it will reach 15 feet in 10 to 12 years. (Because they are in heavy demand, dove trees are seldom available more than 5 feet tall.) The flowers appear in spring and are composed of two parts: the functional blossoms are grouped together in a ball-shaped central cluster that is about 1 inch in diameter; and a surrounding pair of enormous white petallike leaves, or bracts, that, fluttering in the slightest breeze, resemble the wings of a dove. The bracts form a canopy over the true flowers and are of unequal size: the larger bracts are about 7 inches long and 4 inches wide, the smaller ones about 3 to 4 inches long and about 2 inches wide. The blossoms last about two weeks and are followed in early summer by unpalatable pear-shaped green fruit about 1½ inches long. The dove tree has 3- to 6-inch leaves that are covered with short white hairs beneath. Trees do not begin to blossom until they are about 10 years old and even then some trees, apparently healthy, do not blossom every year.

HOW TO GROW. The dove tree grows in the southern half of Area C and in Areas D, I and J. It does best in very light shade and a soil that has been supplemented with peat moss or leaf mold; it will tolerate sun if the soil is kept moist. Plant in early spring in a site sheltered from the wind. Be sure to water it during dry weather. What little pruning is required should be done in winter.

DELONIX

D. regia, also called *Poinciana regia* (royal poinciana, flamboyant, peacock flower, flame tree)

Perhaps the most beautiful of all flowering trees, the fast-growing royal poinciana seems to be crowned with flame in early summer, when massive clusters of yellow-tinged red flowers, 3 to 4 inches across, appear. The tree grows rapidly—3 to 5 feet a year—and begins to blossom when it is four to six years old. Eventually it reaches 20 to 40 feet in height and spreads 30 to 60 feet or even more. The flowers last for a month to six weeks and are followed by enormous flat seed pods—about 2 feet long and 2 inches wide—that cling to the branches for a year or more before dropping. The 2-foot-long fernlike leaves unfold at about the same time that the first flowers appear, and drop late in the year. The royal poinciana is a spectacular lawn ornament and shade tree, but its thick buttress roots may lift up pavements if it is planted near a street.

HOW TO GROW. The royal poinciana grows only in the warmest parts of Area E. It needs full sun, but grows in almost any soil. Pruning is rarely required.

DIOSPYROS

D. kaki (kaki persimmon, Japanese persimmon), *D. virginiana* (common persimmon)

DOVE TREE
Davidia involucrata

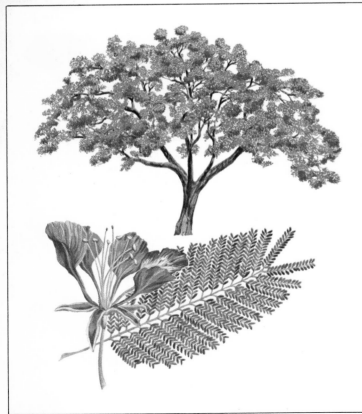

ROYAL POINCIANA
Delonix regia

Persimmons are handsome trouble-free trees that combine beauty and utility. Widely known for their delicious fruit (the Latin name means "food for the gods"), persimmons deserve to be grown more extensively. In case your experience with a persimmon brings back memories of a puckered mouth, it should be said that only unripe fruit causes such an unpleasant reaction; the ripe fruit tastes good. Ripening usually occurs after a frost, but can be hastened if fruit is picked and placed in a plastic bag with a ripe apple for two to four days. Ethylene gas given off by the apple causes the chemical change that removes the astringent quality. Persimmons are members of the ebony family and have hard dark brown or black heartwood that once was widely used to make golf clubs.

Kaki persimmons are native to China and Japan; trees planted when 5 to 6 feet tall become 20 to 25 feet tall in 10 years and eventually reach 20 to 30 feet with an equal rounded spread. The oval leaves, about 4 to 7 inches long, turn brilliant shades of orange, yellow and red in fall. The kaki persimmon usually bears both male and female flowers, yellowish in color, on the same tree, but two or more varieties should be planted to guarantee fruit through cross-pollination, because in this species a single variety is unable to pollinate itself successfully. The highly ornamental 2- to 4-inch yellow or orange fruit usually clings to the trees after the leaves drop. Varieties such as Chocolate, Fuyu, Great Wall, Hachiya, Tamopan and Yokono are recommended for home gardens.

The common persimmon is native to much of the eastern half of the United States and does well in cities. It eventually becomes 35 to 60 feet tall with a spread of 20 to 30 feet. The 3- to 7-inch leaves are coppery when they first open in spring, become dark glossy green above and pale green beneath in summer, then turn yellow, red or pink in fall. Each common persimmon usually produces flowers —small and greenish yellow—that are either male or female; thus trees of both sexes must be planted if the flowers are to be fertilized and produce fruit. There is no obvious difference in appearance between the sexes; ask the nurseryman to make sure you get both. The 1- to 2-inch fruit is yellow or orange in late summer, but often turns purplish when it ripens in fall. Recommended varieties are Garrettson, Early Golden and Killen.

HOW TO GROW. Kaki persimmons grow in the southern part of Area C and throughout Areas D, E, G, I and J. The common persimmon grows throughout Areas C, D, E, G, I and J. Persimmons do best in full sun and need moist soil that is deep enough to accommodate their long roots. Trees bought balled and burlaped—that is, with their roots in their original soil ball wrapped in burlap—should be planted in early spring. What little pruning is necessary is best done in winter.

DOGWOOD See *Cornus*
DOVE TREE See *Davidia*

E

EBONY, GREEN See *Jacaranda*
EBONY, MOUNTAIN See *Bauhinia*

ELAEAGNUS
E. angustifolia (Russian olive, oleaster)

The Russian olive, a fast-growing pest-free tree native to Europe and Asia, ordinarily has several trunks and becomes crooked, gnarled and covered with dark brown shredding bark. If planted at 6 to 8 feet and trained to grow with a single trunk, it reaches about 20 feet in five years, eventually becoming 20 to 25 feet tall with a spread

COMMON PERSIMMON
Diospyros virginiana

RUSSIAN OLIVE
Elaeagnus angustifolia

For growing areas, see map on page 150.

equal to its height. It may also be grown as a multiple-trunked tree or large shrub that, planted when 4 to 6 feet tall, reaches a height of 12 to 15 feet in three to five years. Russian olives are valued for their soft silvery gray leaves, 1½ to 3½ inches long, more than for their fruit or flowers. When the trees grow at the end of a garden, the shimmering of their leaves makes them seem to recede into the distance, creating an illusion of great depth. In early summer the stems of the Russian olive are lined with tiny sweetly fragrant silvery yellow flowers. They are followed in late summer and early fall by edible ½-inch sweet yellow berries that are covered with minute silvery scales. Birds relish them. The Russian olive withstands city conditions, and the multiple-trunked form is a sturdy, useful windbreak in rugged climates such as the western plains of Canada and the United States.

HOW TO GROW. The Russian olive is so adaptable that it grows well in all areas. It needs full sun, but grows in almost any well-drained soil and endures both high winds and drought. Prune young trees in winter or early spring. Small inner branches often die, losing in their competition with the larger outer branches. Remove them at any time; this trimming will show off the handsome form of the trunk to better advantage.

ELDER, BOX See *Acer*
ELM See *Ulmus*
EMPRESS TREE See *Paulownia*
EPAULETTE TREE See *Pterostyrax*

F

FAGUS

F. grandifolia (American beech, red beech, white beech), *F. sylvatica* (European beech)

If the word noble had to be applied to only one kind of tree, the honor would probably go to the beech. Massive and slow growing, eventually reaching heights of 50 to 90 feet with a spread of 50 to 60 feet, it lives for hundreds of years. Many of the magnificent specimens we enjoy today were planted at the turn of the century and are now just reaching maturity. Because of their slow growth, beeches are expensive but well worth the cost. A 6- to 8-foot tree can be expected to be 15 to 20 feet tall in 10 years.

Beeches are at their best on lawns that provide ample room for their development. Their shade is so dense and their feeding roots so close to the surface of the soil that nothing but moss grows beneath them unless lower branches are removed to allow light to enter, as they have been in the drawing at left. They are not suited for planting along roadways, partly because they grow to such large size, but also because they cannot tolerate the hard compacted soil around pavements. There should be a space of 40 feet or more between trees. Beeches have inconspicuous spring flowers followed by ¼-inch triangular edible nuts borne, usually two at a time, in ¾-inch prickly husks. The nuts, collectively called beech mast, ripen in fall and, though sparse on lone cultivated trees, were once fed to swine and were a favorite food of the extinct passenger pigeon. Beechnuts are attractive to squirrels and to blue jays, titmice, grosbeaks, nuthatches and woodpeckers.

The American beech is seldom cultivated by nurserymen; it is extremely difficult to transplant and it lacks the varied leaf colors and shapes found in the European beech. However, where natural stands of American beech occur these handsome trees can easily be preserved—provided the soil beneath them is not disturbed. It is essential that no soil be added over their roots; if it is, the trees will probably die. This species has beautiful pest-free foliage; the 2-

WEEPING EUROPEAN BEECH
Fagus sylvatica pendula

RIVERS PURPLE BEECH
Fagus sylvatica riversii

to 4-inch leaves are silvery when they open from long slender pointed buds early in spring, and have deeply serrated edges; green during the summer, they turn to a golden bronze color in fall and often cling to the branches until late in the winter. The American beech often loses some of its lower limbs, with attractive results, for the loss allows a better view of its handsome smooth gray trunk.

The basic species of the European beech, which has green leaves, is grown less often than its many splendid varieties, which have leaves of unusual colors—shades of purple or copper, or variegated pink, green, yellow and white. There is considerable variation in coloration among plants grown from seeds, and for more certain color it is advisable to buy a named variety propagated by grafting. Leaves of European beeches are 2 to 4 inches long; they turn golden bronze in fall, often clinging until late winter. Many varieties have tortuous branches and deeply indented leaves; all tend to hold their lower branches, which may sweep the ground. One of the most reliable deep purple varieties is the Rivers purple beech, *F. sylvatica riversii*. Two other varieties, the weeping European beech, *F. sylvatica pendula,* and the purple weeping European beech, *F. sylvatica purpurea-pendula,* grow about 50 feet tall with a 40-foot spread and have pendulous branches, often twisted in a most attractive manner. The fern-leaved European beech, *F. sylvatica asplenifolia,* has fern-shaped leaves that are greenish black in color. It eventually reaches a height of about 50 feet and has an equal spread.

HOW TO GROW. Beeches grow in Areas B, C, D, I and the northern part of Area J. They do best when given full sun and well-drained acid soil (pH 5.0 to 6.5) that has been supplemented with peat moss or leaf mold. They are easily harmed by wet or compacted soil, and they are difficult to establish in the garden unless they have been properly root-pruned during their growth in a nursery. Be certain not to plant them any deeper than the level at which they grew previously. Prune young trees in summer or early fall; beeches bleed if cuts are made in winter or spring. Older trees rarely require pruning.

FALSE ACACIA See *Robinia*

FICUS

F. carica (common fig)

The common fruit-bearing fig is a beautiful 20- to 40-foot tree whose branches, spreading to a distance equal to or greater than the tree's height, offer dense shade for patio or garden. The fig grows quickly: a 2- to 3-foot tree will usually reach a height of 10 to 15 feet in five years. Fig trees have smooth gray bark; trunks and branches become picturesquely gnarled as the trees increase in age. Their deeply indented rough-textured rounded leaves, 4 to 8 inches across, have appeared as a motif in art and architecture since ancient times. The fruit is 1 to 3 inches long, and may be brown, purplish or pale shades of yellow or green. Trees begin to bear when they are only three or four years old, and bear two and sometimes three crops annually; the first appears on the previous season's growth, and the others on the current season's growth. In the varieties listed here the fruit is produced without pollination, and the seeds are usually sterile and incapable of producing seedlings. The choice of a specific variety of fig depends upon regional conditions; consult your local nurseryman for those that do best in your growing area. Typical excellent varieties are Brown Turkey, also called Black Spanish; Mission, also called Black Mission; Brunswick; White Genoa; Kadota; Lattarula, also called White Italian; Celeste; and Texas Everbearing.

COMMON FIG
Ficus carica

For growing areas, see map on page 150.

CHINESE PARASOL TREE
Firmiana simplex

FRANKLINIA
Franklinia alatamaha

HOW TO GROW. The common fig grows in the southern part of Area C as well as in Areas D, E, G, I and J. It does best in full sun and well-drained soil. Figs have very shallow root systems—do not cultivate around them or you may cause damage. Figs grow well in windy or dry locations. An excess of moisture or nitrogenous fertilizer reduces fruitfulness anywhere, and the greatest amount of fruit is produced where summers are long and hot. Trees bought bare-rooted or balled and burlaped—that is, with their roots in their original soil ball wrapped in burlap —should be planted in midwinter or early spring. Prune young trees in winter. Old trees rarely need pruning.

FIG See *Ficus*

FIRMIANA
F. simplex, also called *F. platanifolia, Sterculia platanifolia* (Chinese parasol tree, Phoenix tree, varnish tree)

The Chinese parasol tree is a strong disease- and insect-resistant species grown for the immense leaves, up to 12 inches across, that give it its name—a single leaf actually does shed about as much shade as a parasol. This species grows at a moderately fast pace when young: a 5- to 6-foot tree reaches 12 to 15 feet or more in only five years, eventually becoming 20 to 40 feet tall with an equal spread. The trunk and branches are gray green and shiny, and are attractive even when the tree is leafless. In midsummer it bears 12- to 18-inch spikes of greenish white flowers followed in autumn by 4-inch pods that split open into four petallike sections, revealing round, pea-sized seeds along the edges of the sections. The seed pods are often picked for winter decorations. As the pods open, they discharge a brown fluid that looks like varnish—hence one of the species' other common names, varnish tree.

HOW TO GROW. The Chinese parasol tree grows in frost-free parts of Areas E and J, and gardeners willing to cut away branches that have been injured by occasional frosts can grow it elsewhere in these two areas. This tree grows best in full sun and tolerates almost any moist well-drained soil. It should be given a location that is sheltered from the wind. The tree is especially easy to establish in the garden. Pruning is rarely necessary.

FLAMBOYANT See *Delonix*
FLAME TREE See *Delonix*
FLAME TREE, CHINESE See *Koelreuteria*
FRANKLIN TREE See *Franklinia*

FRANKLINIA
F. alatamaha, also called *Gordonia alatamaha* (franklinia, gordonia, Franklin tree)

Franklinia is a fall-flowering tree discovered in the mountains of Georgia by an early American botanist, John Bartram, in the 18th Century, but not seen growing wild since 1790. Its names honor Benjamin Franklin and James Gordon, an English nurseryman who was a friend of Bartram's. The franklinia grows at a slow to moderate pace, depending on climate: in the South or West a 4- to 6-foot tree usually becomes 15 feet tall in 8 to 10 years, eventually reaching 20 to 30 feet with a 10- to 20-foot spread, but in the North it reaches only 6 to 10 feet in about 10 years and rarely grows beyond that. It has reddish brown stems and branches lined with 5-inch bright green shiny leaves, which become red and orange in fall about the time the flowers open. The 3-inch fragrant flowers have centers filled with golden-yellow pollen-bearing stamens.

HOW TO GROW. The franklinia grows in Areas C, D and I and in all but the southern parts of Areas E and J. It will grow in full sun or light shade, but full sun produces brighter autumn foliage and more flowers. This species needs a moist well-drained acid soil (pH 5.0 to 6.0) liberally supplemented with leaf mold or peat moss. Do not cultivate the soil around franklinias. Trees bought balled and burlaped—that is, with their roots in their original soil ball wrapped in burlap—and container-grown trees should be planted in early spring. Pruning is rarely needed.

FRAXINUS

F. americana (white ash), *F. holotricha* 'Moraine' (Moraine ash), *F. ornus* (flowering ash or manna ash), *F. pennsylvanica lanceolata* (green ash), *F. velutina glabra* (Modesto ash)

Ashes grow fast, resist insects and diseases, and cast a light filtered shade in which grass easily grows. Although their ultimate heights and spreads vary, an 8- to 10-foot tree will usually become 25 feet tall in five to eight years. The leaves of ashes are fernlike, and in fall most turn shades of yellow and purple; when they drop, the leaflets crumble and sift into the turf, so that raking is usually unnecessary. Most of the trees listed here bear male and female flowers on separate trees. The inconspicuous greenish yellow flowers appear in early spring, and on female trees are followed within a few weeks by stringy clusters of 1-inch paddle-shaped winged seeds that cling until fall. The seed clusters are not very attractive and eventually produce unwanted seedlings. Both seed clusters and seedlings can be avoided in some varieties that are available in the form of seedless males. These trees are not males selected from a mixed group of seedlings—the sex of such young trees is almost impossible to ascertain—but are propagated from the buds of male trees.

White ashes eventually grow 70 to 90 feet tall with a rounded spread equal to about half their height. Their 8- to 15-inch-long dull green leaves have five to nine leaflets. Two excellent seedless male varieties are Autumn Purple, which has rich purple fall foliage, and Rosehill, which has bronzy red fall coloring.

Moraine ash is an almost seedless variety of the seldom-cultivated species *F. holotricha*. It is a particularly good variety for small gardens because it rarely exceeds 35 feet in height and has a broad oval outline that seldom spreads more than about 20 feet. The 6- to 10-inch-long leaves turn pale yellow in fall.

The flowering ash, unlike the other ashes, bears conspicuous bisexual flowers, each blossom containing both male and female reproductive organs, and all trees bear seeds. The fragrant fluffy whitish blossoms are borne in 3- to 5-inch clusters at the ends of the branches in early summer, followed by masses of brownish seeds that hang on until midwinter. The shiny green leaves are 8 to 10 inches long. The flowering ash usually grows 25 to 35 feet tall with an equal spread.

The green ash is one of the most popular of all ash species because it is suited to many growing conditions. It reaches a height of 50 to 60 feet with a rather narrow spread—only 20 to 30 feet. One of its finest male varieties is Marshall's Seedless ash, with 10- to 12-inch dark green leaves made up of five to nine leaflets. Its foliage turns shades of purple and yellow in fall.

The Modesto ash grows 30 to 50 feet tall with an equal or greater spread. Its dense yellowish green 4- to 6-inch leaves are composed of three to five leaflets and turn a handsome golden yellow in fall.

HOW TO GROW. White and green ashes grow in all areas; Moraine and flowering ashes in Areas C, D, E, G, H, I and J; the Modesto ash in Areas C, D, E, G, I and J. Ashes do

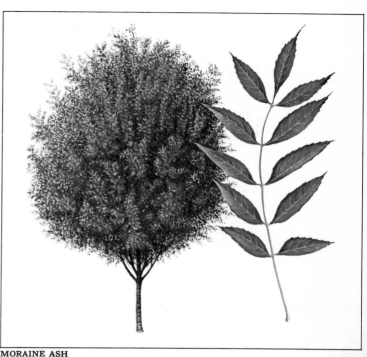

MORAINE ASH
Fraxinus holotricha 'Moraine'

FLOWERING ASH
Fraxinus ornus

For growing areas, see map on page 150.

MARSHALL'S SEEDLESS ASH
Fraxinus pennsylvanica lanceolata 'Marshall's Seedless'

MODESTO ASH
Fraxinus velutina glabra

best in full sun and well-drained average soil that is deep enough to accommodate the trees' long root structures. The flowering ash and the Modesto ash will tolerate dry soil, and the Modesto ash will also withstand alkaline soil. Ashes are particularly easy to establish in the garden. Prune young trees in fall. Older trees rarely need pruning.

FRINGE TREE See *Chionanthus*

G

GINKGO
G. biloba (ginkgo, maidenhair tree)

There are no known forests of ginkgoes, even in China, where Western travelers first found them in the 17th Century growing in temple gardens. These few cultivated trees turned out to be living relics of prehistoric times, among the last survivors of one of the first groups of plants that abandoned spore propagation for the more efficient seed method. The impressions of their ancestors' leaves may be seen in various parts of the world, including the United States, in rocks that are known to be millions of years old. The tree is called maidenhair tree because the 4-inch smooth green leaves resemble those of the maidenhair fern. They are fan-shaped, tough and completely free of insects and diseases, and turn a lovely shade of yellow in fall. The Chinese have another name for the ginkgo that is derived from the shape of its leaves: they call it "the tree with leaves like a duck's foot."

The ginkgo is not the tree for every backyard. One reason is that it eventually reaches a height of 50 to 80 feet with a spread of 40 feet or more, but another factor of importance is that it needs nearly 20 years to get over the gawky stages of adolescence and develop the broadly spreading branches of maturity. Young trees 8 to 10 feet tall may require 10 to 12 years to reach 20 feet in height. When they are young, ginkgoes are characterized by long ascending branches that develop asymmetrically. Strangely, these remnants of bygone ages are among the most satisfactory of all trees to grow in cities, where fumes and dust do not seem to hinder their growth.

Ginkgoes bear male and female flowers on separate trees. It is important to plant only male trees because in late fall the female ones bear bright yellow fruit that has an extremely obnoxious odor. (In the Orient the outer evil-smelling pulp of each fruit is removed to reveal an edible white nutlike seed that is prized as a delicacy.) Nurserymen generally sell only the male trees and have selected several excellent varieties. Among them are Autumn Gold, a handsome broad spreading tree; Fairmount, a conical variety; and the Sentry ginkgo, *G. biloba fastigiata,* a narrow column-shaped type.

HOW TO GROW. Ginkgoes grow in all areas except Area A. They need sun but will grow in almost any soil. They are particularly easy to establish in the garden. Prune the young trees early in the spring. Pruning of older trees is hardly ever necessary.

GLEDITSIA
G. triacanthos inermis (thornless honey locust)

Fortunately for home gardeners, a completely thornless mutation of the common honey locust—which would be considered an excellent shade tree if it were not for its formidable 4-inch thorns and littering seed pods—was found, and from this single plant a whole new strain of trouble-free handsome shade trees has been derived. Many of these trees are seedless, or nearly seedless, as well as thornless, and all do well in the polluted air of cities as well as in the suburbs. Thornless honey locusts grow at a rapid pace:

planted at 6 to 8 feet, they usually become 20 to 25 feet tall in five or six years. At maturity they vary in height from 35 to 70 feet and usually spread to about an equal distance. The fernlike leaves, 6 to 10 inches long, emerge from their buds late in spring; during summer they cast a filtered shade in which it is easy to grow grass. In fall the leaves turn pale yellow and disintegrate as they drop, so that raking is hardly ever necessary. The bark on both the branches and the trunks of thornless honey locusts becomes nearly black as the trees mature, in winter providing a dramatic contrast in a snowy garden.

Although thornless honey locusts grown from seeds are widely sold, the named varieties grown by propagating them from the buds of existing trees are better: they have superior foliage, bear few or no seed pods and have straighter trunks. The following varieties are particularly recommended: Imperial matures at a height of 30 to 35 feet, making it an ideal size for planting in a small plot or along roadways since it will seldom interfere with overhead wires. Majestic, which eventually becomes 60 to 65 feet tall, has few seeds and bears dense dark green foliage. Moraine was the first patented variety of thornless honey locust and is still one of the best. It is seedless and develops a handsome thick crown of foliage. It eventually becomes about 60 feet tall. Rubylace is an unusual tree whose young foliage is wine red until midsummer, then gradually turns green. It is seedless and ultimately reaches a height of 50 to 60 feet. Shademaster eventually grows 50 to 60 feet tall and has dark green leaves that cling later in the fall than do those of most other thornless honey locusts. Skyline grows in a narrow upright shape to a height of 50 to 60 feet, but unlike other types of thornless honey locusts, spreads to only about half its height. It has very few seeds. Sunburst is a seedless variety whose new foliage is a golden yellow until midsummer, then gradually turns green. It eventually reaches a height of 50 to 60 feet and is particularly effective when seen against a background of darker foliage.

HOW TO GROW. Thornless honey locusts grow in all areas except Area A. They require full sun and do best in average well-drained soil that is deep enough to accommodate the trees' long root structures; however, they are tolerant of almost any soil condition and will grow in soil that is quite alkaline. Thornless honey locusts are especially easy to establish in the garden, and because of their ability to grow fast they can be produced economically by nurserymen and are reasonably priced. Large-sized trees can be moved with every expectation of success by nurserymen with the proper tree-moving equipment, and thornless honey locusts are therefore a fine choice for gardeners who want a full-sized tree immediately. Established trees tolerate drought. Prune young thornless honey locusts in fall. Older trees rarely require pruning.

GOLDEN SHOWER See *Cassia*
GOLDEN-CHAIN TREE See *Laburnum*
GOLDEN-RAIN TREE See *Koelreuteria*
GORDONIA See *Franklinia*
GREEN EBONY See *Jacaranda*
GUM, SOUR See *Nyssa*
GUM, SWEET See *Liquidambar*

GYMNOCLADUS

G. dioica (Kentucky coffee tree)
The Kentucky coffee tree is a slow-growing pest-free tree with fernlike leaves casting light filtered shade in which grass grows easily. Planted at 6 to 8 feet, it becomes 20 feet tall in about 10 years, eventually reaching 40 to 90

GINKGO
Ginkgo biloba

MORAINE THORNLESS HONEY LOCUST
Gleditsia triacanthos inermis 'Moraine'

For growing areas, see map on page 150.

KENTUCKY COFFEE TREE
Gymnocladus dioica

CAROLINA SILVER BELL
Halesia carolina

feet with an oval-shaped spread of 20 to 40 feet. The leaves cover the branches late in spring and are pinkish as they emerge, turning blue-green during the summer. Extending to a length of 1½ to 3 feet with a width of 2 feet, they are among the largest leaves borne by any American tree. They do not appear massive, however, because each is made up of 40 to 100 small leaflets. They turn yellow early in fall and drop in two stages: first to go are the leaflets, which disappear into the grass; then the sticklike leafstalks follow, lying on the grass like jackstraws, easy to rake up. The coarse branches appear stark and strong in the dormant season because they have no small twigs, and the trunk has an attractive rough bark. Kentucky coffee trees bear inconspicuous male and female flowers on separate trees, and only the female trees bear seed pods, 6 to 10 inches long and reddish brown, which cling for much of the winter. The ¾-inch seeds within the pods were used by early colonists to make a bitter-tasting beverage, euphemistically called "coffee."

HOW TO GROW. The Kentucky coffee tree grows in Areas B, C, D, F, G, H, I and J. It needs full sun and does best in moist soil that is deep enough to accommodate the tree's long roots, but it will tolerate almost any soil. Give it a spot sheltered from high winds. Prune young trees in winter or early spring. Older trees rarely need pruning.

H

HACKBERRY See *Celtis*

HALESIA
H. carolina, also called *H. tetraptera* (Carolina silver bell); *H. monticola* (mountain silver bell). (Both also called snowdrop tree)

Silver bells are handsome lawn trees noted for their lovely white spring blossoms. As the leaves begin to unfurl, the branches become lined with clusters of flowers shaped very much like snowdrops. The best way to enjoy the flowers is to stand beneath a tree and look up at them glistening in the spring sunshine. The flowers last about one week and are followed by dry four-winged seed pods in the fall. The leaves are 3 to 5 inches long and turn clear yellow in autumn; they are exceptionally pest resistant. Azaleas or rhododendrons grow well beneath silver bells.

The Carolina silver bell and the mountain silver bell grow from 6 to 8 feet to 15 to 20 feet in six to eight years. The Carolina silver bell eventually becomes 20 to 30 feet tall and 15 to 20 feet wide. Its flowers are about ½ to ¾ inch long. The mountain silver bell eventually becomes 40 to 50 feet tall with a spread of 25 to 35 feet. Its white blossoms, about 1 inch long, open from pinkish buds. The pink mountain silver bell, *H. monticola rosea,* is similar to the basic species except that its flowers are pale pink.

HOW TO GROW. Silver bells grow in Areas C, D, E, I and J. They grow in full sun or light shade and do best in a moist well-drained acid soil (pH 5.0 to 6.0) that has been supplemented with peat moss or leaf mold. Older trees rarely need pruning.

HAW, RED See *Crataegus*
HAWTHORN See *Crataegus*
HICORIA See *Carya*
HONEY LOCUST See *Gleditsia*
HOP HORNBEAM See *Ostrya*
HORNBEAM See *Carpinus*
HORSE CHESTNUT See *Aesculus*

I

INDIAN BEAN See *Catalpa*

J

JACARANDA

J. acutifolia, also called *J. ovalifolia* and *J. mimosaefolia*
(sharp-leaved jacaranda, green ebony)

Handsome standing alone, the colorful flowering jacaranda also meets the rigorous requirements for growing
along streets. This Brazilian species is a tree for frost-free
areas. It grows fast: a 6- to 8-foot tree reaches 25 feet in
about five years, eventually becoming 25 to 50 feet tall
with an equal spread. The branching pattern is often irregular, but it is open enough to show the smooth bark of
the trunk and major branches. The jacaranda may grow
with multiple trunks, but can be pruned to have a single
trunk. In late spring and early summer it sends out dense
clusters of 2-inch fragrant flowers; the clusters may contain 40 to 90 flowers and are 8 inches or more long. When
they fall, they do not fade quickly but carpet the ground beneath the tree in a most attractive manner. The flowers
are followed by disk-shaped seed pods about 2 inches long,
which cling most of the year; they are used for indoor decoration. Individual leaves may be 1½ to 2 feet long and
are composed of hundreds of ¼-inch leaflets. They cast a
light filtered shade and cling to the tree most of the year.
Though they fall late in the year, they are soon replaced
by new leaves. The basic species has blue flowers, but there
is also a fine white variety, *J. acutifolia alba.*

HOW TO GROW. Jacarandas grow only in the southern
parts of Areas E and J, and are injured by frost when the
temperature falls to about 27° F. They will grow in full
sun or light shade, but blossom more profusely in sunny
places. They do best in a sandy well-drained acid soil (pH
5.5 to 6.5) and should be planted in a place sheltered
from high winds because the branches are brittle. Established trees tolerate drought. Prune young trees in early
spring to leave a single trunk, if that is desired.

JAPANESE KEAKI TREE See *Zelkova*
JAPANESE SNOWBELL See *Styrax*
JERUSALEM THORN See *Parkinsonia*
JUDAS TREE See *Cercis*

JUGLANS

J. hindsii (Hinds black walnut), *J. nigra* (black walnut),
J. regia (English or Persian walnut)

Walnuts are fine shade trees as well as valuable nut pro-
ducers. Generally fast growing when young, they do best
when set out as 3- to 4-foot trees, becoming about 20 feet
tall in six to eight years. The fern-shaped leaves, made up
of 3- to 5-inch leaflets, generally turn brownish yellow before dropping in autumn. Walnut blossoms are green and
appear with the opening of the leaves; female flowers are
small and inconspicuous, and male flowers are slender scaly
clusters, or catkins, about 3 inches long. Some species of
walnuts begin to bear a few nuts about four years after
planting but most must be established for six to eight years
before producing. Walnuts bear only a few nuts when
grown alone, but the crop is greatly increased if two trees
are planted within 40 to 50 feet of one another to ensure
cross-pollination.

The Hinds black walnut, a West Coast native that eventually grows 30 to 50 feet tall, is handsome standing alone
and meets the stringent requirements for growing along
streets. The 2-inch fruit is thick-shelled. The leaves have
15 to 19 leaflets with fuzzy undersides. The black walnut,
native to the eastern half of the U.S., eventually grows 60
to 80 feet tall. The leaves have 15 to 23 leaflets and are

SHARP-LEAVED JACARANDA
Jacaranda acutifolia

ENGLISH WALNUT
Juglans regia

For growing areas, see map on page 150.

shiny above and fuzzy beneath. Black walnuts have a rich flavor; the nuts from wild trees have hard thick shells, but those from cultivated varieties, usually about 2 inches in size, are easy to crack open. The English walnut eventually grows 40 to 60 feet tall; its dark green shiny leaves have only five to seven leaflets, but because the foliage is dense, the tree casts a heavy shade. The 1½- to 2-inch nuts are easy to shell; they fall from the trees when ripe, and squirrels vie with the gardeners at harvesttime. Many varieties of this species exist, some of which do better in one area than another; consult a local nurseryman for the best type for your area. Of particular interest to gardeners living in northern climates is the variety known as Carpathian walnut; brought to Canada from the Carpathian Mountains of Poland many years ago, it bears heavy crops of nuts even when winter temperatures drop to −40° F.

HOW TO GROW. Hinds black walnuts grow in Areas I and J; black walnuts in Areas B, C, D, F, G, I and J. English walnuts grow in the southern part of Area C and throughout Areas D, G, I and J, but the variety called Carpathian walnut grows in Areas B, C, D, I and J. All need full sun and do best in well-drained soil that is deep enough to accommodate the trees' long roots. Trees bought bare-rooted should be planted early in spring. Prune in summer or fall —walnuts bleed severely if pruned in spring.

JUJUBE See *Zizyphus*
JUNEBERRY See *Amelanchier*

K

KALOPANAX

K. pictus, also called *Acanthopanax ricinifolius* (castor aralia)

The castor aralia is a lush, large-leaved tree with many virtues. The castor aralia is not grown by all nurseries but is worth searching out; it provides shade and is notably free of insects and diseases. It grows relatively fast: a 6- to 8-foot tree reaches 20 feet in seven to nine years, eventually becoming 60 to 80 feet tall with a nearly equal spread. Its five- to seven-lobed leaves range from 7 to 14 inches across and resemble those of the castor-oil plant in shape and size. The leaves, shiny dark green on top with fuzzy gray undersides, turn dull red in fall and are particularly large on young trees. Young trees also have ½-inch thorns, which become less plentiful as the trees increase in size; old trees may be practically thornless. In midsummer the castor aralia produces 1-inch ball-shaped flower clusters composed of many tiny white blossoms, but they are largely hidden by the leaves. The flowers are followed in early fall by 4- to 6-inch clusters of tiny black berries that are relished by birds.

HOW TO GROW. The castor aralia grows in Areas B, C, D, F, G, H and I. It does best when given full sun and moist soil that is deep enough to accommodate the tree's long root structure. Prune young trees at any time during the spring; old trees rarely require pruning.

KATSURA TREE See *Cercidiphyllum*
KEAKI TREE, JAPANESE See *Zelkova*
KENTUCKY COFFEE TREE See *Gymnocladus*

KOELREUTERIA

K. formosana, also called *K. henryii, K. bipinnata* (Chinese flame tree); *K. paniculata* (golden-rain tree)

Golden-rain and Chinese flame trees are handsome trees from the Orient grown for their 12- to 15-inch airy clusters of small yellow flowers, which bloom in early summer. The blossoms are so numerous that they cover the ground

CASTOR ARALIA
Kalopanax pictus

with a gold-colored carpet when they fall. Both species grow at a fairly rapid rate, an 8- to 10-foot tree reaching about 20 feet in five or six years. Leaves 8 to 15 inches long, composed of many 1- to 3-inch leaflets, are reddish as they unfold in spring and become blue-green in summer. Both species are excellent for decorating a lawn or shading a patio; they also meet the rigorous requirements for growing along streets in urban or suburban areas, since they tolerate polluted air.

The Chinese flame tree eventually grows 30 to 40 feet tall with a flat top of equal spread. Its leaves turn yellow late in fall, and its bright orange-red seed pods look like tiny Chinese lanterns. The golden-rain tree, which is much more adaptable to a variety of climates, ultimately grows 20 to 30 feet tall with a spread of 10 to 20 feet. Its flowers are followed by 2-inch balloonlike seed pods that are first green, then pink and finally brown.

HOW TO GROW. The Chinese flame tree grows in Areas E and J, the golden-rain tree in all areas but Areas A and B. Both need full sun, but grow in almost any well-drained soil, including an alkaline soil. Established trees will tolerate drought. Trees up to 12 feet tall can be planted bare-rooted; taller trees should be planted balled and burlaped —that is, with their roots in their original soil ball wrapped in burlap. Prune young trees at any time during the winter; old trees seldom require pruning.

L

LABURNUM

L. alpinum (Scotch laburnum); *L. watererii,* also called *L. vossii* (Waterer laburnum). (Both also called golden-chain tree)

All parts of laburnum trees are poisonous to eat, but for two weeks in midspring laburnums can provide the brightest spot in a garden, sending forth great quantities of bright yellow 1-inch blossoms in hanging clusters that are as much as 20 inches long. The trees grow in a vaselike shape; planted at 6 to 8 feet, they reach 18 to 20 feet in six to eight years, eventually becoming 20 to 25 feet tall. They may have a single trunk or several trunks; multiple-trunked trees spread about as wide as their height while single-trunked trees spread 8 to 10 feet. Laburnums begin to flower the first season after planting. The flowers are followed by 2-inch brown pods that cling until winter. The clover-like leaves consist of three leaflets, each 1 to 2 inches long, that have downy undersides when young. Laburnums are practically pest and disease free when grown in their recommended growing areas.

The Scotch laburnum has flower clusters up to 15 inches long and is the most cold-resistant species. It is well known for its spectacular variety, the weeping Scotch laburnum, *L. alpinum pendulum,* sold in grafted form, with a weeping Scotch laburnum stem grafted to the trunk of the common laburnum, *L. anagyroides.* The common laburnum itself is not recommended because of its smaller flower clusters, but its upright trunk serves as an excellent base for the weeping Scotch laburnum, whose branches hang down on all sides, making it look like a golden waterfall when it blossoms. Waterer laburnum is a hybrid between the Scotch laburnum and the common laburnum. It has larger flower clusters than either of its parents, some reaching as much as 20 inches in length, and is the type most often available in nurseries.

HOW TO GROW. Both laburnums grow in Areas C, D, F, G, H and I and the northern part of Area J. Scotch laburnums also grow in Area B. Both types do best if grown where they get light shade, especially during the hot part of the day. They should also be sheltered from the wind.

GOLDEN-RAIN TREE
Koelreuteria paniculata

WATERER LABURNUM
Laburnum watererii

For growing areas, see map on page 150.

SWEET GUM
Liquidambar styraciflua

TULIP TREE
Liriodendron tulipifera

Laburnums require moist well-drained soil that is deep enough to accommodate their long roots. Trees up to 8 feet tall bought bare-rooted and larger ones bought balled and burlaped—that is, with their roots in their original soil ball wrapped in burlap—should be planted in spring. Since rabbits are fond of the bark of laburnum trees, enclose the lower part of the trunks in a piece of the wire mesh called hardware cloth. To encourage the development of flower-bearing branches for the next season, prune laburnums after they have flowered, removing the seed pods as well as any weak or dead branches.

LILAC See *Syringa*
LINDEN See *Tilia*

LIQUIDAMBAR

L. styraciflua (sweet gum)

An excellent choice for shade or planting along streets, sweet gums grow at a rate that depends upon the amount of moisture in the soil. Planted at 10 to 12 feet, they reach 25 to 30 feet in six to eight years in moist soil but take 10 to 15 years to reach the same height in dry soil, eventually becoming 60 to 70 feet tall. Because they are such moisture lovers, they are particularly useful along river banks and in bottom lands where the soil is always wet. They also withstand seaside conditions but they should be sheltered from wind. They are extremely pest and disease resistant. Sweet gums are conical in shape. They are slender when young but gradually spread to about two thirds of their height. Shiny deep green leaves 4 to 7 inches across open late in spring but cling late in fall, turning yellow, orange, bronze and scarlet, often with several colors on the same tree; in Areas E and J, the leaves usually cling through November or December. The twigs and young branches have corky winglike ridges, while the trunks of old trees have furrowed silvery brown bark. In spring sweet gums bear 1-inch ball-shaped clusters of inconspicuous greenish flowers, which mature in fall into prickly brown seed clusters that are often used for indoor decorations. The seed clusters are easy to rake up in fall along with the leaves. Most nurseries sell only seed-grown sweet gums of the ordinary species, which serve well in nearly all garden situations. A few outstanding varieties have special characteristics: Burgundy has wine-colored fall foliage that clings until January or February in Areas E and J, Festival has a slender columnar shape and Palo Alto grows in a slender conical shape even when mature.

HOW TO GROW. Sweet gums grow in Areas C, D, E, G, I and J. They grow best in full sun in moist soil that has been supplemented with peat moss or leaf mold and that is deep enough to accommodate the trees' long root structures; they also tolerate light shade. Trees bought balled and burlaped—that is, with their roots in their original soil ball wrapped in burlap—should be planted in spring. Prune sweet gums at any time during the winter.

LIRIODENDRON

L. tulipifera (tulip tree, tulip poplar, yellow poplar)

The tulip tree is one of the tallest trees to be found in the eastern regions of North America. It grows at a fairly rapid pace when young: an 8- to 10-foot tree reaches 25 to 30 feet in six to eight years and eventually becomes 70 to 90 feet tall with a spread of 35 to 40 feet. In gardens that are spacious enough, it is an excellent choice for shade. Its 2½- to 5-inch leaves are light green as they unfold in spring, then turn shiny deep green in summer; in autumn they become a clear golden yellow that is sometimes flecked with brown. The tree bears fragrant 2-inch tulip-shaped flowers, but generally not until the tree is 10 to 20 years old; even then their scent and delicate beauty can scarcely be noticed because by that time the branch tips on which they are borne are high in the air, and the leaves, which open first, hide them from view. The flowers are followed by 2- to 3-inch conical light brown seed capsules that cling to the branches after the leaves fall.

HOW TO GROW. The tulip tree grows in Areas B, C, D, E, G, I and J. It needs full sun and does best in moist but well-drained soil that is deep enough to accommodate the tree's long root structure. It tolerates seaside conditions if sheltered from the wind. Trees bought balled and burlaped —that is, with their roots in their original soil ball wrapped in burlap—should be planted only in early spring. Prune in winter; old trees rarely require pruning.

LOCUST See *Robinia*
LOCUST, HONEY See *Gleditsia*

M

MACLURA
M. pomifera (Osage orange)

The Osage orange is a fast-growing, pest-free tree, tolerant of poor growing conditions, that does well in regions where many other trees cannot survive. Planted at 6 to 8 feet, it reaches 15 to 20 feet in three or four years, eventually becoming 25 to 50 feet tall with an equal spread. Mature trees become very densely branched. The 2- to 5-inch leaves are a shiny deep green in summer and turn an attractive yellow in fall. If a leaf is crushed or a leafstalk is broken, however, it exudes a sticky milky juice that irritates the skin of some people. Inconspicuous greenish male and female flowers appear on separate trees of the Osage orange. If both sexes are present, the female trees bear 3- to 6-inch round bumpy unpalatable yellowish green fruit in fall. The twigs and young branches of the Osage orange are lined with sharp thorns up to an inch long. Before the introduction of barbed-wire fences, hedgerows of Osage oranges were often used by farmers to enclose their fields, and today the tree is still used as a hedge plant where an impenetrable barrier is desired. But because it has invasive roots, it should not be planted near sewer or drainage lines. Osage orange posts are very durable when embedded in soil, and the flexible wood is used in archers' bows.

HOW TO GROW. The Osage orange grows in Areas C, D, E, G, I and J. It needs full sun but grows in almost any soil, wet or dry, acid or alkaline. It tolerates desert heat, wind and drought once its far-ranging roots are established. Remove some branches of mature trees to create a more open appearance.

MAGNOLIA
M. acuminata (cucumber tree), *M. cordata* (yellow cucumber tree), *M. denudata* (yulan magnolia), *M. loebnerii* 'Merrill' (Merrill magnolia), *M. soulangiana* (saucer magnolia), *M. stellata* (star magnolia)

A gardener from northern Maine once remarked that he always visited Boston in early May to enjoy the old magnolias in blossom along Beacon Street. He could then go back home and have the patience to wait until Spring came north to his garden. In addition to splendid flowers, all magnolias have strange 2- to 4-inch-long knobby fruit that resemble cucumbers. The fruit are green at first, then usually turn pink or red before opening in early fall to reveal pea-sized bright red seeds. The seeds, which are inedible, often hang suspended from the opened husks on slender threads, but remain colorful for only a week or two. Magnolias have coarse leaves, and the trees are practically free

OSAGE ORANGE
Maclura pomifera

CUCUMBER TREE
Magnolia acuminata

For growing areas, see map on page 150.

YULAN MAGNOLIA
Magnolia denudata

MERRILL MAGNOLIA
Magnolia loebnerii 'Merrill'

of insect pests and tolerate the fumes and grime of cities.

Early-flowering magnolias make useful decorative trees standing alone. Ordinarily they should be placed where they can be enjoyed from the house or street because they come into flower when outdoor temperatures are still quite cool. However, those magnolias that open their blossoms before their leaves unfold present a problem because the flowers sometimes open so early that they are nipped by a late frost. This frost injury is especially common on trees that are grown in protected places because they start into growth at the first sign of warm weather. Exposed locations or those on the north side of a house are preferable —they hold the tree's growth back so that the flowers do not open until danger of severe frosts is past.

The cucumber tree grows rapidly: planted at 8 to 10 feet, it reaches a height of 20 to 25 feet in four to six years, eventually becoming 50 to 80 feet tall with a spread of 25 to 30 feet. It makes a handsome shade tree with huge leaves up to 10 inches long and 5 inches wide. Even though its greenish yellow blossoms are 3 inches tall, they are partially hidden by the luxuriant foliage when they open in early summer. The tree begins to blossom when it is about 20 feet tall.

The yellow cucumber tree grows at about the same rate as the cucumber tree but becomes 25 to 30 feet tall with a spread of 15 to 20 feet. A fine shade tree, it has 3- to 6-inch-long leaves, among which are nestled 2-inch canary-yellow flowers in late spring. The yellow cucumber tree begins blossoming when it is about 15 feet tall.

The yulan magnolia is also good for shade. Planted at 6 to 8 feet, it becomes 20 feet tall in 10 to 12 years, eventually becoming 30 to 40 feet tall with an equal spread. It begins to blossom when 8 to 10 feet tall. The fragrant blossoms, 6 inches across, open before the leaves unfurl; the leaves are about 6 inches long and half as wide.

The Merrill magnolia grows fast: an 8- to 10-foot tree reaches 15 to 20 feet in four to six years, eventually becoming 50 feet tall with a spread of about 20 feet. It begins to blossom when it is 4 to 6 feet tall, bearing 4-inch fragrant flowers that open in early spring before the leaves appear. It is a splendid tree standing alone.

The saucer magnolia grows from 6 feet to 15 to 20 feet in about 10 years, eventually reaching 20 to 25 feet with an equal or greater spread. It has 6-inch leaves that turn an attractive shade of brown in fall. The smooth gray bark and 1-inch fuzzy flower buds tipping the leafless winter branches are attractive even when this species is dormant. It is sometimes grown as a multiple-trunked tree. The saucer magnolia begins to blossom when it is about 4 feet tall; the 6- to 10-inch flowers open in early spring before the leaves appear. Many nurserymen grow saucer magnolias from seeds, but because this type is a hybrid, the seedlings may not resemble their parents and flower color may vary from white to deep rose purple. To be certain of the flower color, buy only named varieties that have been propagated vegetatively. Excellent varieties are the Alexander saucer magnolia, *M. soulangiana alexandrina,* with blossoms whose petals are white on the inside and purplish on the outside; the white saucer magnolia, *M. soulangiana amabilis,* with slightly fragrant pure white flowers; and the Lenne saucer magnolia, *M. soulangiana lennei,* with dark purplish balloon-shaped flowers.

The star magnolia grows from 3 to 4 feet to 6 to 10 feet in five or six years, eventually reaching a height of 15 to 20 feet; it may have one or several trunks and can appear dense and almost shrublike. It begins to blossom when it is about 3 feet tall. The fragrant snowy white flowers are 3 inches across, with each blossom composed of 12 to 19 straplike petals. The flowers open in early spring before the 2½-inch leaves appear. The leaves turn bronzy yellow in fall. A fine variety, the pink star magnolia, *M. stellata rosea,* has similar but nonfragrant flowers; they are pink when they open and fade to white.

HOW TO GROW. The cucumber tree grows in Areas B, C, D, E, H, I and J; the yellow cucumber tree grows in Areas C, D, E, H, I and J; yulan and Merrill magnolias grow in Areas C, D, E, G, H, I and J; and saucer and star magnolias grow in Areas B, C, D, E, G, I and J. Magnolias grow in full sun or light shade (light shade is recommended in Areas D, E, G and J), and do best in moist acid soil (pH 5.0 to 6.0) that has been supplemented with peat moss or leaf mold and is deep enough to accommodate the trees' long root structures. Trees bought balled and burlaped—that is, with their roots in their original soil ball wrapped in burlap—must be planted in early spring when they are beginning active growth; those that blossom before their leaves appear can even be planted with no hazard when they are in full blossom. Be sure to set magnolias at the exact level at which they were growing in the nursery. Pruning should be kept to a minimum but, when needed, should be done immediately after flowering.

MAIDENHAIR TREE See *Ginkgo*

MALUS

M. arnoldiana (Arnold crab apple); *M. atrosanguinea* (carmine crab apple); *M. baccata* (Siberian crab apple); *M.* 'Bob White' (Bob White crab apple); *M. coronaria* 'Charlotte' (Charlotte crab apple); *M.* 'Dolgo' (Dolgo crab apple); *M.* 'Dorothea' (Dorothea crab apple); *M.* 'Flame' (Flame crab apple); *M. floribunda* (Japanese crab apple); *M. halliana parkmanii* (Parkman crab apple); *M. hupehensis,* also called *M. theifera* (tea crab apple); *M.* 'Katherine' (Katherine crab apple); *M.* 'Prince Georges' (Prince Georges crab apple); *M. purpurea lemoinei* (Lemoine purple crab apple); *M.* 'Radiant' (Radiant crab apple); *M.* 'Red Jade' (Red Jade crab apple); *M.* 'Red Silver' (Red Silver crab apple); *M.* 'Royal Ruby' (Royal Ruby crab apple); *M.* 'Royalty' (Royalty crab apple); *M. sargentii* (Sargent crab apple); *M. scheideckerii* (Scheidecker crab apple); *M.* 'Snowdrift' (Snowdrift crab apple); *M. spectabilis riversii* (River's crab apple); *M. zumi calocarpa* (Zumi crab apple)

Crab apples are the easiest to grow and the most resistant to winter cold of all flowering trees. There are varieties that do well in southern Canada and all parts of the United States except the Gulf Coast, Florida and parts of the Southwest. In spring, just before the leaves unfurl, crab apples are smothered in appleblossom-scented flowers, 1 to 2 inches in diameter. The flowers may be either singles, each with one ring of petals, or semidoubles or doubles, with numerous overlapping petals. Trees often begin to blossom the first year after planting. The flowers are borne in clusters that completely conceal the branches regardless of the size of individual blossoms. Except for some double-flowering types that produce additional petals instead of seeds, most crab apples bear great quantities of red, yellow or green fruit ¼ inch to 2 inches in diameter. The fruit clusters along the branches, and can be left on the trees until eaten by birds or used to make jelly. Crab apples have simple 2- to 4-inch sawtooth-edged leaves.

Genetically, crab apples are similar to ordinary apples, but over the years nurserymen have bred seedlings for their deep colors, abundant blossoms and small fruit to produce ornamental rather than fruit trees. Horticulturists define a crab apple as a tree with fruit less than 2 inches

SAUCER MAGNOLIA
Magnolia soulangiana

ARNOLD CRAB APPLE
Malus arnoldiana

For growing areas, see map on page 150.

across; a tree with larger fruit is simply called apple.

Although certain crab apples mature at a height of less than 10 feet and others reach 50 feet, most varieties become 15 to 25 feet tall with an equal spread. They generally grow from 6 to 8 feet to 15 to 20 feet in about five or six years. The height at which they send out their first branches depends on the way they were pruned at the nursery and, in some cases, on the method of propagation. For example, a tree can be pruned so that its branches originate at a point 3 to 4 feet above the ground, or it can have all branches removed up to a height of 6 feet or more. Sometimes a dwarf variety, such as Sargent crab apple, is grafted to the top of a trunk 6 feet tall; this produces a tree beneath which people can walk, yet its ultimate height is that of the 6- to 8-foot Sargent variety added to the height of the stem to which it was grafted. It will never exceed 14 feet. It is possible to buy dwarf crab apples, although relatively few nurseries propagate them because ordinary crab apple trees are suitable for most gardens. Some crab apple varieties are called alternate bearers; they produce a great many flowers one year and relatively few flowers the second year. They are not included here unless they have other qualities that make them especially valuable. Unless so noted, the ones described below can be depended upon to produce enormous crops of flowers each spring. The flowering branches make attractive cut flowers.

The Arnold crab apple grows 12 to 20 feet tall and has red flower buds that open to 2-inch blossoms and produce ⅝-inch fruit. The carmine crab apple grows 15 to 20 feet tall; its 1¼-inch flowers open red but fade to deep pink. They are followed by ⅜-inch dark red fruit. The Siberian crab apple grows 35 to 50 feet tall. It is one of the earliest varieties to blossom and one of the most resistant to winter cold. It bears great quantities of very fragrant 1- to 1½-inch white flowers followed by ⅜-inch red or yellow fruit. The Bob White crab apple grows 15 to 20 feet tall and has multitudes of 1-inch white flowers that are followed by ⅝-inch yellow fruit that cling very late in the year. The Charlotte crab apple grows 15 to 20 feet tall and has 1¼- to 2¼-inch pale pink double flowers and 1¾-inch yellowish green fruit.

Particularly colorful jelly is provided by the fruit of the Dolgo crab apple, which grows 35 to 40 feet tall and bears 1¾-inch white flowers followed by 1¼-inch bright red fruit. This species is an alternate bearer, but is very resistant to winter cold and suitable for far-northern gardens. The Dorothea crab apple grows 20 to 25 feet tall. It bears enormous crops of 1½- to 2-inch pink semidouble flowers followed by ½-inch bright yellow fruit. The Flame crab apple is a very cold-resistant variety that grows 20 to 25 feet tall and has pink flower buds that become white 1-inch blossoms; these are followed by ¾-inch bright red fruit. The Japanese crab apple grows 25 to 30 feet tall; it has deep pink buds that open pink and then fade to white before falling. Because all of the buds do not open or fade simultaneously, the blossoms appear multicolored. The flowers are 1 to 1½ inches across and are followed by ⅜-inch red-and-yellow fruit.

The Parkman crab apple grows in a vase shape and reaches a height of 12 to 15 feet. It has deep pink double flowers about 1¼ inches across followed by pea-sized red fruit. The tea crab apple is an alternate bearer, but it has very graceful pendulous branches and large clusters of deep pink buds that open to 1½-inch pink blossoms and fade to white. It grows 20 to 25 feet tall and has ⅜-inch yellow fruit tinged with red on the branches receiving most sun. The Katherine crab apple grows 18 to 20 feet tall and bears some of the largest double flowers (2 to 2¼ inch-

KATHERINE CRAB APPLE
Malus 'Katherine'

es) of any variety. These pink blossoms fade to white before falling and are followed by ¼-inch red fruit.

The Prince Georges crab apple grows 15 to 20 feet tall and has 2-inch-wide double rose-pink flowers. It is one of the double-flowered types that bear no fruit. Individual blossoms may have as many as 50 petals. The Lemoine purple crab apple grows 20 to 25 feet tall and bears single or semidouble flowers about 1½ inches across. They are followed by ⅝-inch fruit. The leaves of this variety are purplish when they unfold in the spring and become deep green later in the year. The Radiant crab apple grows 25 to 30 feet tall and has masses of red flower buds that open to 1-inch deep pink blossoms followed by ½-inch red fruit. Its young leaves are reddish and turn green during the summer. The Red Jade crab apple is an unusually handsome weeping variety that grows 15 to 20 feet tall. It has 1-inch white flowers followed by enormous crops of ½-inch bright red berries, but may alternate between flowers and fruit, producing mainly blossoms one year, berries another. The berries cling to the pendulous branches until late in fall or early winter. Birds are attracted to them.

The Red Silver crab apple, which grows 25 to 30 feet tall, gets its name from the silvery tinge seen on its reddish leaves as they unfold in spring. Its 1¼-inch rose-pink flowers are followed by ¾-inch deep red fruit. The Royal Ruby crab apple grows 10 to 15 feet tall and has very dark red-pink double flowers about 2 inches across. It produces almost no fruit, but the little that develops is dark red and about ½ inch across. The Royalty crab apple grows 12 to 15 feet tall and has 1-inch purplish crimson flowers followed by ½-inch dark red fruit. The leaves of this unusual variety remain deep purple all summer. The Sargent crab apple is a dwarf tree that rarely grows taller than 6 to 8 feet, but its zigzag branches spread horizontally to a diameter of up to 20 feet. It has ½-inch white flowers followed by ¼-inch red fruit that become colorful early in fall and cling until winter. The Scheidecker crab apple grows 18 to 20 feet tall and has 1½-inch double pale pink flowers followed by ⅝-inch yellow-orange fruit in fall. The Snowdrift crab apple is well named. It grows 20 to 25 feet tall and has pink buds that open to masses of 1-inch white flowers followed by orange-red ⅜-inch fruit. This variety is very cold resistant. The River's crab apple, an old alternate-bearing variety, grows 20 to 25 feet tall and has 2-inch double pink flowers followed by pale yellowish green 1¼-inch fruit. The Zumi crab apple grows 20 to 25 feet tall and has great quantities of 1-inch white flowers followed by ½-inch bright red fruit. Though this variety is an alternate bearer, its fruit is so spectacular and clings so long into fall and early winter that it remains a popular tree with gardeners.

HOW TO GROW. Arnold, carmine, Bob White, Charlotte, Dorothea, Japanese, tea, Katherine, Prince Georges, Lemoine, Radiant, Red Jade, Red Silver, Royalty, Sargent, Scheidecker and River's crab apples grow in Areas B, C, D, F, G, H and I; Parkman, Royal Ruby and Zumi crab apples grow in Areas C, D, G and I; Siberian, Dolgo, Flame and Snowdrift crab apples grow in Areas A, B, C, D, F, G, H and I. All do best when given full sun and a moist well-drained acid soil (pH 5.0 to 6.5). Prune young trees in winter or early spring; old trees seldom require pruning.

MAPLE See *Acer*

MELIA
M. azedarach (chinaberry, pride of India, bead tree)
The chinaberry is a very fast-growing tree. Planted at a height of 2 to 3 feet, it may easily grow 6 to 8 feet a year

LEMOINE PURPLE CRAB APPLE
Malus purpurea lemoinei

TEXAS UMBRELLA TREE
Melia azedarach umbraculiformis

For growing areas, see map on page 150.

and in four or five years become 20 feet tall with an equal spread; ultimately it reaches 35 to 50 feet. In the United States the chinaberry has fallen into disrepute because it is so easy to grow and because its seedlings tend to spring up like weeds. Nevertheless, where fast growth and dense shade are desired or where heat, drought and poor soil are common, it is a highly useful selection. The chinaberry has dense fernlike dark green leaves up to 3 feet long and 1 foot wide with many 1- to 3-inch leaflets. In spring it bears 5- to 8-inch clusters of fragrant lilac flowers at the ends of its branches. The flowers are followed in summer by smooth yellow ¾-inch berries that are poisonous to human beings but are luckily so sour that there is little likelihood anyone would eat them. Birds, however, do eat them, without ill effect. The berries, which become wrinkled and sticky as they ripen, cling to the branches late into fall and often even into winter. Inside each berry is a single pea-sized bony pit that is often used in the making of rosaries—hence, one of the chinaberry's common names, the bead tree. In Persia, India, Ceylon and Malaysia, where the chinaberry is considered to be holy, the berries are strung into garlands and draped over altars.

An interesting mutation of the chinaberry was discovered in Texas in 1894 and is now more widely planted than the ordinary species. This variety is known both as the Texas umbrella tree and as the umbrella chinaberry, *M. azedarach umbraculiformis.* It eventually grows 25 to 30 feet tall and develops a dense mound, or umbrella shape, without having to be trained.

HOW TO GROW. The chinaberry grows in the southern part of Area C and in Areas D, E, G and J. It grows in full sun in almost any soil, including alkaline soil, that is deep enough to accommodate its long root structure but does best in well-drained soil. Because its branches are very brittle, it should be planted in a location where it is protected from wind. Prune in fall.

MESQUITE See *Prosopis*
MEXICAN PALOVERDE See *Parkinsonia*
MIMOSA See *Albizia*

MORUS

M. alba (white mulberry), *M. nigra* (black or Persian mulberry), *M. rubra* (red mulberry)

Mulberries are highly favored in areas with long hot summers or extended droughts, and do well in seaside gardens if sheltered from wind. They grow very rapidly: an 8- to 10-foot tree reaches about 20 feet with an equal spread in four to six years, eventually becoming 30 to 50 feet tall. The 3- to 5-inch leaves have one or more lobes, and multilobed leaves often appear on the same branches with lobeless leaves. The flowers appear in ½-inch scaly clusters in spring and early summer, the female flowers ripening quickly into ½- to 1-inch blackberry-shaped edible fruit. Mulberries sometimes bear male and female flowers on separate trees. Most fruiting trees have flowers of both sexes, but fruitless male trees are the ones most often grown for shade or for planting near paved areas, since the fruit drops and causes stains. However, birds are so fond of the fruit that fruiting mulberries are sometimes planted near more valuable fruit trees, such as cherries, to lure the birds away from the choice crop.

The white mulberry eventually grows up to 50 feet tall and has white, pinkish or purplish fruit that is unpleasantly sweet. Several excellent varieties of white mulberry are *M. alba tatarica,* the Russian mulberry, an especially cold-resistant type; Stribling, also called Mapleleaf, and Kingan, two fruitless types that make fine fast-growing

WHITE MULBERRY
Morus alba

shade trees; *M. alba pendula,* the weeping mulberry, a weeping mutation that is grafted onto the upright stem of a common seedling and forms an 8- to 15-foot-high fountain of slender drooping branches; and Chaparral, a nonfruiting weeping mulberry.

The black mulberry eventually grows about 30 feet tall and bears blackberry-flavored fruit that can be eaten fresh or used for jams.

The red mulberry eventually reaches about 50 feet and has dark red-purple fruit that is relished by birds.

HOW TO GROW. White and red mulberries grow in all areas except Area A; black mulberry grows only in Areas D, E and J. All grow in full sun or light shade in almost any soil, including alkaline soil, but they do best in moist soil that is deep enough to accommodate the trees' long root structures. Once the roots are well established, they will even endure drought. Prune mulberries in winter. Because their branches tend to bend down as they become long, it is often necessary to remove some of the lower ones every few years.

MOUNTAIN ASH See *Sorbus*
MOUNTAIN EBONY See *Bauhinia*
MULBERRY See *Morus*
MULBERRY, PAPER See *Broussonetia*

N

NETTLE TREE See *Celtis*

NYSSA
N. sylvatica (pepperidge, black tupelo, sour gum)

The pepperidge is outstanding in early fall when its 2- to 5-inch shiny green leaves take on warm tones of orange and red. One of the few deciduous trees that have autumn color in mild climates, it is also valuable in wet, swampy areas where few other trees survive. The pepperidge grows from 5 to 6 feet to about 20 feet in 10 to 15 years, usually reaching 30 to 50 feet with a spread equal to half its height. Young trees have a conical shape, but older ones become irregular and flat-topped; young or old, they have distinctive horizontal branches that dip slightly at the tips. This is apparent throughout the year but is especially effective in winter after the leaves have fallen. In early summer pepperidges bear tiny greenish yellow male and female flowers on separate trees. If trees of both sexes happen to be near one another, the flowers on the female trees are followed in early fall by clusters of ½-inch blue-black fruit, which are not very tasty to humans but are eagerly eaten by birds. The pepperidge has notably pest-free foliage and even succeeds in seaside gardens if protected from wind.

HOW TO GROW. The pepperidge grows in Areas B, C, D, E, G, I and J. It does best in full sun and moist acid soil (pH 5.5 to 6.5) but tolerates light shade and ordinary garden soil provided it is watered deeply during dry weather. The pepperidge is notoriously difficult to establish in the garden and must be planted balled and burlaped—that is, with its roots in its original soil ball wrapped in burlap —preferably in early spring. Pruning is seldom required but should be done in fall.

O

OAK See *Quercus*
OLD-MAN'S-BEARD See *Chionanthus*
OLEASTER See *Elaeagnus*
OLIVE, RUSSIAN See *Elaeagnus*
ORANGE, OSAGE See *Maclura*
ORCHID TREE See *Bauhinia*
OSAGE ORANGE See *Maclura*

For growing areas, see map on page 150.

PEPPERIDGE
Nyssa sylvatica

AMERICAN HOP HORNBEAM
Ostrya virginiana

SORREL TREE
Oxydendrum arboreum

JERUSALEM THORN
Parkinsonia aculeata

OSTRYA

O. virginiana (American hop hornbeam, ironwood)

The American hop hornbeam is a graceful small tree with slender spreading branches that are so strong they are seldom injured by wind or ice. It grows very slowly and has the advantage of never outgrowing its place in the yard: a 5- to 6-foot tree may require 15 years or more to reach 20 feet, though it eventually grows up to 40 feet tall with an equal spread. The 2- to 5-inch leaves are notably pest free and are very similar in appearance to elm leaves (*Ulmus, page 146*). They are medium green in summer and turn yellow in fall. The tree bears 1- to 2-inch-long clusters of male flowers and inconspicuous female flowers; both are greenish and both open in early spring. The "hop" part of the name of the American hop hornbeam refers to the 1½- to 2-inch clusters of seed-holding husks, which resemble the fruit of the hop plant, *Humulus lupulus*. The "hornbeam" part of the tree's name alludes to the horny —that is, tough and hard—quality of the wood, which is used for tool handles and was formerly used to make yokes for oxen. Because of its slow growth, the American hop hornbeam is not widely available.

HOW TO GROW. The American hop hornbeam grows in Areas B, C, D, E, F, G and I. It grows in full sun or light shade and does best in a cool moist but well-drained soil. Trees bought balled and burlaped—that is, with their roots in their original soil ball wrapped in burlap—should be planted only in early spring. Prune only in winter or early spring; older trees rarely need pruning.

OXYDENDRUM

O. arboreum (sorrel tree, sourwood)

Many gardeners feel that, among native trees, the sorrel tree is second only to the flowering dogwood in beauty. It is a small tree that grows rather slowly: planted at 5 to 6 feet, it usually takes 12 to 15 years to reach a height of 20 feet and rarely becomes taller than 25 feet with a spread of 10 to 15 feet. It sometimes has a multiple trunk and lower branches that reach down to the ground. The most spectacular season for the sorrel tree is midsummer, when the ends of its branches carry 6- to 8-inch hanging clusters of fragrant bell-shaped tiny white flowers that look much like lilies of the valley. Some nurserymen even call the sorrel tree the lily-of-the-valley tree, a descriptive though incorrect name. The effect of the flowers seems to linger through fall even after the flowers fade, because the seed pods that follow are grayish and, though erect rather than hanging, give much the same appearance as do the flowers. Glossy leathery leaves 5 to 7 inches long are reddish as they unfold in spring, then become deep green in summer before taking on rich red tones in fall; the leaves are notably pest free. The sorrel tree is an attractive lawn ornament, whether it is planted alone or in clusters, and is a natural companion to such shrubs as rhododendrons and azaleas, which require similar growing conditions.

HOW TO GROW. The sorrel tree grows in Areas C, D, E and I and the northern part of Area J. It grows in light shade but produces the most flowers and the brightest autumn colors when grown in full sun. It does best in moist well-drained acid soil (pH 5.5 to 6.5) that has been liberally supplemented with peat moss or leaf mold. Pruning is almost never required.

P

PAGODA TREE See *Sophora*
PAPAW See *Asimina*
PAPER MULBERRY See *Broussonetia*
PARASOL TREE, CHINESE See *Firmiana*

PARKINSONIA

P. aculeata (Jerusalem thorn, Mexican paloverde)

The Jerusalem thorn is grown for its feathery foliage, fragrant yellow flowers and irregularly arranged branches, which are especially attractive when seen against the sky. It grows very rapidly when young, a 5- to 6-foot tree reaching 15 feet with an equal spread in about three years. Older trees grow more slowly, eventually becoming up to 30 feet tall. The Jerusalem thorn makes a handsome lawn decoration but casts only light shade because of its strange delicately formed leaves. They are 8 to 12 inches or more long with leaflets only 1⁄8 inch long. The leaves drop during drought as well as in cold weather, but the green twigs, rich with chlorophyll and set with thorns, continue the process of photosynthesis that is normally carried on by the leaves. Because the Jerusalem thorn casts filtered rather than dense shade, a lawn is easy to grow beneath it. In spring and early summer and intermittently during the rest of the year, the Jerusalem thorn produces loose 3- to 8-inch clusters of 3⁄4-inch yellow flowers, which can easily be seen through the thin veil of the foliage. The flowers are followed by brown seed pods 2 to 5 inches long. The Jerusalem thorn is sometimes grown as a spiny barrier hedge because of its thorns, its fast growth and its ability to withstand shearing. The flowering branches can be cut for use as indoor decorations.

HOW TO GROW. The Jerusalem thorn grows in Areas D, E and J. It does best in full sun but tolerates nearly any well-drained soil and is at home in deserts and on seacoasts as well as in average gardens. Prune young trees in spring. Older trees seldom need pruning.

PARROTIA

P. persica (Persian parrotia)

The Persian parrotia is grown primarily for its handsome autumn foliage. The 3- to 4-inch shiny dark green leaves turn yellow, orange, pink and red in fall; they are virtually pest free. The Persian parrotia grows from 5 to 6 feet to about 15 feet in six to eight years, eventually becoming up to 30 feet tall with an equal spread. It may have a single or multiple trunk, but its graceful branches are often allowed to grow to the ground, obscuring the trunk. The flowers, which appear in early spring before the leaves unfurl, are small and petalless, but their red pollen-bearing stamens make them interesting at close hand. They are followed by 1⁄2-inch dry brown seed capsules. In winter the smooth gray trunks are attractively blotched with white where the outer bark flakes off.

HOW TO GROW. The Persian parrotia grows in Areas C, D, E, I and J. It does best and has most colorful foliage in full sun, but tolerates light shade. It grows in almost any well-drained acid soil (pH 6.0 to 6.5) if sheltered from wind. Trees bought balled and burlaped—that is, with their roots in their original soil ball wrapped in burlap—should be planted in early spring. Remove side branches in winter if a relatively tall tree is wanted; unpruned, the tree is apt to be short and shrubby.

PAULOWNIA

P. tomentosa, also called *P. imperialis* (empress tree, royal paulownia)

The empress tree is amazingly beautiful in blossom. In spring, just before the leaves open, its 3⁄4-inch fuzzy buds, which hang like clusters of tiny brown pears at the tips of the bare winter branches, develop into 8- to 15-inch clusters of vanilla-scented 2-inch blue flowers. The flowers are followed by 1- to 1½-inch dry seed pods that cling for at least a year. The empress tree grows very rapidly when

PERSIAN PARROTIA
Parrotia persica

EMPRESS TREE
Paulownia tomentosa

For growing areas, see map on page 150.

young, sometimes making 8 feet or more of growth during its first year. Planted at 5 to 6 feet, it reaches 20 feet in about four years. As it approaches maturity, it grows more slowly, eventually becoming 35 to 40 feet tall with an equal spread. The leaves of the empress tree are normally quite large—5 to 12 inches long and up to 8 inches wide—but on young plants or on fast-growing stems, they may become as much as 2 to 3 feet long and nearly as wide. The empress tree is seldom troubled by pests. It withstands the pollution of urban and suburban areas and does well in seaside locations. But it also has some drawbacks. It produces dense shade, in which grass and other ground covers are difficult to grow, and it litters the ground with faded flowers, seed pods and, in fall, its huge leaves. And in northern regions its flower buds are sometimes killed by cold winters, even when the tree itself resists the winter cold.

HOW TO GROW. The empress tree grows in the southern part of Area C and in Areas D, E, G, I and J. It grows in full sun in almost any kind of soil but does best in light shade and moist well-drained soil that is deep enough to accommodate the tree's long root structure. Large trees are especially difficult to establish in the garden, so purchase young trees no taller than 5 to 6 feet. Trees bought balled and burlaped—that is, with their roots in their original soil ball wrapped in burlap—should be planted in early spring. Prune trees in winter.

PAWPAW See *Asimina*
PEACH See *Prunus*
PEACOCK FLOWER See *Delonix*
PEAR See *Pyrus*
PECAN See *Carya*
PEPPERIDGE See *Nyssa*
PERSIMMON See *Diospyros*

PHELLODENDRON

P. amurense (Amur cork tree)

Notable for its deeply ridged soft bark, the Amur cork tree is an easy-to-establish pest-free shade tree that is excellent in urban areas because it withstands polluted air and meets the rigorous requirements for growing along streets. It is relatively fast growing when young: an 8- to 10-foot tree reaches about 20 feet in five to seven years, eventually becoming 30 to 50 feet tall with branches spreading an equal or greater distance. Its 10- to 15-inch dark green leaves have 5 to 13 leaflets, 2 to 4 inches long. The leaves, which turn yellow before dropping in autumn, cast such a delicate shade that grass is easy to grow beneath the trees in summer. The leaves have a pleasant turpentinelike fragrance when crushed. Only female trees bear fruit, ¼-inch black berries that cling late into the fall and winter and are eventually eaten by birds. The berries have the same fragrance as the leaves.

HOW TO GROW. The Amur cork tree grows in Areas A, B, C, D, F, G, H and I and the northern part of Area J. It needs full sun but will grow in almost any soil. Prune young trees in winter; older trees seldom require pruning.

PHOENIX TREE See *Firmiana*
PISTACHE See *Pistacia*

PISTACIA

P. chinensis, also called *P. sinensis* (Chinese pistache)

The Chinese pistache is one of the most beautiful shade trees for the Southwest, Florida and the Gulf Coast, and for both desert and seaside locations. It grows rather fast when young. Planted at 8 to 10 feet, it reaches 20 feet in five to seven years, eventually becoming 40 to 50 feet tall

AMUR CORK TREE
Phellodendron amurense

CHINESE PISTACHE
Pistacia chinensis

with an equal spread. Exceptionally pest-free 12- to 16-inch leaves made up of 10 or more slender shiny leaflets, each 2 to 4 inches long, are bright green in summer but take on handsome tones of orange and red in fall. Young shoots are eaten as a vegetable in the tree's native China. Inconspicuous male and female flowers grow on separate trees. If both sexes are present, the female flowers are followed in fall by 6-inch-long clusters of ¼-inch nutlike but inedible red fruit that turn purplish when ripe. However, male trees are preferable because they have denser foliage. A fine variety is Keith Davey.

HOW TO GROW. The Chinese pistache grows only in Areas E and J. It does best in full sun in well-drained soil that is deep enough to accommodate the tree's long root structure, but tolerates almost any kind of soil, including the alkaline ones. Prune young trees in winter; older trees will seldom require pruning.

PLANE TREE See *Platanus*

PLATANUS

P. acerifolia (London plane tree); *P. occidentalis* (American plane tree); *P. orientalis* (Oriental plane tree); *P. racemosa*, also called *P. californica* (California plane tree). (All also called sycamore, buttonball and buttonwood)

Plane trees are among the easiest of all large shade trees to grow and one of them, the London plane tree, is considered to be the world's most reliable tree for city planting because of its high resistance to air pollution. Although the larger-growing types are popular because they provide such desirable shade, their use is best reserved for large lawns and avenues; planted in small yards or along narrow streets, they soon become overwhelming. Plane trees grow rapidly and furnish quick shade: a 10- to 12-foot tree reaches 20 feet in about five years and eventually becomes 40 to 100 feet tall, depending on its species, with an equal spread. The 4- to 8-inch-wide leaves usually have three to five shallow lobes and resemble maple leaves, but do not turn color in autumn. Ball-shaped seed pods 1 to 1½ inches in diameter are green in summer, turn brown in fall and cling most of the year. The American plane tree bears its seed balls singly, but the other species usually have groups of two or more than dangle from the branches as though they were on strings. The bark of all plane trees flakes off, revealing an inner bark of greenish yellow or white that gives the trunk a distinctive appearance even in winter when the leaves have fallen. Plane trees are susceptible to attacks by leaf blights, anthracnose and twig cankers; for controls, see page 149.

The London plane tree, a hybrid between the American plane and the Oriental plane trees, not only withstands the polluted air of cities but also is more disease resistant than other plane trees. It eventually grows 70 to 100 feet tall and is the species most widely available in nurseries. The American plane tree also grows 70 to 100 feet tall but does not tolerate urban air well and is best planted in country settings. The Oriental plane tree grows 70 to 90 feet tall and, though often listed by nurserymen as Oriental plane, is in many cases actually London plane tree. The California plane tree grows 40 to 50 feet tall, sometimes with multiple trunks that may be picturesquely gnarled.

HOW TO GROW. The London plane tree grows in Areas C, D, E, F, G, I and J; the American plane tree in all areas except Area A; the Oriental plane tree in the southern part of Area C and in Areas D, E, G, I and J; and the California plane tree in Areas I and J. All grow in full sun or light shade in almost any soil, including alkaline soil, but do best in moist soil that is deep enough to accommodate

LONDON PLANE TREE
Platanus acerifolia

CALIFORNIA PLANE TREE
Platanus racemosa

For growing areas, see map on page 150.

BOLLEANA POPLAR
Populus alba pyramidalis

LOMBARDY POPLAR
Populus nigra italica

their long root structures. To build up the trees' resistance to disease, it is especially important to fertilize them every year or two and water them deeply during spells of dry weather. Prune plane trees in winter.

PLUM See *Prunus*
POINCIANA See *Delonix*
POPLAR See *Populus*
POPLAR, TULIP See *Liriodendron*
POPLAR, YELLOW See *Liriodendron*

POPULUS
P. alba (white poplar); *P. deltoides,* also called *P. deltoidea* (eastern poplar, cottonwood); *P. nigra italica* (Lombardy poplar)

Some gardeners, aware of the way the roots of poplars search out and plug drainpipes or heave up the pavements of sidewalks, are likely to condemn the entire genus. But this attitude is usually based on experience with one particularly annoying poplar, the Carolina poplar, *P. canadensis,* which, though once a favorite, is now prohibited by law in some communities. The other species must also be treated with caution—they should never be planted near paving or drains and, because their wood is weak, they should not be placed where broken branches may be a nuisance. Yet it must be admitted that these fast-growing trees are extremely beautiful and that there are places where the needs of gardeners are best served by them. In arid areas, for instance, they are among the few trees that grow without coddling, and on ground that has no trees at all, they grow so quickly that they soon give a garden an established look. By the time they have outlived their usefulness—in 25 to 30 years—other, more permanent species will have grown tall enough to be effective. Poplars often average 3 to 5 feet or more of growth each year, an 8- to 10-foot tree reaching about 20 feet in two or three years. They bear undistinguished male and female flowers on separate trees. The female trees produce an abundance of fluffy white seeds that accumulate on the ground like bits of cotton—hence the name cottonwood, as the poplar is frequently called in the West.

The white poplar eventually grows 50 to 60 feet tall with an equal spread. Its 3- to 5-inch leaves have three to five lobes and are gray green on top with chalky white undersides. The slightest breeze causes them to turn and show their white surface. The leaves become reddish in fall. A handsome columnar variety is the Bolleana poplar, *P. alba pyramidalis,* also called *P. alba bolleana;* a 50-foot tree usually spread only 15 to 20 feet.

The eastern poplar grows 75 to 100 feet tall, spreading 50 to 75 feet in a broad vaselike shape. Its triangular 4- to 7-inch shiny dark green leaves have the scent of balsam when crushed and turn yellow before dropping in autumn. Nurserymen sell the male trees of this species, calling them "cottonless cottonwoods" because they have no seeds and produce no seedlings. One of the best is the variety Siouxland, whose leaves are particularly dark green in color and resistant to disease.

The Lombardy poplar is the species that comes to most minds when the name poplar is mentioned. It grows 70 to 90 feet tall with a spread of only 10 to 15 feet. Its lofty spires of dark green 3- to 4-inch leaves turn golden and then drop in fall, leaving its masses of vertical branches etched against the winter sky. It is quickly effective when grown in groups, but is very susceptible to a canker disease that causes branches to die from the top down and generally kills the tree in 25 to 30 years.

HOW TO GROW. The poplars listed here grow in all areas.

They tolerate light shade and almost any soil, but make fastest growth in full sun and moist well-drained soil that is deep enough to accommodate the trees' long root structures. Prune in summer or fall—winter and spring pruning causes poplars to bleed.

PRIDE OF INDIA See *Melia*

PROSOPIS

P. glandulosa, also called *P. glandulosa torreyana*, *P. juliflora glandulosa* and *P. chilensis* (honey mesquite, algaroba, cashaw)

In hot and arid climates the honey mesquite, which grows wild from the southeastern part of the United States to Chile, offers airy, welcome shade. Honey mesquites grow fast when young: a 5- to 6-foot tree reaches 20 feet with an equal spread in four or five years and eventually becomes 20 to 60 feet tall, depending upon the amount of moisture that is available. These trees have main roots, or taproots, that, on mature desert trees, may reach as much as 50 to 60 feet into the ground, ranging wide in search of moisture and making the trees very tolerant of drought and heat. Honey mesquites usually have multiple trunks but can be pruned to grow with a single trunk. The 3- to 6-inch fernlike leaves fall late in the year. The branches are lined with ½- to 2-inch spines. The small 2- to 4-inch flowers, which blossom in spring and summer, are delightfully fragrant and are a favorite of bees; as a result, mesquite honey is commonly sold wherever these trees can be grown. The flowers are followed by 2- to 6-inch beanlike pods, which are often used as fodder because of their high sugar content. The trunks of old trees become attractively gnarled and develop a rich brown bark.

HOW TO GROW. The honey mesquite grows in Areas G and J as well as in the western parts of Areas D and E. It does best when given full sun and well-drained soil that is deep enough to accommodate the tree's long root structure. It will tolerate alkaline and dry soils and, once the honey mesquite is established, will even endure drought. Pruning should be done in the winter.

PRUNUS

P. avium plena (double-flowered mazzard or sweet cherry); *P. blireiana* (Blireiana or purple-leaved plum); *P. cerasifera atropurpurea*, also called *P. pissardii* (Pissard plum); *P. persica*, also called *Amygdalus persica* (peach); *P. sargentii*, also called *P. serrulata sachalinensis* (Sargent cherry); *P. serrula* (paperbark or birchbark cherry); *P. serrulata* (Oriental cherry, Japanese flowering cherry); *P. subhirtella* (Higan cherry, rosebud cherry); *P. yedoensis* (Yoshino cherry)

When cherries, plums and peaches are in bloom, it is easy to believe that they are the most spectacular flowering trees in the world, particularly if they are species, like the ones listed here, they have been bred for their blossoms rather than for their fruit. The pink or white flowers are 1 to 2 inches in diameter and are borne in great clusters that mass along the stems or droop beneath them. The flowers come in single forms, each with one ring of petals; doubles, with numerous overlapping petals; or semidoubles. They blossom quite early in the spring before or at the same time the leaves begin to unfold. Double-flowered trees do not produce fruit, but single-flowered types will bear edible miniature versions of the same kinds of fruit produced by species that are cultivated primarily for their fruit. Most flowering cherry trees have sawtooth-edged leaves 3 to 5 inches long. The plums listed all have slender purple leaves that are 2½ to 3½ inches long. Flowering

HONEY MESQUITE
Prosopis glandulosa

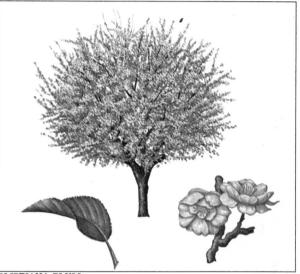

BLIREIANA PLUM
Prunus blireiana

THUNDERCLOUD PLUM
Prunus cerasifera atropurpurea 'Thundercloud'

For growing areas, see map on page 150.

PEACH
Prunus persica

SARGENT CHERRY
Prunus sargentii

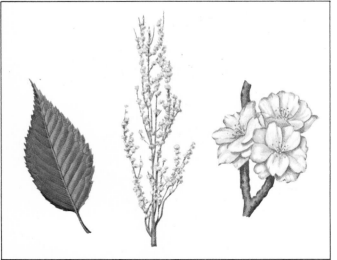

AMANOGAWA ORIENTAL CHERRY
Prunus serrulata 'Amanogawa'

peach trees have 4- to 5-inch-long bright green leaves.

Most of the trees recommended here grow fast. An Oriental cherry, for instance, grows from about 8 feet to 20 feet in six to eight years. These trees generally begin to blossom their first year but are short lived, living only 20 to 25 years. All make handsome lawn ornaments and many of them become large enough to shade a patio. Their flowers are most effective when contrasted against a dark background of evergreens.

The double-flowered mazzard cherry grows in a conical shape, eventually reaching a height of 30 to 35 feet with an equal spread. It bears clusters of 1½-inch double white flowers early in spring, slightly before the more familiar Oriental cherry comes into blossom. The double-flowered mazzard cherry is quite resistant to winter cold and is especially recommended for gardeners who live too far north to be able to grow the Oriental species.

The Blireiana plum, a hybrid, reaches a height of 15 to 20 feet and bears fragrant double pink flowers about an inch across. Its many branches are densely set with dark purplish red leaves that keep their color throughout the summer. A particularly choice variety, Newport, has slender graceful branches and many flowers.

Varieties of Pissard plum have far surpassed the ordinary species, which is seldom grown nowadays. The varieties grow 15 to 20 feet tall and have deep reddish purple foliage throughout the summer. Thundercloud has single pink-to-white flowers and occasional small red fruit that is eagerly eaten by birds. Vesuvius, also called Krauter Vesuvius, has extremely dark leaves; it bears only a few 1-inch single pink flowers and hardly any fruit.

Flowering peaches, unlike flowering plums and cherries, are genetically similar to the trees that are grown primarily for their fruit; single-flowered peaches bear reasonably good fruit, although the flavor may not equal that of varieties grown only for fruit. Most, however, are nonfruiting types with double flowers, 1½ to 2½ inches across, in white, pink or red. The trees grow 15 to 25 feet tall if left unpruned, but are generally cut back to force new growth. The trees are short lived, usually lasting only 10 to 15 years. A delightful variety, Peppermint Stick, has white petals marked with pink and red stripes. The branches of flowering peaches can be cut while they are still in flower and used as excellent indoor decorations.

The Sargent cherry is one of the most useful combination flowering and shade trees available to the home gardener. It grows 40 to 50 feet tall and spreads to a distance roughly equal to its height. In early spring its branches are lined with single pink flowers more than an inch across that are soon followed by 3- to 5-inch reddish tinged leaves. The shiny leaves turn a dark green in the summer and then become red in the fall. The pea-sized cherries, which are first red, then black, are quickly eaten by birds.

The paperbark cherry is not easy to find in nurseries, but its gleaming, peeling dark red bark is so handsome that it is worth hunting for. The bark is effective throughout the year, but is especially so in winter when the trunk and branches of the tree are fully exposed. For this reason, the paperbark cherry is best planted where it can be seen from inside the house. The tree grows 20 to 30 feet tall with an equal rounded spread and bears clusters of single white flowers about ¾ inch in diameter. The flowers appear in early spring before the 2- to 4-inch slender leaves unfold and are followed in early summer by ¼-inch oval red cherries that are tart but edible.

The Oriental cherry is one of the types of cherry tree that make up the famous spring display around the tidal basin in Washington, D.C. The Japanese have bred this species for hundreds of years, and there are many varieties whose flowers differ only slightly from one another. The ones listed here are among the most satisfactory and are widely available from nurseries. Like most other *Prunus* varieties, they are grafted—that is, the stem is made to grow onto the upright trunk of another species with strong roots—and in the case of the Oriental cherry, the height at which the graft connection is made determines the tree's use in the garden. Stems that are grafted on 4-foot trunks make low bushy trees with branches that sweep the ground. Those grafted on 6- to 8-foot trunks produce their lowest branches high up enough for people to walk beneath them. Amanogawa is an unusual variety whose upright branches form a columnar tree 15 to 25 feet tall but only 3 to 6 feet across. Its fragrant semidouble pink blossoms are slightly less than 2 inches across. Fugenzo, also called Kofugen and James H. Veitch, grows 20 to 25 feet tall with an equal spread. Its buds are deep pink and open into lighter pink double flowers 2 to 2½ inches across. The leaves of Fugenzo unfold reddish bronze when the last of the flowers fade. Kwanzan, also called Sekiyama, is the most popular of all flowering cherries. It grows 15 to 25 feet tall and has stiffly upright branches that spread as the tree ages. It bears an abundance of deep pink double flowers about 2½ inches across. Its foliage is reddish when new and turns dark green in summer. Shirofugen grows 20 to 25 feet tall with an equal rounded spread and has reddish foliage in spring. It is one of the last of the Oriental cherries to open its flowers, usually five to seven days after other varieties are already in blossom. The buds are dark pink but open into 2- to 2½-inch double pink flowers that fade to white. Shirotae, also called Mount Fuji, is generally agreed to be the finest variety for double white flowers. It grows 15 to 20 feet tall with a spread that is equal to or greater than its height. Its fragrant 2½-inch flowers open from pale pink buds, and the leaves often turn yellow in fall. Shogetsu, a low-growing variety, rarely becomes more than 12 to 15 feet tall and spreads its arching branches to an equal or greater distance. It bears an abundance of 2-inch pale pink double flowers.

The Higan cherry is seldom cultivated in its basic form, but the variety *P. subhirtella pendula,* the weeping Higan cherry, is the most popular weeping tree in spring gardens. The weeping variety is grafted to the upright stem of a straight-growing type at a height of about 6 feet, and eventually becomes 25 to 30 feet tall, bearing cascades of 1-inch single light pink flowers in spring. There is also a double-flowered weeping Higan cherry, *P. subhirtella* 'Yae-shidare-higan,' also called *P. subhirtella pendula flore pleno* and *P. subhirtella plena,* but it produces fewer blossoms than the single-flowered type. Another excellent variety, the autumn-flowering Higan cherry, *P. subhirtella autumnalis,* sends out semidouble flowers that are less than an inch across. They bloom not only in spring but also in autumn if the weather is warm at that time.

Yoshino cherries make up most of the trees that delight spring visitors to Washington. Its slightly fragrant 1-inch single flowers are so plentiful that they seem to smother the branches. The colors are pale pink or white and not, as many highly colored postcards show, bright pink. The intensified color applied by the printers does not do justice to the subtle shades the blossoms have in reality. The Yoshino cherry grows 20 to 40 feet tall with an equal spread. An outstanding variety is called Akebono or Daybreak; it grows 20 to 25 feet tall and has soft pink double flowers.

HOW TO GROW. The double-flowered mazzard cherry and the Pissard plum grow in all areas except Area A; the Blireiana plum grows in Areas B, C, D, E, F, G, I and J; the Sar-

KWANZAN ORIENTAL CHERRY
Prunus serrulata 'Kwanzan'

SHIROTAE ORIENTAL CHERRY
Prunus serrulata 'Shirotae'

DOUBLE-FLOWERED WEEPING HIGAN CHERRY
Prunus subhirtella 'Yae-shidare-higan'

For growing areas, see map on page 150.

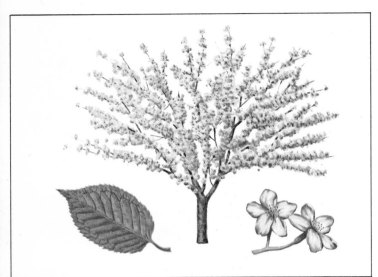

YOSHINO CHERRY
Prunus yedoensis

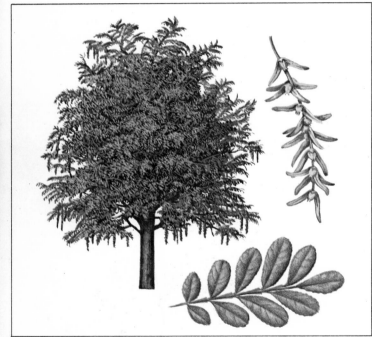

CHINESE WINGNUT
Pterocarya stenoptera

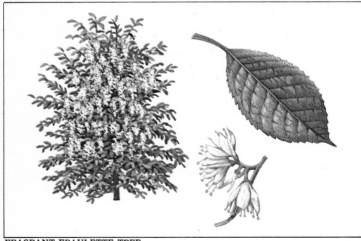

FRAGRANT EPAULETTE TREE
Pterostyrax hispida

gent cherry in Areas B, C, D, F, G, H, I and J; the paperbark, Oriental and Higan cherries in Areas C, D, I and J; and the Yoshino cherry in Areas B, C, D, I and J. All do best in full sun in average soil. Trees bought bare-rooted or balled and burlaped—that is, with their roots in their original soil ball wrapped in burlap—should be planted in early spring. Prune immediately after flowering. About half the growth on flowering stems of peaches must be pruned each year to force new branches and fresh buds for the following year. Pruning of plums and cherries should be kept to a minimum; when pruning is necessary, cut small lateral branches flush to the main stems—if branches are left stubby, they do not heal easily.

PTEROCARYA
P. fraxinifolia, also called *P. caucasica* (Caucasian wing-nut); *P. stenoptera* (Chinese wingnut)

Wingnuts are Asian trees that in summer bear 6- to 20-inch pendulous racemes—strings of winged seeds that account for the common name. They hang down beneath the branches and are somewhat reminiscent of Spanish moss; during the summer they are green, but they gradually turn brown as they ripen and drop to the ground in fall. A 6- to 8-foot wingnut will reach 20 feet in about eight years, eventually becoming 30 to 50 feet tall with broadly spreading branches that extend to a distance at least equal to the tree's height. Wingnuts meet the stringent requirements for growing along streets. The Caucasian species has leaves 8 to 24 inches long and racemes of winged seeds that vary from 12 to 20 inches in length. The Chinese wingnut has 6- to 12-inch leaves and seed clusters 6 to 12 inches long. Both species have a tendency to develop more than one trunk or to have several low branches unless trained by being pruned.

HOW TO GROW. The Caucasian wingnut grows in Areas C, D, E, G, I and J, and the Chinese wingnut grows in Areas E, I and J. Both need full sun and grow best in moist soil that is deep enough to accommodate the trees' long root structures. They will tolerate wind, drought and hard soil if the roots are well established, but these species are at their finest when grown in relatively moist soil, as beside a pond or stream. Trees bought balled and burlaped—that is, with their roots in their original soil ball wrapped in burlap—should be planted in spring. Prune in summer to prevent the bleeding that occurs when cuts are made in winter or spring.

PTEROSTYRAX
P. hispida (fragrant epaulette tree, wisteria tree)

The fragrant epaulette tree spreads forth pendulous branched sprays of tiny fragrant flowers, each branch vaguely resembling the epaulette on a military uniform. A 6- to 8-foot tree reaches 20 feet with an equal spread in about eight years; its ultimate height is 20 to 45 feet. The oval light green leaves, 3 to 8 inches long, are silvery underneath. Trees begin to blossom when 8 to 10 feet tall. Flowers appear in early summer after the leaves are fully grown, and are most impressive when seen from beneath the tree. They are followed by small hairy seed pods that cling until midwinter.

HOW TO GROW. The fragrant epaulette tree grows in the southern part of Area C and throughout Areas D, E, G, I and J. It does best in full sun and a moist well-drained soil. Trees bought balled and burlaped—that is, with their roots in their original soil ball wrapped in burlap—should be planted in spring. Prune young trees during the winter to remove low-growing side branches, which are borne unusually close to the ground.

PYRUS

P. calleryana (Callery pear)

Seeds of the thorny wild Callery pear of China were sent to North America years ago in the hope that the tree's resistance to fire blight—a bacterial disease that sometimes kills entire limbs of pear trees and is difficult to control —might be bred into orchard fruiting varieties. Among the early hybrid seedlings was a thornless tree that is one of the finest new ornamental trees available to gardeners. Called Bradford, it grows from 6 to 8 feet to about 20 feet tall in eight years, eventually reaching 30 to 50 feet with a conical spread of 15 to 30 feet. In spring profuse clusters of 1-inch flowers open before the leaves appear and are followed by pea-sized rust-colored inedible pears that are hidden by the leaves and eventually eaten by birds. The 1½- to 3-inch leaves cling late in fall, turning deep red to scarlet with a look of polished leather. The Bradford pear withstands pollution and meets the stringent requirements for planting along roadways. The variety Chanticleer is very similar to Bradford and matures at about 30 feet with a spread of 15 feet.

HOW TO GROW. Bradford and Chanticleer pears grow in all areas except Area A. They need full sun and will grow in any average garden soil. Pruning, when necessary, should be done in winter or early spring; generally it is needed only to remove lower branches of young trees so that there is headroom beneath them.

Q

QUERCUS

Q. alba (white oak); *Q. borealis*, also called *Q. rubra* (red oak); *Q. coccinea* (scarlet oak); *Q. imbricaria* (shingle oak, northern laurel oak); *Q. kelloggii*, also called *Q. californica* (California black oak); *Q. nigra* (water oak); *Q. palustris* (pin oak); *Q. phellos* (willow oak); *Q. prinus*, also called *Q. montanus* (chestnut, rock or mountain oak); *Q. robur* (English oak)

The deciduous oaks native to the United States and southern Canada include widely differing trees. Some grow fast, others slow, and leaves vary immensely in size and form, not necessarily conforming to the so-called oak-leaf pattern. However, most oak trees share a common shape: rounded and broadly spreading. All have tough branches that are resistant to damage from wind or ice, and their life span is measured in centuries. The foliage of most turns red, scarlet or yellow in fall, and the acorns, which may require one or two years to mature, drop in the fall. Oak trees cast a filtered shade in which grass can grow, and the area beneath the outer branches is one of the best places for rhododendrons and azaleas—the subdued light suits them, and fallen leaves, after decaying, provide the acid that these plants need. Many species of oaks become too massive for small backyards, but they are very useful where space is available.

The white oak is imposing when old—50 to 80 feet tall with a spread equal to or greater than its height—but it grows slowly: an 8- to 10-foot tree reaches 20 to 25 feet in 10 to 12 years. Moreover, trees taller than 14 feet are difficult to establish in the garden unless they were carefully prepared in the nursery when young. The strong horizontal branches carry 5- to 9-inch leaves that turn purplish red in fall and cling to the tree until late in winter.

The red oak grows rapidly: an 8- to 10-foot tree reaches a height of 20 feet in five or six years and eventually becomes 60 to 75 feet tall with a spread of 40 to 50 feet. Its 5- to 9-inch leaves turn red in autumn. The red oak is an excellent large shade tree that is able to withstand the polluted air of cities.

BRADFORD PEAR
Pyrus calleryana 'Bradford'

WHITE OAK
Quercus alba

For growing areas, see map on page 150.

RED OAK
Quercus borealis

CALIFORNIA BLACK OAK
Quercus kelloggii

The scarlet oak has deeply lobed leaves shaped like those of the red oak, but they turn brilliant scarlet in fall. Leaves usually are 3 to 7 inches long and have five to nine lobes. An 8- to 10-foot tree reaches 20 to 25 feet in seven or eight years, eventually becoming 60 to 75 feet tall and spreading 40 to 50 feet. Since this species grows moderately fast, fairly small trees can be bought; those taller than 14 feet are difficult to establish in the garden unless carefully prepared in a nursery when young.

The shingle oak grows from 8 to 10 feet to 20 to 25 feet in 10 to 12 years, eventually becoming 50 to 60 feet tall with an equal spread. The species is broadly conical when young, but becomes rounded as it matures. It has slender unlobed leaves, 4 to 6 inches long and 1 to 2 inches wide, that are pointed at both ends. The leaves, bright red when they first open in spring, turn a deep shining green in summer; in fall they become russet red and cling well into winter. The shingle oak is useful as a windbreak or tall hedge because it tolerates shearing and because it holds its lower branches unless they are removed to allow headroom. Its symmetrical shape and dense foliage also make it a handsome lawn or street tree. The name shingle oak was applied to this species by pioneers, who found the straight-grained wood split easily into shingles.

The California black oak grows from 8 to 10 feet to about 20 feet tall in six to eight years, eventually reaching 40 to 80 feet with an equal spread. It has 3- to 8-inch leaves that are reddish as they open in spring and become yellowish before dropping in the fall.

The water oak grows fast: an 8- to 10-foot tree reaches 20 to 25 feet in five or six years. It eventually becomes 60 to 75 feet tall with a 40- to 50-foot spread. Its 2- to 4-inch leaves cling until late in the year, finally turning an inconspicuous yellow before falling.

The pin oak grows rapidly: an 8- to 10-foot tree reaches 20 to 25 feet in five or six years, eventually becoming 60 to 70 feet tall with a 25- to 40-foot spread. It usually has great numbers of slender branches that reach upward near the top of the tree, are horizontal in the middle and somewhat pendulous lower down. If this tree is planted in the open, it will often retain all of its branches to ground level; it is sometimes grown this way in parks, but home gardeners usually prune the lower limbs to allow headroom.

The willow oak is a fast-growing tree that grows well in a wide variety of soils; an 8- to 10-foot tree reaches 20 to 25 feet in five or six years. It eventually becomes 40 to 60 feet tall with a spread of 30 to 40 feet. Its shiny 4-inch leaves are shaped like those of the willow; bright green during the summer, they turn pale yellow in fall.

The chestnut oak, native to sandy or rocky hillsides from Maine to Alabama, is a fine choice for the gardener whose soil is dry or exceptionally well drained. Planted at 8 to 10 feet, it reaches 20 to 25 feet in 7 to 10 years, eventually becoming 60 to 70 feet tall with an equal but irregular spread. The thick deeply furrowed bark of old trees becomes nearly black in color and is broken into distinctive flat-topped ridges. The leaves, 5 to 9 inches long and 1½ to 4 inches wide, have shallow-scalloped lobes around their edges. Shiny bright green in summer, they turn orange yellow or yellowish brown in fall and give the tree its common name —they resemble the leaves of the American chestnut, a species of *Castanea* no longer widely grown.

The English oak grows quite rapidly, an 8- to 10-foot tree reaching 20 feet in six to eight years. The basic species is rarely sold by nurseries, but the pyramidal English oak, *Q. robur fastigiata,* is widely grown for use in restricted areas because of its durability and its slender columnar shape (a mature tree may be 50 to 60 feet tall but only 20 feet in diameter). Where this shape is desired it provides a more permanent landscape accent than the similarly formed but disease-prone Lombardy poplar. The 2- to 5-inch leaves have 6 to 14 shallow rounded lobes and are dark green with pale green undersides.

HOW TO GROW. White, scarlet and pin oaks grow in all areas except Area A; the red oak grows in all areas; the shingle oak grows in Areas C, D and I; the California black oak grows in Areas I and J; the water oak grows in Areas D and E; the willow oak grows in the southern part of Area C and throughout Areas D, E, G, I and J; the chestnut oak grows in Areas B, C, D, H and I; and the English oak grows in Areas C, D, I and J. All oaks do best in full sun and grow in average garden soil that is acid (pH 5.5 to 6.5); water and willow oaks do well in wet soil, and the chestnut oak tolerates dry soil. Prune young trees in winter or early spring; old trees seldom need pruning.

R

RED HAW See *Crataegus*
REDBUD See *Cercis*

ROBINIA
R. 'Idaho' (Idaho locust), *R. pseudoacacia* (black or yellow locust, false acacia)

Locusts are especially valuable because of their ability to do well in poor dry soil and in sandy, salty conditions by the seashore. These native trees have 4- to 14-inch fernlike leaves, made up of many 1- to 2-inch leaflets, and cast a very light shade in which grass grows easily. The leaves appear late in spring, cling until late autumn and turn pale yellow before dropping. In early summer, soon after the leaves become full-sized, locusts bear pendulous flower clusters. The trees grow fast: an 8- to 10-foot tree reaches 20 feet with a 10- to 15-foot spread in four or five years.

The Idaho locust, a hybrid that eventually grows 25 to 35 feet tall and spreads to a width of 15 to 20 feet, has 6- to 8-inch clusters of 1-inch reddish purple flowers. It is a very popular tree in semiarid parts of the West that suffer extremes of heat and cold, and it meets the stringent requirements for growing along streets.

The black locust eventually grows 40 to 80 feet tall and is fairly narrow. Though the branches will usually spread horizontally when the tree is young, mature trees have ascending branches that spread to a width of only 20 to 40 feet. This species has a pair of ½-inch thorns set at the base of each leaf and has great numbers of sweet-scented ¾-inch white blossoms in hanging clusters 4 to 8 inches long. Bees favor the flowers, from which they produce a delicious honey. Locust blossoms are followed by 4-inch flat seed pods that cling most of the winter. When the trees are about 20 years old—even younger if they are planted in deep moist soil—the bark becomes furrowed with curious deep ridges. The Decaisne locust, *R. pseudoacacia decaiseana,* has fragrant pink flowers, and the umbrella black locust or the globe locust, *R. pseudoacacia umbraculifera,* forms a dense umbrellalike canopy 20 feet tall and 20 feet across but bears few or no flowers. It is increasingly planted along roadways because it seldom grows tall enough to interfere with overhead wires.

HOW TO GROW. Locusts grow in all areas. They do best in full sun and will grow in almost any well-drained soil, including alkaline soil. Established trees are tolerant of drought. Pruning is best done in late summer or fall, since locusts bleed when pruned in the spring. The branches are brittle, and the trees have a tendency to send up a number of suckers, which should be removed as soon as they appear so as to force all growth to a single trunk.

WATER OAK
Quercus nigra

PIN OAK
Quercus palustris

WILLOW OAK
Quercus phellos

For growing areas, see map on page 150.

IDAHO LOCUST
Robinia 'Idaho'

BLACK LOCUST
Robinia pseudoacacia

BABYLON WEEPING WILLOW
Salix babylonica

ROWAN TREE See *Sorbus*
RUSSIAN OLIVE See *Elaeagnus*

S

SALIX

S. alba tristis (golden weeping willow), *S. babylonica* (Babylon weeping willow), *S. blanda* (Wisconsin weeping willow, Niobe weeping willow), *S. elegantissima* (Thurlow weeping willow)

All weeping willows have a distinctive drooping form that is much admired, although some "weep" more than others. They are very fast growing: an 8- to 10-foot tree should reach 20 feet with an equal spread in about three years. Willows are also among the most satisfactory of trees for growing in wet places; but because their wide-ranging roots search out moisture, they should not be planted within 50 feet of sewer or drain lines, or their roots will plug them. Willows are usually the first trees to send out fresh new leaves in spring and among the last to lose them in fall, when the foliage turns yellow before dropping. The long pendulous branches move in the slightest breeze. Although the branches are brittle and easily broken by high winds or ice storms, the graceful willow remains one of the most widely planted trees.

The golden weeping willow eventually grows 50 to 75 feet tall. Its young branches are bright yellow and covered with 1½- to 4-inch medium green leaves about ½ inch wide; the leaves are fuzzy when young but become smooth in summer. The Babylon weeping willow ultimately grows 25 to 40 feet tall and has the most pendulous branches of any species. The most beautiful of all weeping willows, it is not as resistant to winter cold as the other types listed here. Its young branches, yellowish green in color, are thickly set with 3- to 6-inch leaves about ½ inch wide. The Wisconsin or Niobe weeping willow is a hybrid that grows 30 to 50 feet tall. It has green twigs and dark green shiny leaves 3 to 6 inches long and about ½ inch wide. The branches are pendulous, but not so long as those of the other willows listed. The Thurlow weeping willow grows 30 to 50 feet tall and has dull green leaves 3 to 6 inches long and about ½ inch wide. It is a hybrid rather similar to the Wisconsin weeping willow, except that its pendulous branches are about twice as long.

HOW TO GROW. The golden weeping willow grows in Areas A, B, C, D, F, G, H, I and J; the Babylon weeping willow grows in the southern part of Area C and throughout Areas D, E, G, I and J; the Wisconsin and Thurlow weeping willows grow in Areas B, C, D, F, G, H, I and J. All willows do best in full sun in moist or wet soils, but they can be grown perfectly well in most average soils if watered during dry weather. Because their weeping boughs are often long enough to touch the ground, it is important to trim off the lower branches of young trees so that the first limbs will be high enough off the ground to allow headroom. Pruning should be done in the summer or fall, since willows bleed when pruned in the winter or spring.

SAPIUM

S. sebiferum (Chinese tallow tree)

The Chinese tallow tree grows fast: a 5- to 6-foot tree grows to 20 feet with an equal spread in about six years, eventually becoming 35 to 40 feet tall. The unusually pest-free leaves, 1 to 3 inches long, quake in the breeze like those of the aspen; before the leaves drop in late autumn, they turn deep red or yellow with occasional touches of orange and purple. This species casts moderate shade in which grass will grow. In spring the tree puts out little yellow catkinlike flowers followed by hard ½-inch capsules, which split open to reveal waxy white seeds that cling for months. These are used for indoor decoration in this country but are a source of tallow and soap in China.

HOW TO GROW. The Chinese tallow tree grows in Areas E and J. It needs full sun but grows in almost any soil. Prune young trees in winter; old trees rarely need pruning.

SASSAFRAS
S. albidum, also called *S. officinale* and *S. variifolium* (sassafras)

The sassafras is appealing even in winter because of the way its side branches stretch out horizontally, then bend upward like a candelabra. It grows from 8 to 10 feet to about 20 feet in five to seven years, eventually becoming 30 to 60 feet tall with a spread of 15 to 30 feet. In spring, just as the leaves unfurl, it bears 2-inch clusters of fragrant ¼-inch yellow blossoms. Male and female blossoms are usually borne on separate trees; in early fall the female trees bear ½-inch dark blue inedible berries on red stems. The leaves, 3 to 6 inches long and 2 to 4 inches wide, may have a single lobe, two lobes or none at all, and are shiny green on top with pale green undersides. In fall the outer leaves become orange and red, while the leaves on the inside turn yellow, creating the appearance of an inner glow. All parts of the tree are aromatic; early settlers made sassafras tea as a spring tonic from the bark of the roots.

HOW TO GROW. The sassafras grows in Areas B, C, D, E, G, I and J, in full sun or light shade. It does best in moist well-drained soil that is deep enough to accommodate the tree's long root structure. If you want fruit, ask the nurseryman for at least one male and one female tree. The sassafras is difficult to establish in the garden unless its wide-ranging roots have been pruned at regular intervals in the nursery; this pruning produces a more compact root system that can more easily be dug up intact in the nursery field. Trees bought balled and burlaped—that is, with their roots in their original soil ball wrapped in burlap—should be planted in early spring. Prune in winter, but cut away any shoots, or suckers, that spring up around the tree as soon as they appear.

SCHOLAR TREE See *Sophora*
SENNA See *Cassia*
SERVICEBERRY See *Amelanchier*
SHAD-BLOW See *Amelanchier*
SHOWER OF GOLD See *Cassia*
SILK TREE See *Albizia*
SILVER BELL See *Halesia*
SNOWBELL See *Styrax*
SNOWDROP TREE See *Halesia*

SOPHORA
S. japonica (Japanese pagoda tree, Chinese scholar tree)

The Japanese pagoda tree, cultivated in Oriental temple grounds for more than 1,000 years, is nevertheless able to flourish in polluted urban air. On a lawn, this outstanding shade tree grows from 8 to 10 feet to about 20 feet in five or six years, eventually becoming 50 to 75 feet tall with an equal spread. In the compacted soil along roadways, however, it grows more slowly, ultimately reaching only 30 to 40 feet. The 6- to 10-inch fernlike leaves are notably pest free. Trees usually begin to blossom when they are 10 to 15 years old. In late summer and early fall the end of each branch bears a 10- to 15-inch cluster of tiny flowers; they last for about a month and are followed by 3- to 4-inch yellow pods that cling long into winter. The variety Regent is fast growing; it is prized because of its deep green shiny leaves and its ability to blossom when

CHINESE TALLOW TREE
Sapium sebiferum

SASSAFRAS
Sassafras albidum

For growing areas, see map on page 150.

JAPANESE PAGODA TREE
Sophora japonica

KOREAN MOUNTAIN ASH
Sorbus alnifolia

EUROPEAN MOUNTAIN ASH
Sorbus aucuparia

younger than the basic species, usually at six to eight years.

HOW TO GROW. The Japanese pagoda tree grows in Areas B, C, D, F, G, H, I and J. It needs full sun and does best in a moist well-drained soil that is deep enough to accommodate the tree's long root structure, but it will grow in almost any soil. Prune young trees in fall, removing lower branches if necessary to provide headroom; this tree has a greater tendency than most other kinds to send out branches close to the ground.

SORBUS
S. alnifolia (Korean mountain ash), *S. aucuparia* (European mountain ash, rowan tree), *S. cashmiriana* (Kashmir mountain ash), *S.* hybrids (hybrid mountain ash)

Mountain ashes are especially decorative in two seasons: in early summer they bear great clusters of small flowers, and in early fall the fruit hangs in 5-inch clusters so heavy the branches bend under their weight. The fruit is favored by migrating birds, such as robins and evening grosbeaks. Mountain ashes grow rapidly: an 8- to 10-foot tree reaches 20 feet in about five years. Most species have fernlike leaves that turn deep shades of red and orange in fall. However, all but the Korean mountain ash are sometimes attacked by borers that enter the trunk near the ground. (See page 148 for methods of borer control.)

The Korean mountain ash eventually grows 40 to 50 feet tall; it is cone-shaped when young but becomes rounded with a spread of 20 to 30 feet when mature. It is unusual in its genus because the leaves are not fernlike but simple 2- to 4-inch leaves with saw-toothed edges. The Korean mountain ash has ¾-inch white blossoms that mature into loose clusters of ½-inch berries. Handsome standing alone as a lawn decoration, the tree is also able to grow along streets if the air is not heavily polluted.

The European mountain ash is the species most often planted in gardens and is known for its heavy crop of white flowers, which are followed by great clusters of berries. The leaves are 5 to 10 inches long. This species eventually grows 20 to 40 feet tall with an equal spread.

The Kashmir mountain ash is conical and eventually grows 30 to 40 feet tall with an equal spread. Its flowers are an unusual pinkish white and its great clusters of white berries contrast dramatically with its red autumn leaves. European nurserymen have been experimenting with the hybridization of mountain ashes, and some of these are now offered in America. Typical hybrids, all about 20 to 40 feet tall when mature, are Carpet of Gold, yellow berries; Kirsten Pink, dark pink berries; and Maidenblush, pale pink berries.

HOW TO GROW. Korean, European, Kashmir and hybrid mountain ashes grow in Areas B, C, D, F, G, H and I and the northern part of Area J, but in the East, south of Washington, D.C., are satisfactory only in mountainous regions; the European mountain ash grows in Area A as well. All do best in full sun and grow in nearly any well-drained soil. Prune young trees in winter or early spring; older trees rarely need pruning.

SORREL TREE See *Oxydendrum*
SOUR GUM See *Nyssa*
SOURWOOD See *Oxydendrum*
STERCULIA See *Firmiana*

STYRAX
S. japonica (Japanese snowbell)

The Japanese snowbell is a choice little flowering tree. It grows rather slowly: a 5- to 6-foot tree reaches about 15 feet in 7 to 10 years. Eventually it grows up to 30 feet tall, spreading its branches horizontally to a distance at least equal to its height. Its shiny 1½- to 3-inch leaves are particularly pest free; they often turn reddish or yellow in fall. In early summer, shortly after the leaves are fully grown, the Japanese snowbell bears sprays of three to six faintly fragrant ¾-inch white flowers with prominent yellow pollen-bearing stamens. The flowers are suspended from the tree's slender branches, with the leaves above them. Because of this positioning, the flowers are noticeable, particularly when they are seen from beneath the tree, making the Japanese snowbell an excellent choice for a patio or a slope above a walk. The flowers are followed in fall by ½-inch gray inedible fruit.

HOW TO GROW. The Japanese snowbell grows in the southern part of Area C and in Areas D, E, I and J. It does well in full sun or light shade in moist well-drained soil supplemented with peat moss or leaf mold. Trees bought balled and burlaped—that is, with their roots in their original soil ball wrapped in burlap—should be planted in early spring. Prune young trees during the winter. Older trees rarely require any pruning.

SUGARBERRY See *Celtis*
SWEET GUM See *Liquidambar*
SYCAMORE See *Platanus*

SYRINGA

S. amurensis japonica (Japanese tree lilac)

Although most lilacs are shrubs, the Japanese tree lilac is indeed a tree that grows 20 to 30 feet tall, spreading its branches to a distance equal to its height. A 6- to 8-foot tree reaches 15 to 20 feet with an equal spread in about eight years. The leaves are 3 to 6 inches long and sometimes turn pale yellow in autumn, but may also drop without changing color. In midsummer, about a month after ordinary lilacs have faded, this species bears masses of small flowers in thick conical clusters as much as 12 inches long at the ends of its stems; the white clusters contrast strikingly with the dark leaves. Unfortunately, the blossoms have a penetrating scent similar to that of privet, which some people find objectionable at close range. The flowers are followed by tiny dry seed capsules that are not particularly ornamental but cling through winter unless pruned off. The Japanese tree lilac is an excellent choice for lawn decoration and also meets the stringent requirements for growing along streets.

HOW TO GROW. The Japanese tree lilac grows in Areas A, B, C, D, F, G, H and I, and is especially useful because it can withstand very cold winters. It does best in full sun in moist well-drained soil supplemented with peat moss or leaf mold, but will tolerate very light shade. If pruning is necessary, wait until after the flowers have faded.

T

TALLOW TREE See *Sapium*
THORN, JERUSALEM See *Parkinsonia*
THORN, WASHINGTON See *Crataegus*

TILIA

T. americana (American linden, basswood); *T. cordata* (little-leaved linden); *T. euchlora* (Crimean linden); *T. tomentosa,* also called *T. alba, T. argentea* (silver linden)

Lindens are longtime favorites as shade trees. They are handsome standing alone and some types meet the stringent requirements for growing along streets. In midsummer lindens bear tiny, extremely fragrant flowers followed by pea-sized inedible fruit that cling until midwinter. Bees are extremely fond of the blossoms, and basswood honey

JAPANESE SNOWBELL
Styrax japonica

JAPANESE TREE LILAC
Syringa amurensis japonica

LITTLE-LEAVED LINDEN
Tilia cordata

For growing areas, see map on page 150.

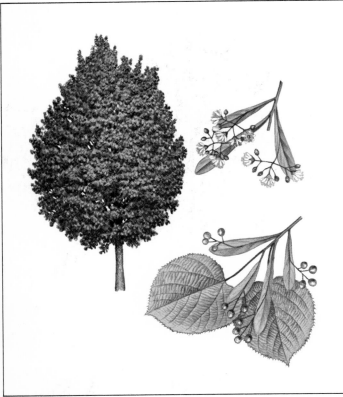

SILVER LINDEN
Tilia tomentosa

is a delicacy in some places. The lopsided heart-shaped leaves appear early in spring and cling to the branches until late in the fall; in some years the leaves turn yellow before dropping, but in mild autumns they remain green until they are killed by frost.

The American linden grows fast: an 8- to 10-foot tree reaches 20 feet in four or five years, ultimately becoming 60 to 80 feet tall with a spread equal to about half its height. Its coarsely saw-toothed leaves are 4 to 6 inches long and 3 to 4 inches wide. It cannot tolerate the polluted air of cities. The little-leaved linden, on the other hand, is one of the most satisfactory trees for cities. An 8- to 10-foot tree grows to 20 feet in about five years, eventually reaching 50 to 70 feet with a spread of 25 to 35 feet. The leaves are 1½ to 3 inches long. Its variety Greenspire is recommended for its rapid erect growth and symmetry. The hybrid Crimean linden grows from 8 to 10 feet to 20 feet in about five years, eventually becoming 40 to 60 feet tall and spreading to half that distance. It has 2- to 4-inch bright green shiny leaves. The excellent variety Redmond has a dense conical shape. The silver linden is fast growing: an 8- to 10-foot tree reaches 20 feet in four or five years, eventually becoming 50 to 70 feet tall with a spread equal to half the height. Its 2- to 4-inch leaves are dark green above and silvery white underneath. This symmetrical species is handsome standing alone and meets the rigorous requirements for growing along streets.

HOW TO GROW. American and little-leaved lindens grow in Areas A, B, C, D, F, G, H, I and the northern part of Area J; Crimean and silver lindens grow in Areas B, C, D, F, G, H, I and the northern part of Area J. All do well in full sun or light shade and do best in moist well-drained soil that is deep enough to accommodate the trees' long root structures. Little pruning is required.

TREE OF HEAVEN See *Ailanthus*
TULIP POPLAR See *Liriodendron*
TULIP TREE See *Liriodendron*
TUPELO See *Nyssa*

U

ULMUS
U. carpinifolia (smooth-leaved elm), *U. parvifolia* (Chinese elm), *U. pumila* (Siberian elm)

The stately elms that graced the village streets of 19th Century America are almost gone now, victims of Dutch elm disease or an infection called phloem necrosis, and it is foolhardy to plant elms today—with a few exceptions. The species listed here, while not totally immune to the diseases, resist them. Elms grow rapidly: an 8- to 10-foot tree reaches 20 feet in about five years.

A variety of the smooth-leaved elm called Christine Buisman is particularly recommended because of its fast, uniform growth. It eventually becomes 50 to 60 feet tall with a 30- to 40-foot spread. The dark green glossy 3-inch leaves turn yellow in fall. The Chinese elm eventually reaches 40 to 50 feet and has pendant branches spreading to an equal distance. Its leaves are 1 to 2 inches long and in cold climates turn purplish red in fall. A number of its varieties have evergreen or nearly evergreen foliage, and are suited to gardens in Areas E and J. This species has unusual grayish brown bark that flakes off, creating a mottled effect on trunks and large limbs. Its flowers and fruit appear in fall rather than in spring. The Siberian elm grows 50 to 75 feet tall with an equal spread and has ¾- to 3-inch smooth dark green leaves that turn yellow in fall. This species is widely grown in the central and northern plains because it can tolerate wind and drought. One of its

CHRISTINE BUISMAN ELM
Ulmus carpinifolia 'Christine Buisman'

excellent varieties is called Coolshade and has darker green foliage and stronger branches than the ordinary species.

HOW TO GROW. The smooth-leaved elm grows in all areas except Area A; the Chinese elm grows in Areas C, D, E, G, I and J; and the Siberian elm in all areas. Elms do best in full sun and moist well-drained soil deep enough to accommodate the trees' long root structures, but the Siberian elm is tolerant of dry soil. Prune in fall.

UMBRELLA TREE, TEXAS See *Melia*

V

VARNISH TREE See *Firmiana*

W

WALNUT See *Juglans*
WASHINGTON THORN See *Crataegus*
WILLOW See *Salix*
WINGNUT See *Pterocarya*
WISTERIA TREE See *Pterostyrax*

Y

YELLOW POPLAR See *Liriodendron*
YELLOWWOOD See *Cladrastis*

Z

ZELKOVA

Z. serrata (Japanese zelkova, Japanese Keaki tree)

The Japanese zelkova grows rapidly: an 8- to 10-foot tree reaches 20 feet with a 10-foot vase-shaped spread in four to six years. It eventually becomes 50 to 80 feet tall and spreads to an equal distance. The tree has slender branches and may have a single trunk or multiple trunks. It is widely used as a replacement for the American elm, now nearly wiped out by Dutch elm disease, because its leaves have a somewhat similar appearance. Leaves are 1 to 2½ inches long near the tops of the trees, where the branches bear fertile flowers, and 2 to 5 inches long on lower branches, which bear only male flowers. The leaves have saw-toothed edges and are rough-surfaced and dark green during summer, but become deep red in fall. Village Green is a very cold-resistant variety of Japanese zelkova.

HOW TO GROW. The Japanese zelkova grows in the southern part of Area C and in Areas D, E, G, I and J. It needs full sun, but will grow in almost any soil, including alkaline soil. Trees that are established tolerate wind as well as drought. Prune young trees in the fall; older trees seldom require pruning.

ZIZYPHUS

Z. jujuba (jujube, Chinese date)

The jujube, or Chinese date, is not a true date tree, but bears 1- to 2-inch fruit that look like dates and may be eaten fresh, dried or preserved. An 8- to 10-foot jujube reaches 15 to 20 feet with an equal spread in six to eight years, eventually becoming 15 to 25 feet tall. It has spiny zigzag branches lined with ¾- to 2½-inch pest-resistant leaves, dark green above and pale green underneath, that cast a light filtered shade. In early summer new branches carry clusters of tiny yellow flowers, followed by fruit that ripen in late fall. This tree usually begins to bear fruit the first year it is set into the garden.

HOW TO GROW. The jujube grows in Areas D, E, G and J, and does best where the growing season is long and hot. It grows in full sun or light shade in almost any soil, including alkaline soil. Established trees tolerate heat and drought. Prune young trees in the winter; old trees seldom require pruning.

CHINESE ELM
Ulmus parvifolia

JAPANESE ZELKOVA
Zelkova serrata

JUJUBE
Zizyphus jujuba

For growing areas, see map on page 150.

A guide to pests and diseases

The best protection for a tree is proper care to ensure vigorous good health. Feed trees properly, especially during their peak growing season (generally in the spring), and water them if necessary —do not expect them to weather severe drought on their natural vitality alone. Guard against injury from such things as lawn mowers and the girdling cuts of guy wires, for wounds are an open

PEST	DESCRIPTION	METHODS OF CONTROL
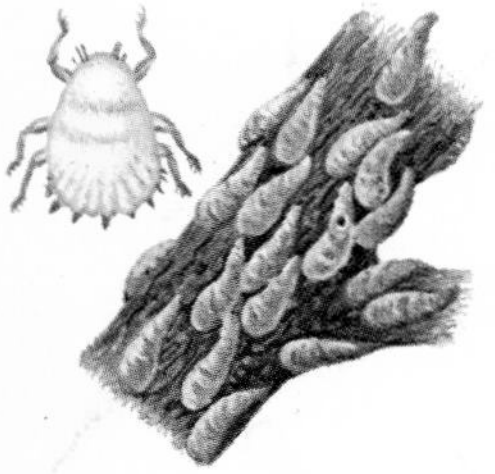	**SCALE INSECTS** Only female scales are harmful; their mouths, needlelike tubes almost as long as their ⅛- to ½-inch bodies, penetrate wood to suck the sap, killing branches and even whole trees. Crawlers, the wingless young *(far left)*, select a permanent position on a twig and encrust the surface. As they mature, many, like the oyster-shell scale *(left)*, develop a waxy shell. Some secrete honeydew that attracts sooty-mold fungus. VULNERABLE TREES: ALDER, BAUHINIA, CHERRY, CRAB APPLE, DOGWOOD, MAGNOLIA, MOUNTAIN ASH, PLUM, POPLAR, SILK TREE, TULIP TREE, WILLOW	Most infested trees can be sprayed in early spring with dormant oil to smother the female scales and their eggs, but Japanese and sugar maples are harmed by oil. In early summer, when crawlers appear, spray with malathion. Repeat twice more at two-week intervals. Remove badly infested branches.
	**LEAF MINERS** Many types of leaf miners exist, each attacking a specific host, but the most common and most troublesome is the birch-leaf miner shown at left. Birch trees rarely escape infestation by this pest. In spring it emerges from the soil as a tiny sawfly that lays eggs in half-grown leaves; the hatched larvae feed between the leaf surfaces, tunneling out the tissue. Blisters appear first, then the entire leaf turns brown and drops. VULNERABLE TREES: ALDER, BIRCH, BLACK LOCUST, ELM, HAWTHORN, LINDEN, OAK, POPLAR, SERVICEBERRY	In spring, as soon as the leaves begin to open, spray with diazinon, carbaryl, malathion or dimethoate. Repeat the application twice at 10-day intervals, and again three times at similar 10-day intervals beginning about five weeks later.
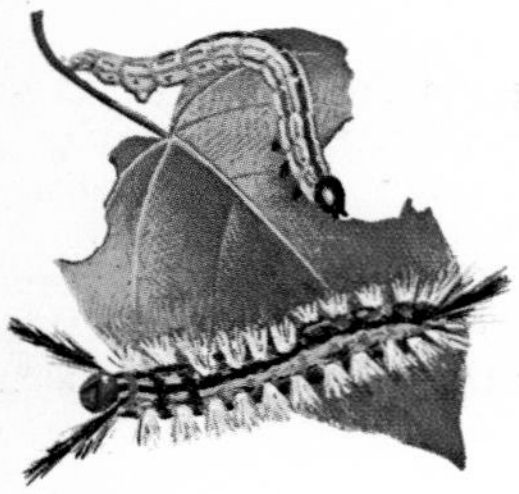	**CATERPILLARS** Caterpillars, the grublike, often hairy, larvae of moths and butterflies, come in many sizes and colors and chew up foliage and sometimes fruit. The larvae of the spring cankerworm *(top)*, also called the inchworm or measuring worm because of its looping forward motion, hatch in early spring from egg clusters laid on the bark. The tussock moth *(bottom)* produces two and sometimes three generations in a year. VULNERABLE TREES: BUCKEYE, CHERRY, CRAB APPLE, ELM, HORSE CHESTNUT, LINDEN, MAPLE, OAK, PLANE TREE, PLUM, POPLAR, WILLOW	Apply dormant oil in early spring, but not to Japanese or sugar maples, or spray in spring and midsummer with carbaryl or *Bacillus thuringiensis*. Trap egg-laying females by encircling the trunk with a 2-inch-wide band of cotton batting, tar paper and the sticky tape called "bug barrier."
	**APHIDS** These pear-shaped insects, also known as plant lice, are seldom more than ⅛ inch long. They attack the leaves, stems and buds of trees, sucking the plant juices. They usually congregate at the tips of new growth, causing malformed foliage. Aphids alone rarely cause lasting harm, but they spread disease and excrete honeydew, which attracts the black fungus, sooty mold, that may turn leaves yellow. VULNERABLE TREES: ALDER, ASH, BEECH, BIRCH, CHERRY, CRAB APPLE, ELM, HACKBERRY, HAWTHORN, LINDEN, MAPLE, OAK, PECAN, PLUM, WILLOW	Knock aphids from trees with a stream of water from a hose, or release ladybugs at the base of the tree. For heavy infestations, spray with pyrethrum or malathion. Dormant oil, sprayed before leaves open, is a good preventive. Do not use oil on Japanese or sugar maples, birches or beeches.
	**BORERS** Borers feed unseen inside the roots, trunks, branches and twigs of many trees; usually sawdust around their holes betrays their presence. They are particularly destructive to newly planted trees and trees in poor health. The dogwood borer, shown here, is a menace to dogwood and pecan trees. Its ½-inch grublike larvae hatch in early spring from eggs laid in crevices on the bark, bore into the wood and may kill the tree. VULNERABLE TREES: ALDER, ASH, BIRCH, BLACK LOCUST, CRAB APPLE, DOGWOOD, ELM, LINDEN, MAPLE, MOUNTAIN ASH, OAK, PECAN, PLUM, POPLAR	To prevent egg-laying on the bark, cover the trunks of newly planted trees with tree wrap *(drawing, page 31)*. Spray established trees four times with methoxychlor at weekly intervals in midspring. If borers attack, probe their holes with wire to kill them, or inject a pest killer containing lindane.

invitation to pests. Though most trees will survive mild infestations of such things as aphids and may recover unaided from a single defoliation by caterpillars, repeated attacks weaken trees and leave them vulnerable to further injury.

In dealing with insects and diseases, use the least toxic method first. One ladybug (they are sold by the pint in garden stores and by mail) may eat up to 50 aphids a day. Enmesh insects in sticky tree bands; smother eggs and hibernating insects by applying nonpoisonous dormant oil sprays in early spring. Remove diseased leaves and branches and dispose of them to prevent reinfecting the trees. When you must turn to one of the chemical pesticides, use it with caution and exactly as directed on the label.

DISEASE	DESCRIPTION	METHODS OF CONTROL
ANTHRACNOSE	A number of tree species suffer from the fungus disease called anthracnose, but sycamores are most severely affected. When the malady attacks in early spring, the tips of year-old twigs die; this stage is called twig blight. The disease then attacks and kills the buds. In the next stage, shoot blight *(far left)*, leaves wilt on the current season's shoots. In the final stage, called leaf blight *(left)*, the leaves turn brown and drop. VULNERABLE TREES: BLACK WALNUT, BOX ELDER, ELM, MAPLE, OAK, PLANE TREE, SYCAMORE	Spray with zineb, thiram, maneb or captan just before the leaves unfurl, again when the leaves are half grown and a third time when they are fully grown. To avoid reinfection, prune dead branch tips. Dispose of dead leaves in fall by burying them at least 6 inches deep (do not add them to compost).
CANKER	Cankers are oval dead patches on twigs, branches or trunks, ranging in length from an inch to over a foot; some are caused by bacteria, some by fungus. The infection enters through wounds or borer holes. A canker may develop as a deeply sunken area with raised callous tissue around the edge, or as a flat discoloration on the bark; occasionally the only sign of cankers is the presence of small raised bumps on the bark. VULNERABLE TREES: ASH, BIRCH, BLACK WALNUT, CHERRY, DOGWOOD, ELM, MAPLE, MOUNTAIN ASH, OAK, PLUM, POPLAR, WILLOW	Cut away infected branches. After each cut, dip tools in 70 per cent denatured alcohol to avoid spreading the disease. To kill bacterial cankers, cover the cuts with an antibiotic chemical such as streptomycin sulfate and coat them with tree paint. To treat fungus cankers, use tree paint alone.
LEAF SPOT	Leaf spot in its many forms is the most common disease affecting trees and usually strikes in cool moist weather. Caused by various fungi and bacteria, the spots usually develop as small lesions with brown centers, often sprinkled with the black dots of fungus spores. If the spots become numerous, they join to form large dead areas. Although unsightly, leaf spot seldom causes permanent injury to trees. VULNERABLE TREES: ASH, BLACK WALNUT, BUCKEYE, DOGWOOD, ELM, HACKBERRY, HORSE CHESTNUT, LINDEN, MAPLE, OAK, POPLAR	Spray foliage with ferbam, zineb or captan several times in late spring and early summer, especially when leaves are unfolding and damp weather is expected. In fall rake up infected leaves and dispose of them by burying them at least 6 inches deep (do not add them to compost).
ROOT ROT	Poor growth, yellowing leaves that drop early, rotting bark at the base of the tree and a distinct mushroomlike odor are early signs of this disease. The spores enter at ground level through wounds or borer holes, thin strands develop and grow down into the roots, causing them to decay. Later, white fibrous fans of the fungus *(inset)* appear near the base of the trunk. In the final stage—often too late to save the tree—honey-colored mushrooms grow around the base of the tree. VULNERABLE TREES: CATALPA, DOGWOOD, OAK, SASSAFRAS	Be certain that drainage is good; trees in wet soil are especially vulnerable. Do not water directly around the trunk. Cut away diseased sections and apply tree paint to wounds. Professional soil fumigation can sometimes control the disease, but not if it reaches the sapwood or is widespread.
LEAF SCORCH	Leaf scorch afflicts trees when the leaves give off more moisture than the roots can replace; the leaves turn brown, curl and sometimes fall. The condition occurs in summer, usually after a rainy period has produced lush growth, when temperatures above 90° F. are accompanied by drying winds. Newly planted trees are susceptible; so are trees in paved areas and in places where the ground level has been changed. VULNERABLE TREES: ASH, BEECH, CRAB APPLE, DOGWOOD, ELM, HAWTHORN, HORSE CHESTNUT, LINDEN, MAPLE, OAK	Water trees deeply during droughts and mulch around them to help conserve moisture. Fertilize in spring to stimulate the roots. Plant sensitive species in locations sheltered from wind. Spray susceptible trees in late spring or early summer with a chemical antitranspirant to slow water loss.

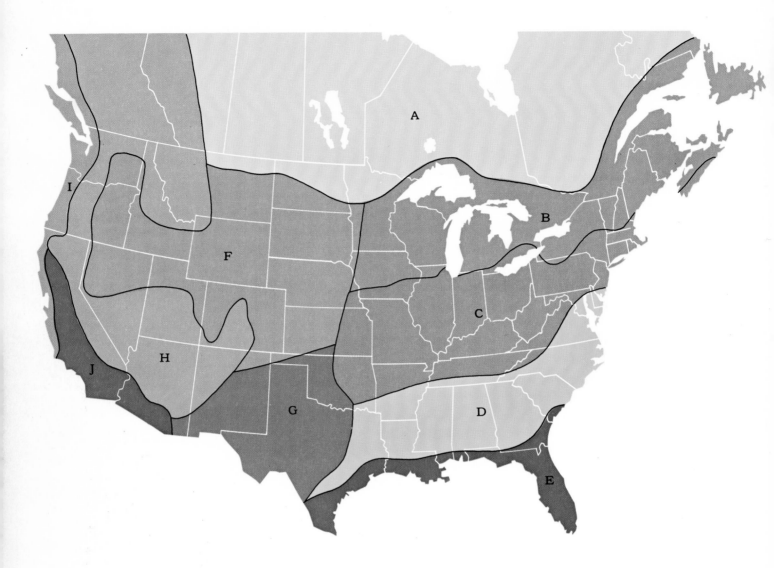

Where to plant deciduous trees

The map above is designed for use in conjunction with the encyclopedia entries in Chapter 5 and is planned to help you determine if a particular tree is likely to prosper where you live. The map divides the United States and southern Canada into 10 areas on the basis of temperature, rainfall, altitude and soil; each of the entries in the encyclopedia indicates by letters that are keyed to the map the areas in which the tree described grows best. If you look up the entry for the ginkgo, for instance, you will discover that it is a highly adaptable tree that can be grown in all areas except Area A; the white alder, on the other hand, has a far more restricted range and is recommended only for Areas I and J. Many trees will also thrive outside of their recommended areas if they are given extra care.

Even within an area, however, conditions sometimes vary dramatically, and it is advisable to consult your local nurseryman to find out whether the particular tree you are considering is likely to do well in your garden. In the large expanse of Area C, for example, some of the mountainous regions tend to be colder than regions that are at sea level, while temperatures in areas near the sea fluctuate less than they do in inland areas.

Characteristics of 188 deciduous trees

Unless varietal names are given, the chart includes the characteristics of all recommended varieties of the species listed.

	SHAPE					MATURE HEIGHT			RATE OF GROWTH			USES			NOTABLE TRAITS				GROWING CONDITIONS					
	Rounded	Weeping	Spreading	Conical	Columnar	Under 25 feet	25-50 feet	Over 50 feet	Slow	Medium	Fast	Shade tree	Ornamental tree	Street tree	Flowers	Fruit	Leaf color*	Bark	Full sun	Light shade	Dry soil	Moist soil	Acid soil**	Alkaline soil**
ACER BUERGERIANUM (trident maple)	•				•		•			•			•	•			•		•					
ACER CAMPESTRE (hedge maple)	•				•		•			•			•						•	•				
ACER CIRCINATUM (vine maple)			•		•					•			•	•	•	•	•			•		•		
ACER GINNALA (Amur maple)	•				•					•			•	•	•	•	•		•	•				
ACER GRISEUM (paperbark maple)	•				•		•						•				•	•	•					
ACER NEGUNDO (box elder)	•			•	•			•			•					•			•		•			
ACER PALMATUM (Japanese maple)	•				•	•				•			•				•			•	•			
ACER PLATANOIDES (Norway maple)	•	•	•	•	•		•	•		•		•		•			•		•	•				
ACER PSEUDOPLATANUS (sycamore maple)	•				•			•		•		•					•		•				
ACER RUBRUM (red maple)	•		•	•				•		•		•	•	•	•	•		•			•		
ACER SACCHARINUM (silver maple)	•		•					•		•		•					•		•		•		
ACER SACCHARUM (sugar maple)	•			•			•	•		•		•					•		•				
AESCULUS CALIFORNICA (California buckeye)	•				•		•		•		•		•	•	•	•	•						
AESCULUS CARNEA BRIOTII (ruby horse chestnut)	•				•		•		•		•	•	•	•	•	•							
AESCULUS GLABRA (Ohio buckeye)	•				•		•		•		•		•	•	•	•							
AESCULUS HIPPOCASTANUM (common horse chestnut)	•				•			•	•		•	•	•	•	•	•							
AILANTHUS ALTISSIMA (tree of heaven)	•				•	•		•		•			•	•									
ALBIZIA JULIBRISSIN (silk tree)			•		•	•				•	•		•	•	•								•
ALNUS CORDATA (Italian alder)			•		•			•		•			•	•			•		•	•			
ALNUS RHOMBIFOLIA (white alder)	•			•				•		•			•	•			•		•	•			
ALNUS RUBRA (red alder)	•				•	•		•		•		•	•	•	•	•		•	•			
AMELANCHIER CANADENSIS (downy serviceberry)	•			•	•					•		•		•	•							
AMELANCHIER GRANDIFLORA (apple serviceberry)	•	•			•					•			•		•	•						
AMELANCHIER LAEVIS (Allegheny serviceberry)	•				•					•			•	•	•	•						
ASIMINA TRILOBA (papaw)	•				•					•			•	•	•	•		•				
BAUHINIA VARIEGATA (Buddhist bauhinia)	•			•					•	•	•	•	•	•			•	•				
BETULA PAPYRIFERA (canoe birch)	•				•			•		•			•	•	•		•	•				
BETULA PENDULA (European white birch)		•		•	•	•		•		•			•			•	•	•	•			
BETULA POPULIFOLIA (gray birch)			•		•			•		•			•		•	•	•	•				
BROUSSONETIA PAPYRIFERA (paper mulberry)	•				•		•			•		•	•			•	•	•		•		
CARPINUS BETULUS (European hornbeam)	•		•		•	•	•			•			•		•		•	•				
CARPINUS CAROLINIANA (American hornbeam)	•				•	•	•						•			•	•	•				
CARYA ILLINOENSIS (pecan)	•							•		•			•	•								
CASSIA FISTULA (golden shower)	•				•					•		•	•	•	•		•	•				
CASTANEA MOLLISSIMA (Chinese chestnut)			•		•				•	•	•		•	•	•		•	•	•		
CATALPA BIGNONIOIDES (common catalpa)	•				•			•		•		•		•	•			•				•
CATALPA SPECIOSA (western catalpa)	•				•				•	•		•		•	•			•				
CELTIS AUSTRALIS (European hackberry)	•				•		•		•			•			•	•	•	•	•		•
CELTIS LAEVIGATA (sugarberry)	•		•				•			•			•			•	•	•	•		
CELTIS LAEVIGATA RETICULATA (net-leaved hackberry)	•			•				•		•		•			•	•	•	•	•		
CELTIS OCCIDENTALIS (common hackberry)	•		•					•		•		•		•	•	•	•	•	•	•
CERCIDIPHYLLUM JAPONICUM (katsura tree)	•			•				•	•	•	•		•		•	•					
CERCIS CANADENSIS (eastern redbud)	•		•		•					•			•	•	•		•	•			
CERCIS OCCIDENTALIS (California redbud)	•			•						•			•	•	•		•	•			
CERCIS RENIFORMIS (Texas redbud)	•				•					•			•	•	•		•	•			
CHIONANTHUS VIRGINICUS (fringe tree)	•				•								•	•	•	•	•	•			
CLADRASTIS LUTEA (yellowwood)	•				•			•	•	•	•	•		•		•	•			•
CORNUS FLORIDA (flowering dogwood)	•	•	•		•	•				•			•	•	•	•		•	•		
CORNUS KOUSA (Kousa dogwood)			•		•				•			•		•	•		•	•		•	

*Included are leaves that are distinctively colored in spring or summer as well as those that turn notable colors in fall.

**Most trees grow best in soil that is slightly acid to neutral (pH 6.0 to 7.0). Trees that prefer greater acidity are listed here under "acid soil," and those that tolerate alkalinity are listed under "alkaline soil."

CHARACTERISTICS OF TREES: CONTINUED

	SHAPE					MATURE HEIGHT			RATE OF GROWTH			USES			NOTABLE TRAITS				GROWING CONDITIONS					
	Rounded	Weeping	Spreading	Conical	Columnar	Under 25 feet	25-50 feet	Over 50 feet	Slow	Medium	Fast	Shade tree	Ornamental tree	Street tree	Flowers	Fruit	Leaf color*	Bark	Full sun	Light shade	Dry soil	Moist soil	Acid soil**	Alkaline soil**
CORNUS NUTTALLII (Pacific dogwood)			•			•				•			•	•	•	•		•		•		•	•	
CRATAEGUS ARNOLDIANA (Arnold hawthorn)	•					•	•				•	•	•	•	•	•			•		•	•		•
CRATAEGUS CRUS-GALLII (cockspur hawthorn)			•			•	•				•	•	•	•	•	•		•		•	•		•
CRATAEGUS LAVALLEI (Lavalle hawthorn)	•			•	•		•				•	•	•	•	•			•		•	•		•
CRATAEGUS MOLLIS (downy hawthorn)	•					•	•				•	•	•	•	•	•		•		•	•		•
CRATAEGUS MONOGYNA (single-seeded hawthorn)	•			•		•					•	•	•	•	•	•		•		•			•
CRATAEGUS MORDENENSIS 'TOBA' (Toba hawthorn)	•			•		•					•	•	•	•	•			•		•			•
CRATAEGUS NITIDA (glossy hawthorn)	•			•	•		•				•	•	•	•	•	•		•		•	•		•
CRATAEGUS OXYACANTHA (English hawthorn)	•					•	•				•	•	•	•	•	•		•		•	•		•
CRATAEGUS PHAENOPYRUM (Washington hawthorn)			•			•					•	•	•	•	•	•		•		•	•		•
DAVIDIA INVOLUCRATA (dove tree)	•		•			•				•		•	•	•	•			•				•		
DELONIX REGIA (royal poinciana)			•			•			•	•	•	•	•		•	•			•			•		
DIOSPYROS KAKI (kaki persimmon)	•				•			•			•	•	•			•		•					•	
DIOSPYROS VIRGINIANA (common persimmon)			•		•	•	•				•	•	•			•		•					•	
ELAEAGNUS ANGUSTIFOLIA (Russian olive)	•			•				•			•	•	•	•		•	•				•			
FAGUS GRANDIFOLIA (American beech)			•				•	•		•		•	•			•	•	•		•			•	
FAGUS SYLVATICA (European beech)	•	•	•				•	•		•		•	•			•	•	•		•			•	
FICUS CARICA (common fig)	•					•	•			•	•		•			•		•						
FIRMIANA SIMPLEX (Chinese parasol tree)			•			•				•	•		•	•		•	•	•		•				
FRANKLINIA ALATAMAHA (franklinia)			•		•	•	•					•		•	•	•	•	•		•	•		
FRAXINUS AMERICANA (white ash)	•						•			•	•	•				•		•			•			
FRAXINUS HOLOTRICHA 'MORAINE' (Moraine ash)	•					•				•	•	•				•		•			•			
FRAXINUS ORNUS (flowering ash)	•					•				•	•	•		•	•			•		•			
FRAXINUS PENNSYLVANICA LANCEOLATA (green ash)			•			•				•	•	•				•		•		•				
FRAXINUS VELUTINA GLABRA (Modesto ash)	•					•				•	•	•				•		•			•		•
GINKGO BILOBA (ginkgo)			•	•	•		•	•				•		•			•		•			•		
GLEDITSIA TRIACANTHOS INERMIS (thornless honey locust)	•		•			•		•		•	•	•		•			•	•		•			
GYMNOCLADUS DIOICA (Kentucky coffee tree)	•					•	•	•		•		•				•	•	•		•			
HALESIA CAROLINA (Carolina silver bell)	•			•		•			•			•		•			•		•	•		•	•	
HALESIA MONTICOLA (mountain silver bell)	•					•			•			•		•			•		•	•		•	•	
JACARANDA ACUTIFOLIA (sharp-leaved jacaranda)			•			•				•	•	•	•	•	•		•		•	•	•		•	
JUGLANS HINDSII (Hinds black walnut)	•					•				•	•	•	•		•			•			•		
JUGLANS NIGRA (black walnut)	•						•			•	•	•			•			•			•		
JUGLANS REGIA (English walnut)	•					•	•			•	•	•			•			•			•		
KALOPANAX PICTUS (castor aralia)			•	•			•			•		•				•	•	•			•		
KOELREUTERIA FORMOSANA (Chinese flame tree)			•			•				•	•	•	•	•	•	•		•					•
KOELREUTERIA PANICULATA (golden-rain tree)			•			•				•	•	•	•	•	•	•		•					•
LABURNUM ALPINUM (Scotch laburnum)		•			•			•			•	•	•			•		•	•		•		
LABURNUM WATERERII (Waterer laburnum)	•				•			•			•	•	•			•		•	•		•		
LIQUIDAMBAR STYRACIFLUA (sweet gum)				•			•	•	•	•		•		•			•	•	•			•	•	
LIRIODENDRON TULIPIFERA (tulip tree)	•						•			•		•	•			•		•			•		
MACLURA POMIFERA (Osage orange)			•			•				•	•			•		•		•		•			•
MAGNOLIA ACUMINATA (cucumber tree)			•			•	•			•		•	•			•		•	•		•	•	
MAGNOLIA CORDATA (yellow cucumber tree)			•			•				•		•	•			•		•	•		•	•	
MAGNOLIA DENUDATA (yulan magnolia)	•					•				•			•		•			•	•			•	•	
MAGNOLIA LOEBNERII 'MERRILL' (Merrill magnolia)	•					•				•			•		•			•	•			•	•	
MAGNOLIA SOULANGIANA (saucer magnolia)	•			•		•				•			•		•	•	•	•	•			•	•	
MAGNOLIA STELLATA (star magnolia)	•			•		•				•			•		•	•		•	•			•	•	
MALUS ARNOLDIANA (Arnold crab apple)	•			•		•				•			•	•			•		•			•	•	

Included are leaves that are distinctively colored in spring or summer as well as those that turn notable colors in fall.

** *Most trees grow best in soil that is slightly acid to neutral (pH 6.0 to 7.0). Trees that prefer greater acidity are listed here under "acid soil," and those that tolerate alkalinity are listed under "alkaline soil."*

	SHAPE					MATURE HEIGHT			RATE OF GROWTH			USES			NOTABLE TRAITS				GROWING CONDITIONS					
	Rounded	Weeping	Spreading	Conical	Columnar	Under 25 feet	25-50 feet	Over 50 feet	Slow	Medium	Fast	Shade tree	Ornamental tree	Street tree	Flowers	Fruit	Leaf color*	Bark	Full sun	Light shade	Dry soil	Moist soil	Acid soil**	Alkaline soil**
MALUS ATROSANGUINEA (carmine crab apple)	●					●				●			●	●	●	●			●			●	●	
MALUS BACCATA (Siberian crab apple)			●				●			●			●	●	●	●			●			●	●	
MALUS 'BOB WHITE' (Bob White crab apple)	●					●				●			●	●	●	●			●			●	●	
MALUS CORONARIA 'CHARLOTTE' (Charlotte crab apple)			●	●		●				●			●	●	●	●			●			●	●	
MALUS 'DOLGO' (Dolgo crab apple)			●				●			●			●	●	●	●			●			●	●	
MALUS 'DOROTHEA' (Dorothea crab apple)	●		●			●				●			●	●	●	●			●			●	●	
MALUS 'FLAME' (Flame crab apple)	●					●				●			●	●	●	●			●			●	●	
MALUS FLORIBUNDA (Japanese crab apple)	●					●				●			●	●	●	●			●			●	●	
MALUS HALLIANA PARKMANII (Parkman crab apple)			●	●		●				●			●	●	●	●			●			●	●	
MALUS HUPEHENSIS (tea crab apple)			●	●		●				●			●	●	●	●			●			●	●	
MALUS 'KATHERINE' (Katherine crab apple)			●	●		●				●			●	●	●	●			●			●	●	
MALUS 'PRINCE GEORGES' (Prince Georges crab apple)			●	●		●				●			●	●	●	●			●			●	●	
MALUS PURPUREA LEMOINEI (Lemoine purple crab apple)			●			●				●			●	●	●	●			●			●	●	
MALUS 'RADIANT' (Radiant crab apple)				●		●				●			●	●	●	●	●		●			●	●	
MALUS 'RED JADE' (Red Jade crab apple)		●				●				●			●		●	●			●			●	●	
MALUS 'RED SILVER' (Red Silver crab apple)	●						●			●			●	●	●	●	●		●			●	●	
MALUS 'ROYAL RUBY' (Royal Ruby crab apple)	●					●				●			●		●				●			●	●	
MALUS 'ROYALTY' (Royalty crab apple)	●					●				●			●	●	●	●	●		●			●	●	
MALUS SARGENTII (Sargent crab apple)	●					●				●			●	●	●	●			●			●	●	
MALUS SCHEIDECKERII (Scheidecker crab apple)			●	●		●				●			●	●	●	●			●			●	●	
MALUS 'SNOWDRIFT' (Snowdrift crab apple)	●					●	●			●			●	●	●	●			●			●	●	
MALUS SPECTABILIS RIVERSII (River's crab apple)			●			●	●			●			●	●	●	●			●			●	●	
MALUS ZUMI CALOCARPA (Zumi crab apple)				●		●	●			●			●	●	●	●			●			●	●	
MELIA AZEDARACH (chinaberry)	●		●			●				●	●	●	●					●	●		●	●		●
MORUS ALBA (white mulberry)	●	●				●	●			●	●	●				●			●		●	●	●	●
MORUS NIGRA (black mulberry)	●					●				●		●				●			●		●	●		●
MORUS RUBRA (red mulberry)	●					●				●	●	●	●			●			●		●	●		●
NYSSA SYLVATICA (pepperidge)			●	●			●		●			●	●				●	●	●	●		●	●	
OSTRYA VIRGINIANA (American hop hornbeam)			●	●		●			●			●	●			●		●	●	●	●	●		
OXYDENDRUM ARBOREUM (sorrel tree)			●	●	●	●			●				●		●		●	●	●	●		●	●	
PARKINSONIA ACULEATA (Jerusalem thorn)			●			●				●	●		●		●	●			●		●			
PARROTIA PERSICA (Persian parrotia)			●	●		●				●			●				●	●	●	●		●	●	
PAULOWNIA TOMENTOSA (empress tree)	●					●				●	●	●	●	●	●	●			●			●		
PHELLODENDRON AMURENSE (Amur cork tree)			●				●			●	●	●	●		●	●	●	●	●		●	●		
PISTACIA CHINENSIS (Chinese pistache)	●					●				●		●	●				●		●		●	●		
PLATANUS ACERIFOLIA (London plane tree)	●		●					●		●	●	●	●	●				●	●		●	●		●
PLATANUS OCCIDENTALIS (American plane tree)	●							●		●	●	●	●					●	●			●		●
PLATANUS ORIENTALIS (Oriental plane tree)	●							●		●	●	●						●	●			●		●
PLATANUS RACEMOSA (California plane tree)	●						●	●		●		●		●				●	●			●		●
POPULUS ALBA (white poplar)				●				●		●		●	●				●	●	●		●			
POPULUS DELTOIDES (eastern poplar)			●					●		●		●						●	●			●		
POPULUS NIGRA ITALICA (Lombardy poplar)					●			●		●			●						●	●	●			
PROSOPIS GLANDULOSA (honey mesquite)			●	●	●	●	●		●		●		●		●	●			●		●		●	●
PRUNUS AVIUM PLENA (double-flowered mazzard cherry)			●				●			●			●		●				●					
PRUNUS BLIREIANA (Blireiana plum)	●					●				●			●		●		●		●					
PRUNUS CERASIFERA ATROPURPUREA (Pissard plum)	●					●				●			●		●	●	●		●					
PRUNUS PERSICA (peach)			●			●				●			●		●	●			●					
PRUNUS SARGENTII (Sargent cherry)	●						●	●		●		●	●	●	●		●		●					
PRUNUS SERRULA (paperbark cherry)	●					●				●			●	●	●			●	●					

153

CHARACTERISTICS OF TREES: CONTINUED

Column groups: **SHAPE** (Rounded, Weeping, Spreading, Conical, Columnar) · **MATURE HEIGHT** (Under 25 feet, 25-50 feet, Over 50 feet) · **RATE OF GROWTH** (Slow, Medium, Fast) · **USES** (Shade tree, Ornamental tree, Street tree) · **NOTABLE TRAITS** (Flowers, Fruit, Leaf color*, Bark) · **GROWING CONDITIONS** (Full sun, Light shade, Dry soil, Moist soil, Acid soil**, Alkaline soil**)

Tree	Rounded	Weeping	Spreading	Conical	Columnar	Under 25 feet	25-50 feet	Over 50 feet	Slow	Medium	Fast	Shade tree	Ornamental tree	Street tree	Flowers	Fruit	Leaf color*	Bark	Full sun	Light shade	Dry soil	Moist soil	Acid soil**	Alkaline soil**
PRUNUS SERRULATA (Oriental cherry)	●	●		●	●					●			●	●	●				●					
PRUNUS SUBHIRTELLA (Higan cherry)		●			●					●			●	●					●					
PRUNUS YEDOENSIS (Yoshino cherry)			●		●	●				●			●	●					●					
PTEROCARYA FRAXINIFOLIA (Caucasian wingnut)			●					●			●	●		●					●			●		
PTEROCARYA STENOPTERA (Chinese wingnut)			●					●			●	●		●					●					
PTEROSTYRAX HISPIDA (fragrant epaulette tree)	●							●					●		●	●			●					
PYRUS CALLERYANA 'BRADFORD' (Bradford pear)				●				●		●			●	●	●	●	●		●					
QUERCUS ALBA (white oak)			●				●	●	●			●		●					●				●	
QUERCUS BOREALIS (red oak)	●		●					●		●	●	●		●					●				●	
QUERCUS COCCINEA (scarlet oak)	●		●					●	●			●		●					●				●	
QUERCUS IMBRICARIA (shingle oak)	●		●				●	●					●	●					●				●	
QUERCUS KELLOGGII (California black oak)	●							●		●		●		●					●				●	
QUERCUS NIGRA (water oak)	●							●			●			●					●				●	
QUERCUS PALUSTRIS (pin oak)	●		●	●				●			●			●					●				●	
QUERCUS PHELLOS (willow oak)	●		●	●				●			●			●					●			●	●	
QUERCUS PRINUS (chestnut oak)	●		●					●		●			●	●	●	●		●		●			●	
QUERCUS ROBUR (English oak)			●					●		●			●	●					●				●	
ROBINIA 'IDAHO' (Idaho locust)			●		●			●		●			●	●					●		●			●
ROBINIA PSEUDOACACIA (black locust)	●		●	●				●		●	●	●	●	●	●	●			●		●			●
SALIX ALBA TRISTIS (golden weeping willow)		●						●			●		●					●	●			●		
SALIX BABYLONICA (Babylon weeping willow)		●				●					●		●					●	●			●		
SALIX BLANDA (Wisconsin weeping willow)		●						●			●		●					●	●			●		
SALIX ELEGANTISSIMA (Thurlow weeping willow)		●						●			●		●					●	●			●		
SAPIUM SEBIFERUM (Chinese tallow tree)	●		●				●	●			●		●				●	●	●		●	●		
SASSAFRAS ALBIDUM (sassafras)			●				●		●				●	●	●		●		●	●			●	
SOPHORA JAPONICA (Japanese pagoda tree)	●						●	●	●	●		●	●	●	●				●		●			
SORBUS ALNIFOLIA (Korean mountain ash)			●					●		●		●	●	●	●	●	●		●					
SORBUS AUCUPARIA (European mountain ash)	●	●						●		●			●	●	●	●			●					
SORBUS CASHMIRIANA (Kashmir mountain ash)			●					●		●			●		●	●			●					
SORBUS HYBRIDS (hybrid mountain ash)			●					●		●			●		●	●			●					
STYRAX JAPONICA (Japanese snowbell)	●		●				●	●	●				●		●		●		●	●		●		
SYRINGA AMURENSIS JAPONICA (Japanese tree lilac)	●		●				●	●		●			●	●	●				●					
TILIA AMERICANA (American linden)			●					●	●	●		●	●						●	●		●		
TILIA CORDATA (little-leaved linden)			●					●	●	●		●	●	●					●	●		●		
TILIA EUCHLORA (Crimean linden)			●					●		●		●		●					●	●				
TILIA TOMENTOSA (silver linden)			●					●		●		●	●	●	●	●	●		●	●				
ULMUS CARPINIFOLIA 'CHRISTINE BUISMAN' (Christine Buisman elm)				●				●		●				●				●	●	●				
ULMUS PARVIFOLIA (Chinese elm)		●			●			●		●		●	●	●			●	●	●	●	●			
ULMUS PUMILA (Siberian elm)	●							●		●		●						●	●	●	●			
ZELKOVA SERRATA (Japanese zelkova)	●							●		●		●		●			●		●	●	●			●
ZIZYPHUS JUJUBA (jujube)			●		●			●			●		●	●	●	●			●	●	●	●		●

Included are leaves that are distinctively colored in spring or summer as well as those that turn notable colors in fall.

Most trees grow best in soil that is slightly acid to neutral (pH 6.0 to 7.0). Trees that prefer greater acidity are listed here under "acid soil," and those that tolerate alkalinity are listed under "alkaline soil."

Picture credits

The sources for the illustrations that appear in this book are listed below. Credits for pictures from left to right are separated by semicolons, from top to bottom by dashes. Cover—Bill Binzen. 4—Keith Martin courtesy James Underwood Crockett. 6—Courtesy New York Botanical Garden. 12,13—Drawings by Vincent Lewis. 17 through 23 —Illustrations by Davis Meltzer. 24—A. E. Bye Landscape Architect. 27, 29, 31, 32, 33—Drawings by Vincent Lewis. 35 —Malak, Ottawa. 36—Julius Shulman; P. H. Brydon courtesy Strybing Arboretum Collection. 37—Costa Manos from Magnum; Ralph D. Cornell—James J. Cox. 38—Evelyn Hofer. 39—Clarence E. Lewis except bottom center Sonja Bullaty, bottom right Costa Manos from Magnum. 40 —Molly Adams. 41—Clarence E. Lewis—Gottlieb Hampfler. 42—Malak, Ottawa; Grant Heilman—Ralph D. Cornell. 43—A. E. Bye Landscape Architect except bottom right Costa Manos from Magnum. 44—Clarence E. Lewis except bottom left Dean Brown. 45—Richard Parker from National Audubon Society—Malak, Ottawa; Sonja Bullaty.

46—Clarence E. Lewis except top right A. E. Bye Landscape Architect. 47—Angelo Lomeo; Gottlieb Hampfler. 48 —Bartlett Tree Expert Co. 53,54,56,58,61—Drawings by Vincent Lewis. 65—Sonja Bullaty. 66—Angelo Lomeo. 67 —Antoinette Jongen—Clarence E. Lewis—Dr. Bruce Hamilton. 68—Sonja Bullaty. 69—Clarence E. Lewis. 70,71 —Sonja Bullaty and Angelo Lomeo. 72—Humphrey Sutton. 73—Clarence E. Lewis. 74,75—Gottlieb Hampfler; Sonja Bullaty. 76—Sonja Bullaty. 77—Clarence E. Lewis except center Humphrey Sutton. 78—Angelo Lomeo. 79—Jim Kielbaso, Forestry Dept., Michigan State U.—A. E. Bye Landscape Architect—Sonja Bullaty. 80—Bartlett Tree Expert Co. 84,85,86—Drawings by Vincent Lewis. 88—Illustration by Don Moss. 90 through 147—Illustrations by artists listed in alphabetical order: Norman Adams, Adolph E. Brotman, Walter Hortens, Mary Kellner, Donald Mac Kay, Harry McNaught, Rebecca Merrilees, Raoul Minamora, John Murphy, Eduardo Salgado. 148,149—Illustrations by Rebecca Merrilees. 150—Map by Adolph E. Brotman.

Acknowledgments

For their help in the preparation of this book, the editors wish to thank the following: Robert A. Bartlett, President, The F. A. Bartlett Tree Expert Co., Stamford, Conn.; Walter Carpenter, Nassau County Cooperative Extension Service, Agricultural Division, Mineola, N.Y.; T. Brian Carter, Robert E. Clancy Associates, New York City; Dr. J. Cedric Carter, Plant Pathologist, Illinois Natural History Survey, Urbana, Ill.; Dr. E. L. Chandler, Physiologist, Bartlett Tree Research Laboratories, Charlotte, N.C.; Mrs. Edith Crockett, Librarian, The Horticultural Society of New York, Inc., New York City; Dr. William B. Davis, U. of California at Davis, Dept. of Environmental Horticulture, Davis, Calif.; Bob De Cicco, Manager, Marketing Services, Thompson-Hayward Chemical Co., Kansas City, Kans.; Derek Fell, W. Atlee Burpee Co., Philadelphia, Pa.; Dr. James Feucht, Denver Botanical Gardens, Denver, Colo.; Miss Marie Giasi, Librarian, Brooklyn Botanic Garden, Brooklyn, N.Y.; Adele Greenbaum, Nassau County Extension Service, Mineola, N.Y.; Miss Elizabeth Hall, Senior Librarian, The Horticultural Society of New York, Inc., New York City;

Dr. Richard Henley, Dept. of Horticulture, U. of Kentucky, Lexington, Ky.; Dr. Richard Klein, Horticulture Dept., U. of Vermont, Burlington, Vt.; Dean F. Lindgren, Regional Manager, International Minerals and Chemical Corp., Libertyville, Ill.; Robert R. Peek, Hastings, Atlanta, Ga.; Richard Pinder, Green Thumb Nursery, Canoga Park, Calif.; Dr. Pascal P. Pirone, Senior Plant Pathologist, The New York Botanical Garden, Bronx Park, N.Y.; Ross Daniels, Inc., West Des Moines, Iowa; Edward H. Scanlon; Edward H. Scanlon & Associates, Inc., Olmsted Falls, Ohio; Bob and John Siebenthaler, Siebenthaler Co., Dayton, Ohio; George H. Spalding, Botanical Information Consultant, Los Angeles State and County Arboretum, Los Angeles, Calif.; Dan Speer, President, Dan Speer Nursery, Inc., Hillsboro, Ore.; C. Powers Taylor, President, Rosedale Nurseries, Inc., Hawthorne, N.Y.; Itsuro Uenaka, President, Cupertino Nursery, Inc., Cupertino, Calif.; Dr. Jack Valdovinos, Lehman College, Bronx, N.Y.; Mrs. Sonia Wedge, Reference Librarian, The New York Botanical Garden, Bronx Park, N.Y.; Brayton F. Wilson, U. of Massachusetts, Forestry Dept., Amherst, Mass.

Bibliography

American Association of Nurserymen, Inc., *U.S.A. Standard for Nursery Stock*. American Association of Nurserymen, Inc., 1969.

Baumgardt, John Philip, *How to Prune Almost Everything*. M. Barrows and Company, Inc., 1968.

Collingwood, G. H., *Knowing Your Trees*. The American Forestry Association, 1937.

Collis, John Stewart, *The Triumph of the Tree*. William Sloane Associates, 1954.

Flemer, William, III, *Shade and Ornamental Trees in Color*. Grosset and Dunlap, Inc., 1965.

Free, Montague, *Plant Pruning in Pictures*. Doubleday and Company, Inc., 1961.

Harrison, Richard E. and Charles R., *Know Your Garden Series, Trees and Shrubs*. Charles E. Tuttle Company, 1965.

International Shade Tree Conference, Inc., *Shade Tree Evaluation*. International Shade Tree Conference, Inc., 1970.

Ketchum, Richard M., *The Secret Life of the Forest*. American Heritage Press, 1970.

Maino, Evelyn and Frances Howard, *Ornamental Trees*. University of California Press, 1955.

Martin, John Stuart, *The Home Owner's Tree Book*. Bantam Books, Inc., 1962.

Murphy, Richard C. and William E. Meyer, *The Care and Feeding of Trees*. Crown Publishers, Inc., 1969.

Perkins, Harold O., *Ornamental Trees for Home Grounds*. E. P. Dutton and Company, Inc., 1965.

Pirone, Pascal P., *Diseases and Pests of Ornamental Plants*. The Ronald Press Company, 1970.

Pirone, Pascal P., *Tree Maintenance*. Oxford University Press, 1959.

Rodale, J. I. and Staff, *How to Landscape Your Own Home*. Rodale Books, Inc., 1963.

Steffek, Edwin F., *The Pruning Manual*. Van Nostrand Reinhold Company, 1969.

Sunset Books, *Sunset Western Garden Book*. Lane Magazine and Book Company, 1967.

Taggart, George H., *The Wonderful World of Trees*. Review and Herald Publishing Association, 1970.

Taylor, Norman, *The Guide to Garden Shrubs and Trees*. Houghton Mifflin Company, 1965.

Taylor, Norman, *Norman Taylor's Encyclopedia of Gardening*. Houghton Mifflin Company, 1961.

Westcott, Cynthia, *The Gardener's Bug Book*. Doubleday and Company, Inc., 1964.

Wyman, Donald, *Trees for American Gardens*. The Macmillan Company, 1965.

Index

foliage of, 13, *73, map* 73; growth rate of, *13;* as ornamental tree, 13; pest resistance of, 13; pollution tolerance of, 13; spring-flowering, 13, 40. *See also Pyrus*

Pecan, 44, 83, *chart* 148. *See also Carya*

Pepperidge, 13, 28, 37, 38, 64, *69, map* 69, 83. *See also Nyssa;* Tupelo

Persimmon, 28. *See also Diosporus*

Pesticides, *chart* 148, 149

Pests, 61-63, 148-149, *chart 148;* biological controls of, 63, *chart* 148, 149; care of trees to prevent, 60, 61, 148-149; resistance to damage by, 9, 13, 61-62; spraying to prevent, *48,* 49, 62, 63

pH, 30-31, 89; adjusting, 30-31

Phellodendron, 132, chart 153. *See also* Cork tree

Phloem, *20-21*

Phoenix tree. *See Firmiana*

Phosphorus: bone meal as source of, 31; as fertilizer ingredient, 51, 52; to increase cold resistance, 51; to stimulate formation of flower buds, 51; to stimulate root growth, 51

Photosynthesis, 23

Pistache, Chinese, 44. *See also Pistacia*

Pistacia, 132-133, chart 153. *See also* Pistache, Chinese

Plane tree, *12,* 14, 38, 44, 46, 83, *chart* 148-149. *See also Platanus*

Plant lice, *chart 148*

Planting, *27,* 30-32; balled-and-burlaped trees, *27,* 31-32; bare-rooted trees, 30, 32; and building saucer for water, 32; container-grown trees, *27,* 32; depth, 27, 31, 32; mulching after, 32; preparation for, *27,* 30-31; season for, 30

Platanus, 133-134, chart 153. *See also* Plane tree; Sycamore

Plum, *13,* 38, 40, *chart* 148-149. *See also Prunus*

Pods, 9, *44*

Poinciana, 36, 43. *See also Delonix*

Poison ivy, 81, 82

Pollution tolerance, 10, 13, 77

Poplar, 14, 31, 34, 36, *37,* 83, 86; bark of, 46; diseases of, *chart 149;* growth rate of, 14; leaves of, 38; Lombardy, *37,* 59, 88, 89; pests of, *chart 148;* pruning, 59; shape of, 34, 36, *37,* 59; white, 38, 46. *See also Populus*

Poplar, tulip. *See Liriodendron*

Poplar, yellow. *See Liriodendron*

Populus, 134, 135, *chart* 153. *See also* Poplar

Potassium: as fertilizer ingredient, 51, 52; to increase resistance to breakage and disease, 51; to strengthen trees, 51

Praying mantis, 63

Pride of India. *See Melia*

Primary branches, 16, *17*

Propagation, by rooting branches, 14-15

Prosopis, 135, chart 153

Pruning, 10, 50, 55-61, 62, 81, 85, 87, 89; basic steps in, *56;* big branches, special technique for, 60, *61;* and care of wounds, 57, 60-61; damaged branches, 56, 57; high branches, 56, 59, 60, *80,* 81, 87; initial, 32, 58; low branches, 55-56, 59, 60; objectives of, 56, 57, 59, 60; older trees, 59-61, 81; professional, 60, 87; root, 25, *27;* second, 58; time for, 57; tools for, 57-*58,* 61

Prunus, 135-138, chart 153-154. *See also* Cherry; Peach; Plum

Pterocarya, 138, chart 154. *See also* Wingnut

Pterostyrax, 138, chart 154. *See also* Epaulette tree

Pyrethrum, *chart* 148

Pyrus, 139, chart 154. *See also* Pear

quercus, *139-141, chart* 154. *See also* Oak

rabbits. *See* Rodents

Red haw. *See Crataegus*

Redbud, *13,* 15, 40, *41, 73;* fall foliage of, *73, map* 73; fruit of, 44; growth rate of, *13;* leaf of, 38, *39;* as ornamental tree, 13, 15; spring-flowering, 40, *41,* 73. *See also Cercis*

Retaining wall, 83-84, *85,* 87

Ribs, of leaf, *23*

Rings, of trunk, 21

Robinia, 141, 142, chart 154. *See also* Locust

Rodents, protection from, *31,* 33

Root feeder, 54

Root girdling, 85-*86*

Root pruning, 25, *27*

Root rot, *chart 149*

Root system, 16, *17, 18-19;* and choice of trees for transplanting, 25; damage to from construction, 62, 81, 82, 83, 85; danger to sewer and water lines, 31; effect of change of soil level on, 81; effect of compressed soil on, 83; effect of paving on, 50, 82; examination of when buying trees, 29; functions of, 16, 17, 18-19; indications of damage to, 62; need for air and water of, 62, 81, 82, 83, 85; parts of, *18-19;* pruning, 25, *27;* ratio to crown of tree, 16. *See also* Feeding; Watering

Root tips, *18*

Root-zone applicator, 54

Rowan tree. *See Sorbus*

Russian olive, 46. *See also Elaeagnus*

Salix, *142, chart* 154. *See also* Willow

Sapium, 142-143, chart 154

Sapwood, *20-21*

Sassafras, 38, 46, *88,* 89, *143, chart* 149, *chart* 154

Saucer, around tree, 27, 32

Sawfly, *chart* 148

Scale insects, 49, 62, 63, *chart 148*

Scholar tree. *See Sophora*

Screens, 8, 11

Seaside conditions, trees for, 13

Secondary branches, 16, *17*

Seeds, 9, *44*

Senna. *See Cassia*

Serviceberry, 40, 44, 46, *67, map* 67, *chart* 148. *See also* Amelanchier

Shad-blow. *See* Amelanchier; Serviceberry

Shade trees, 7, 8, 11, 14, *chart* 151-154; fast-growing, 14, 89; foliage of, and kind of shade, 11, 38; late-flowering trees as, 42; location of, 11; ornamental trees as, 11, 34; for specific areas, 8, 11, 34

Shape, natural, 34, *36-37,* 59

Shower of gold. *See Cassia*

Silk tree, 11, *36,* 38, *39,* 43, 44, *chart* 148. *See also Albizia*

Silkworms, 59

Silver bell, 40. *See also Halesia*

Slow-growing trees, 14, *chart* 151-154

Snowbell, 43. *See also Styrax*

Snowdrop tree. *See Halesia*

Soil: compacted, 77, 83; and drainage, 13, 29, 31; effects of construction on, 81; erosion of, 8; fumigation of, *chart* 149; insufficient, 50; pH level of, 30-31, 89; preferences, 8, 13, 26, 30-31, *chart* 151-154; testing, 30, 31

Sooty-mold fungus, *chart* 148

Sophora, 143-144, chart 154. *See also* Pagoda tree

Sorbus, 144, chart 154. *See also* Mountain ash

Sorrel tree, *37,* 43. *See also Oxydendrum*

Sour gum. *See Nyssa*

Sourwood, 38, *68, map* 68. *See also Oxydendrum*

Spacing, 9, 10-11

Spongy layer, of leaf, 23

Spraying, 10, 62-63, *chart* 148-149; equipment for, *48,* 49, 55, 62; to prevent insect attack, *48,* 49, 62-63, 149; season for, 49, 62; temperature for, 62, 63

Spring-flowering trees, 34, *35,* 40-*41*

Staking, *32,* 33

Sterculia. See Firmiana

Sterilization, as insect control, 63

Sticky tape, *chart* 148, 149

Street trees, *chart* 151-154

Streptomycin sulfate, *chart* 149

Styrax, 144-145, chart 154. *See also* Snowbell

Sugarberry. *See Celtis*

Sulfur, ground, 30-31

Summer-flowering trees, 42-43

Sunlight: effect on fall foliage, 64, 68, 69, 74; and photosynthesis, 16, 23; protection of trunk from, *31,* 33

Sunscald, 25-26, 85

Sweet gum, 13, 38, 45, 69; adaptability of, 13; bark of, 46; fall foliage of, *69, map* 69; fruit of, 44, *45;* growth rate of, *12;* leaves of, 38; shape of, 37. *See also Liquidambar*